Dick Goddard's
ALMANAC
for NORTHEAST OHIO

Also by Dick Goddard:

Dick Goddard's Weather Guide

Dick Goddard's
ALMANAC
for NORTHEAST OHIO

GRAY & COMPANY, PUBLISHERS
CLEVELAND

A portion of the proceeds from the sale of this book will benefit animal charities in Northeast Ohio.

Illustrations by the author except where noted.
Photographs courtesy of the author or contributors except where noted.

Gray & Company, Publishers
1588 E. 40th St., Cleveland, OH 44103
(216) 431-2665
www.grayco.com

ISBN 1-886228-64-7

Printed in the United States of America

First Printing

CONTENTS

Introduction 6

2002–03 Forecast 8

WINTER 9

January 13

Notes from the Field, *by Bob Hinkle* 16

Ohio's Magnificent Seven (Well, Sort of),
by Dick Goddard 20

Warren G. Harding, 29th President
1921–1923, *by Dick Goddard* 22

February 27

Police Blotter Oddities 31

William Howard Taft, 27th President
1909–1913, *by Dick Goddard* 36

NEO's 2001 Weather Year in Review 34

Poop Patrol, *by Chuck Schodowski* 39

SPRING 45

March 47

The Ohio Country Myth, *by Dick Goddard* 51

Our Tale of Cassandra: Mythology Comes
to Our Lives, *by Wilma Smith* 55

April 59

William McKinley, 25th President
1897–1901, *by Dick Goddard* 62

Pet of the Year 65

Know What's Bugging You, *by Dick Goddard* 66

The Making of a Weatherman, *by A. J. Colby* ... 69

May 73

Coronation of the Carnation, *by Dick Goddard* ... 76

The Dog and Cat Protection Act,
by Dick Goddard 78

Animal Adoption Success Stories,
by Kate Malarney 80

NEO Animal Shelters 84

Happy Trails To Me!, *by Janice the Pig* 86

SUMMER 91

June 93

Benjamin Harrison, 23rd President
1889–1893, *by Dick Goddard* 96

Dick & Mick, *by Michael Stanley* 99

Cleveland's Killer Twister, *by Dick Goddard* 103

July 107

Of Cardinal Importance, *by Dick Goddard* 111

2003 Eclipses: By the (Rosy) Light of the Silvery
Moon, *by Clyde Simpson* 113

Record Fish 118

August 121

James A. Garfield, 20th President
(1881), *by Dick Goddard* 124

Northeast Ohio County Fairs 126

Oh, Those White Tails, *by Dick Goddard* 129

Tales from the News Desk, *by Tim Taylor* 131

More Tang Toungelers, *by Dick Goddard* 136

AUTUMN 139

September 141

Rutherford B. Hayes, 19th President
1877–1881, *by Dick Goddard* 145

Distance Learning, *by Dan Coughlin* 148

City-by-City Weather Statistics 153

October 157

Go Bucks!, *by Dick Goddard* 160

National or International Award Winners from
Northeast Ohio 162

Zoos in the Future, *by Steve Taylor* 164

November 169

Ulysses S. Grant, 18th President
1869–1877, *by Dick Goddard* 172

Why I Live in Cleveland, *by Robin Benzle* 175

Winners of Annual Northeast
Ohio Awards 178

December 179

In the Name of Religion, *by Dick Goddard* 182

Northeast Ohio County Stats 185

A Christmas Story, *by Neil Zurcher* 189

INTRODUCTION

More than 30,000 books are published each year in the United States. I can say with great confidence that this is one of them. As with my previous efforts, if you don't like it you have my 100 percent guarantee that I'll buy it back.

This 2003 edition of the Almanac for Northeast Ohio again features essays by a dozen authors who call this part of the Buckeye State home. Since 2003 is the bicentennial year for Ohio statehood, I did considerable research into the lives of United States presidents that Ohio claims as native sons. A more disparate assortment of chief executives you cannot imagine.

While both Ohio and Virginia claim to be the Mother of Presidents, with eight apiece, this cannot be so. The wild card is our ninth president, William Henry Harrison. Harrison was born and spent his youth in Virginia, but he was elected president while living in Ohio.

You'll learn about all of the Ohio state symbols, from buckeyes and lady-bugs to trilobites (which proves that I am NOT the state fossil). No state caterpillar is recognized, but I strongly urge consideration for *Isia isabella*, the comely and nondestructive banded woollybear caterpillar (known as a "woolly worm" south of Interstate 70).

Among the contributors in this edition is Tim Taylor, who regales us with tales of the FOX 8 anchor ladies over the years. Wilma Smith delights us with a story of the most recent addition to her family of furry friends. Neil Zurcher tells about the quaint Lorain County community where Santa Claus has been making individual house calls for the past 30 years. Meteorologist A.J. Colby (Anthony Joseph, by the way) whose smile can outshine the sun, gives hope to all youthful weather buffs considering weather-guessing as a career. "Jaguar" Danny Coughlin, FOX 8's staff leprechaun, enthralls us with his youthful deeds of derring-do as he taught Mario Andretti how to handle the brickyard at Indy (clue: always turn left). Big Chuck hilariously recounts the time he and his trustworthy companion, Rowdy the Ridgeback, nearly asphyxiated an admiring bagboy. Rock music icon Michael Stanley creates a science fiction analogy involving the still-Rolling Stone, Mick Jagger. Robin Benzle's story is truly phantasmagoric as she becomes a woman for all seasons in praising the constantly changing Northeast Ohio weather. Annette Fisher, a wonderful humanitarian, lets Janice the pig tell in her own words how she founded the Sanctuary for (unwanted) Farm Animals in Ravenna. The Cleveland Metroparks Zoo guru, Steve Taylor, impresses us with the problems and opportunities that all zoological facilities will be facing in the 21st century.

This almanac will provide some great reading as we head through the steadily darkening and colder days of autumn and winter, before the brightening skies and warmth of spring return.

Speaking of winter, if the early indications are correct, our weather will again be influenced by the phenomenon known as El Niño. This "suggests" that the Northeast Ohio winter will not be especially cold, with snowfall being normal in most places. But, let us not forget the forecaster's timeless mantra: heavier amounts in the snowbelt.

THE OHIO STATE FLAG:

Ohio has the only state flag that is not rectangular. Shaped like a swallow's tail, the flag is known as a burgee (a pennant with two points). The flag was designed by architect John Eisemann in 1901 for the Ohio Building at the Pan American Exposition in Buffalo, New York. (Ironically, it was at this event that President William McKinley of Ohio lost his life to an assassin.)

The flag's white circle stands for the "O" in Ohio, while the red center portrays the eye of the male deer, a buckeye. The tips of the flag acknowledge the state's hills and valleys, while the red and white stripes stand for waterways and roadways.

Seventeen stars represent Ohio's entrance into the Union as the 17th state.

2002–2003 FORECAST*

Our pleasant and mild weather of early October will give way in early November to increasingly stronger cold fronts. Winds will become gusty and early snow will often be mixed with rain near Lake Erie. In December we will notice the days are becoming darker earlier and the nights are becoming much longer. The unique phenomenon known as lake-effect snow will develop and continue off and on through January—and February as well—if Lake Erie and Lake Huron remain unfrozen, as they often do. Daylight will become noticeably longer as we reach February, although cold temperatures and occasional snow will continue. March snows will be wet and soggy, and, by month's end, the "gatekeepers" of spring, the tiny cricket frogs known as spring peepers, will be serenading us with their sleighbell chorus. Spring will soon appear, and by early April the Cleveland Indians will be playing baseball at Jacobs Field. During April and May the weather will become warmer and more turbulent, with thunder being heard. Temperatures will continue to steadily rise, becoming very warm to frequently oppressive as we move through the month of June and into the dog days of July and August. By late August and September children will return to school. At this time almanacs will again appear in drug and book stores where nice, but gullible, people will spend countless dollars to find out what the following year will hold. Just as they have for several hundred years.

---

* Purists demand that an almanac should forecast the weather for a year in advance. Such extended forecasts are notoriously inaccurate, but after serious consultation with local squirrels, caterpillars, and groundhogs, I offer the above with great confidence. D.G.

Winter

Some call the Ohio winter "invigorating." Others prefer the word "interminable."

NORTHEAST OHIO'S WARMEST AND COLDEST WINTERS
(by Median Temp)

....

WARMEST
Cleveland: 38.7° / 1931–32
Akron/Canton: 38.2° / 1889–90

....

COLDEST
Cleveland: 19.8° / 1976–77
Akron/Canton: 20.7° / 1976–77

At the time of the winter solstice in December, the sun appears at it's lowest point on the horizon. In Ohio's northeast counties, the shortened daylight combined with the heavy lake-effect cloudiness makes December the dimmest and darkest month of the year. On average, Greater Cleveland receives only 26 percent of possible sunshine during December.

By early January, much of Ohio is usually a study in frozen motion as we are firmly locked into the season of silence. During the latter part of January the legendary thaw often pays a fleeting, but welcome, visit. It's soon back to numb's-the-word, however, as the icy tyrant King Winter returns to use the state for his throne room.

By mid-February, spring will have begun its inexorable march northward from the Gulf of Mexico. At a rate of 15 miles each day, the frost line pushes closer to Ohio. At each point it passes, the insects emerge from their wintering places and the migrant birds follow this food supply northward. Spring will soon be touching all growing things with the magic of rebirth.

If there were such a thing as a Hall of Infamy for Ohio's winters, these would have to be considered the most difficult in terms of cold, snow, or both: 1995–96; 1977–78; 1976–77; 1962–63; 1935–36; 1917–18; and 1898–99.

Winter Glossary

Flurries indicates relatively brief, intermittent periods of snow. The flurry may be light or heavy, but it passes quickly.

Heavy Snow for most of Ohio is four inches or more in a 12-hour period, or six inches or more in a 24-hour period. In the snowy northern third of Ohio, heavy snow is considered to be six inches or more in a 12-hour period.

Snow in a forecast indicates the possibility of a steady fall with amounts of anywhere from one to three inches over the forecast period.

Snow Squalls are bursts of heavy snow accompanied by gusty winds. A squall can drop several inches of snow in one spot and leave nearby areas untouched.

Winter Storm Warning means that a storm is imminent. Estimates of snowfall will be included in the warning.

Winter Storm Watch means that a storm is approaching. It could slide by and miss the area, so stay up on the latest advisory.

Winter Weather Advisory alerts you to an important event such as freezing rain, sleet, blowing snow, strong winds, or fog but is below the level of a warning category.

NORTHEAST OHIO'S WETTEST AND DRIEST WINTERS
(Liquid)

WETTEST
Cleveland: 14.95" / 1949–50
Akron/Canton: 15.09" / 1949–50

DRIEST
Cleveland: 3.27" / 1900–01
Akron/Canton: 2.86" / 1905–06

NORTHEAST OHIO'S SNOWIEST AND LEAST SNOWIEST SEASONS

SNOWIEST
Cleveland: 101.1", 1995–96
Akron/Canton: 82.0", 1977–78

LEAST SNOWIEST
Cleveland: 8.8", 1918–19
Akron/Canton: 10.8", 1932–33

STATE SYMBOLS:

Flower: scarlet carnation (1904)
Tree: buckeye (1953)
Bird: cardinal (1933)
Insect: ladybug (1975)
Gemstone: flint (1965)

Song: "Beautiful Ohio" (1969)
Beverage: tomato juice (1965)
Fossil: trilobite (1985)
Animal: white-tailed deer (1988)
Wildflower: large white trillium (1987)

Ohio has a **state beverage**: tomato juice, declared as such in 1965.

IN THE
✳ Northeast Ohio Sky ✳
THIS SEASON

ALDEBERAN

BETELGEUSE

BELLATRIX

ORION

RIGEL

SAIPH

SIRIUS

Winter

Our sky has twice as many bright stars in winter than in any other season. It's not because of cold, clear nights; it's simply because the earth is turned to its most favorable position for the viewing of stars.

Arguably the most beautiful constellation of them all, Orion—The Mighty Hunter—rules the frigid, brittle skies of winter. The red-orange superstar Betelgeuse (BET-el-jooz) is one of the largest known stars. (Sorry, kids, it isn't pronounced "beetle juice.") When fully expanded Betelgeuse may be 1,000 times as large as our sun. Blue-white Rigel (RYE-jel) is one of the brightest stars visible to us.

The three stars that make up the belt in the middle of Orion are Mintaka (min-TAK-ah), Alnilam (al-NIGH-lam), and Alnitak (al-nih-TAK).

Yapping at Orion's heels is Sirius, the Dog Star, the brightest star in our sky. To the upper right is cool-yellow Aldeberan (al-DEB-ah-ran), the ninth-brightest jewel in our heavens.

FIRST & LAST FREEZES

Location	Average date of first freeze	Average date of last freeze	Location	Average date of first freeze	Average date of last freeze
Akron/Canton	Oct 20	Apr 30	Lancaster	Oct 14	Apr 28
Alliance	Oct 17	May 3	Lima	Oct 11	May 1
Ashland	Oct 11	May 7	Lorain	Oct 17	Apr 29
Ashtabula	Nov 2	Apr 22	Mansfield	Oct 10	May 6
Athens	Oct 10	Apr 28	Marietta	Oct 18	Apr 22
Bellefontaine	Oct 15	Apr 29	Marion	Oct 17	Apr 30
Bowling Green	Oct 10	May 5	Massillon	Oct 20	Apr 30
Bucyrus	Oct 9	May 5	Medina	Oct 18	May 3
Cadiz	Oct 14	May 1	Millersburg	Oct 15	May 3
Cambridge	Oct 15	Apr 28	Millport	Sep 30	May 18
Canfield	Oct 4	May 15	Mineral Ridge	Oct 6	May 11
Celina	Oct 8	May 3	Mt. Vernon	Oct 16	Apr 29
Chardon	Oct 15	May 10	Napoleon	Oct 9	May 3
Chillicothe	Oct 17	Apr 25	New Philadelphia	Oct 15	Apr 30
Chippewa Lake	Oct 6	May 10	Newark	Oct 17	Apr 28
Cincinnati	Oct 25	Apr 15	Newcomerstown	Oct 14	Apr 29
Circleville	Oct 15	Apr 26	Norwalk	Oct 11	May 4
Cleveland, inland	Oct 22	May 1	Oberlin	Oct 17	May 3
Cleveland, shore	Nov 2	Apr 25	Painesville	Oct 28	Apr 28
Columbus	Oct 21	Apr 21	Pandora	Sep 28	May 10
Conneaut	Nov 2	Apr 22	Portsmouth	Oct 23	Apr 18
Coshocton	Oct 16	May 1	Put-In-Bay	Nov 6	Apr 15
Dayton	Oct 19	Apr 23	Ravenna	Oct 12	May 15
Defiance	Oct 6	May 2	Sandusky	Oct 30	Apr 18
Delaware	Oct 9	May 1	Sidney	Oct 8	May 5
Dorset	Sep 29	May 19	Springfield	Oct 18	Apr 24
Elyria	Oct 20	May 1	Steubenville	Oct 18	Apr 29
Findlay	Oct 11	May 3	Tiffin	Oct 11	May 2
Fremont	Oct 12	May 1	Toledo	Oct 20	Apr 27
Gallipolis	Oct 19	Apr 26	Upper Sandusky	Oct 11	May 2
Geneva	Oct 28	Apr 29	Van Wert	Oct 9	May 6
Hiram	Oct 15	May 5	Warren	Oct 7	May 10
Ironton	Oct 25	Apr 16	Wooster	Oct 5	May 8
Jefferson	Oct 16	May 5	Youngstown	Oct 4	May 15
Kent	Oct 15	May 10	Zanesville	Oct 15	Apr 28
Kenton	Oct 8	May 7			

JANUARY STATISTICS

SUNSHINE % 30

DRIEST MONTH .... 0.31"/1871

WARMEST MONTH .... 40.2°/1932

COLDEST MONTH .... 11.0°/1977

LIQUID PCPN AVG. .... 2.04"

RAINIEST DAY .... 2.93"/1995

RAINIEST MONTH .... 7.01"/1950

THUNDERY DAYS 0

SNOWIEST DAY .... 10.8"/1996

SNOWIEST MONTH .... 42.8"/1978

LEAST SNOWFALL .... 0.5"/1932

DAYS ONE INCH SNOW 5

January is named after the Roman god Janus, the two-faced Keeper of the Gates. Janus usually shows us only his cold and snowy countenance, however. Paradoxically, in early January Planet Earth is three million miles closer to the sun than in July. It is the angle of the incoming solar radiation—acute in winter and more direct in summer—that makes our winter cold and our summer hot. In many Januaries a welcome small reward comes in the form of the legendary January thaw, usually during the third week. The milder weather quickly leaves and Northeast Ohio plunges back into the depths of winter. Another psychological up-lift comes as the seed catalogs arrive—like the one that has the guy on the cover holding up an 80-pound rutabaga and saying, "You can imagine my surprise...."

On the 26th day of the month in 1978, Ohio's deepest storm, literally a white hurricane, ravaged the state from south to north. On the 19th day of 1994, Cleveland's temperature fell to an all-time record 20 degrees below zero; temperatures remained below zero for a benchmark string of 56 hours. Our coldest January was in 1977, our warmest in the El Niño year of 1932. Depending on the strength of the cold, the first flower of the year, the snowdrop, will appear by month's end. Mosquitoes are never a problem this month.

JAN FEB MAR APR MAY JUN JUL AUG SEP OCT NOV DEC

DAILY DATA FOR JANUARY

Date	Moon Phase	Day	Day of Year	Days Left in Year	Sunrise	Sunset	Length of Day	Avg. Hi	Avg. Lo
1		Wed	1	364	7:53	5:07	9:14	33	20
2	●	Thu	2	363	7:53	5:08	9:15	33	19
3		Fri	3	362	7:53	5:09	9:16	33	19
4		Sat	4	361	7:53	5:10	9:17	32	19
5		Sun	5	360	7:53	5:11	9:18	32	19
6		Mon	6	359	7:53	5:12	9:19	32	18
7		Tue	7	358	7:53	5:13	9:20	32	18
8		Wed	8	357	7:53	5:14	9:21	32	18
9		Thu	9	356	7:53	5:15	9:22	32	18
10	◑	Fri	10	355	7:53	5:16	9:23	32	18
11		Sat	11	354	7:52	5:17	9:25	32	18
12		Sun	12	353	7:52	5:18	9:26	32	18
13		Mon	13	352	7:52	5:19	9:27	32	17
14		Tue	14	351	7:51	5:20	9:29	32	17
15		Wed	15	350	7:51	5:22	9:31	32	17
16		Thu	16	349	7:50	5:23	9:33	32	17
17		Fri	17	348	7:50	5:24	9:34	31	17
18	○	Sat	18	347	7:49	5:25	9:36	31	17
19		Sun	19	346	7:49	5:26	9:37	31	17
20		Mon	20	345	7:48	5:28	9:40	31	17
21		Tue	21	344	7:48	5:29	9:41	31	17
22		Wed	22	343	7:47	5:30	9:43	31	17
23		Thu	23	342	7:46	5:31	9:45	31	17
24		Fri	24	341	7:46	5:33	9:47	32	17
25	◐	Sat	25	340	7:45	5:34	9:49	32	17
26		Sun	26	339	7:44	5:35	9:51	32	17
27		Mon	27	338	7:43	5:36	9:53	32	17
28		Tue	28	337	7:42	5:37	9:55	32	17
29		Wed	29	336	7:41	5:39	9:58	32	17
30		Thu	30	335	7:41	5:40	9:59	32	17
31		Fri	31	334	7:40	5:41	10:01	32	17

JAN FEB MAR APR MAY JUN JUL AUG SEP OCT NOV DEC

Rec. Hi°	Rec. Lo°	Avg. Lake°	On This Date ...
69/1876	-4/1968	35	Actor Don Novello ("Father Guido Sarducci") born in Ashtabula (1943)
66/1876	-12/1879	34	Green Bay Packers beat Browns 23-12 in NFL champ. game (1966)
65/1874	-16/1879	34	Cavaliers retire jersey #34, Austin Carr (1981)
65/1874	-7/1679	34	Football coach Don Shula born in Grand River (1930)
66/1939	-13/1884	34	Football coach Chuck Noll born in Cleveland (1932)
66/1946	-9/1884	34	WKBN TV 27 in Youngstown begins broadcasting (1953)
63/1907	-9/1884	34	First issue of the *Cleveland Plain Deale*r published (1842)
66/1937	-10/1968	34	The State Convention of Baptists in Ohio was formed (1954)
61/1937	-13/1875	34	-87°F (-66°C), Northice Station, Greenland (Greenland record) (1954)
61/1939	-12/1875	34	Race car driver Bobby Rahal born in Medina (1953)
67/1890	-9/1899	34	Atlanta, Georgia's temperature goes below zero° F (1982)
65/1916	-9/1886	34	NFL champion Cleve. Rams given permission to move to L.A. (1946)
69/1890	-10/1977	34	Congress changes U.S. flag to 15 stars & 15 stripes (1794)
70/1932	-6/1893	33	Musician Dave Grohl born in Warren (1969)
68/1932	-7/1972	33	Actor Chad Lowe born in Dayton (1968)
57/1889	-15/1977	33	18th Amendment (prohibition) becomes law of the land (1920)
60/1973	-17/1982	33	Actor Oscar Apfel born in Cleveland (1878)
64/1996	-15/1994	33	Ghoulardi debuts on "Shock Theater" on WJW TV 8 (1963)
67/1907	-20/1994	33	Cleveland's WKBF TV, channel 61, begins broadcasting (1968)
65/1906	-18/1985	33	Holmes County incorporated (1824)
71/1906	-17/1985	33	Golfer Jack Nicklaus born in Columbus, OH (1940)
71/1906	-10/1936	33	Temperature rises 49°F in 2 minutes in Spearfish, SD (1943)
68/1967	-17/1963	33	Indians' Bob Feller elected to Baseball Hall of Fame (1962)
35/1909	-19/1963	33	Cavs biggest margin of victory, 43 points, vs. Milwaukee 132-89 (1976)
73/1950	-15/1897	33	Browns' Lou "The Toe" Groza born (1924)
69/1950	-9/1897	33	Actor Paul Newman born in Cleveland (1925)
69/1916	-6/1966	33	Browns/Ravens kicker Matt Stover born (1968)
62/2002	-10/1977	33	25th Space Shuttle (51L)-Challenger 10 explodes (1986)
65/1914	-17/1873	33	William McKinley born in Niles (1843)
62/1916	-4/1873	33	"The Lone Ranger" premieres on ABC radio (1933)
62/1989	-5/1971	32	Coshocton County incorporated (1810)

JAN FEB MAR APR MAY JUN JUL AUG SEP OCT NOV DEC

Notes from the Field

BOB HINKLE

One of the joys of a naturalist's life is learning to see nature as an endlessly changing cycle, repeatable and predictable throughout the years. In my half-century on the planet, I have gone from a view of nature as utter randomness and chaos to one of embracing the cycles of life, and finding pleasure in the repetition of a myriad of little happenings that taken together can be called a year.

I think the idea first really came to me one spring in a pasture in Michigan. I was working late at the office, and the local farm caretaker noticed the lights in the window as dusk fell. "Are you still here?" he asked. "Your day's long enough—come out back and see the Timberdoodles fly!" "Whatberdoodles?" I replied, as he dragged me out of the office and along the lane to the edge of an old farm field recently overgrown with dogwoods and other shrubs. "Listen!" he said, and the still night air was pierced with a sharp "Bzzzzt! Bzzzzt!" as the pasture's woodcock began its mating dance. It was April 9. The snows were a month gone, and the air was heavy with the damp smells of wet earth. "Bzzzt!" the woodcock said, and "Bzzzt!" again. Then stillness. In seconds, the silence was broken by a flutter of wings, as the male woodcock flew up in a long low takeoff, then circled above us, higher and higher, fluttering changing to a wavering warble, until a point was reached when he suddenly seemed to collapse in midflight, plummeting toward the ground. Amazed, I watched him fall, sure of his death, but just before he crashed into the damp spring earth, he popped out his little round wings, daintily set down on the same spot he'd arisen from, and exclaimed "Bzzzzt! Bzzzzt!" We watched and listened to the Timberdoodle woodcock's mating dance and flights until darkness fell. It was the same the next night, and the next, until mid-May when, either satiated with females or disheartened beyond measure, he quit.

The next April he returned, and the next April, and the next, always to the same place, always flying at the same time each evening, until darkness fell. He danced the dance of woodcocks—ancestral, reaching back through thousands of woodcock generations into a deep past when the Great Ice had just left, and hopefully also reaching forward into a dim future that we can only hope holds woodcocks and damp spring sights and smells forever. Spring equals woodcocks, and the amazing sky dance that they perform every evening (and morning, as I later discovered) from their return to the dancing grounds until mid-May.

I stayed at that job long enough to see three springs of woodcock dances, waves of bufflehead ducks, and the deafening choruses of tree frogs, spring peepers, and wood frogs. For three summers I walked through fields covered with ox-eye daisies, black-eyed Susans, blue sailors (chicory), and Deptford pinks. When fall came, I recognized its pace by the sounds of migrating geese and the subtle glow of reds and yellows in the staghorn sumac and sassafras. I began to see the cycle. One evening with an old bearded farmer had changed my whole life.

One evening with an old bearded farmer had changed my whole life.

The seemingly unrelated disciplines of ornithology and sky-watching sealed my understanding of the cycles of nature. I had spent half my adult life never knowing that the stars flowed slowly across the sky in an absolutely orderly and predictable sequence each day, each month, each year, repeating the pattern over and over for millennia. When I watched the constellation Scorpio rise in the summer sky in mid-July, it was the same view my father saw, and my grandfather, and his grandfather, going back for generations, farther than we could measure. On the same date each year, the sky would slip back to its exact configuration for that date. The stars would be in exactly the same place. Only the wandering planets would make the sky look any different. It was the sky of my ancestors, and yours, and the sky of our great-great-grandchildren as well. In a world of human chaos, something was finally orderly and predictable.

The following year, I was taking a course in ornithology. Up till then, as far as I was concerned, there were only six kinds of birds on the planet—chirp birds, tweet birds, hoot birds, hiss birds, honk

JAN FEB MAR APR MAY JUN JUL AUG SEP OCT NOV DEC

birds, and barbecue birds—and I favored the latter. Bird-watchers were little old people in pith helmets and sneakers, with binoculars around their scrawny necks and butterfly nets in their right hands. I didn't want to be one, or even to be associated with them. Then I met a remarkable man named George Wallace, one of the mid–20th century's most regarded names in the science of bird biology. He took us into the field and made the first sighting of a starling as exciting as if it had been an eagle.

I began to notice birds, and then to seek them out. As orderly as the stars, each spring they returned to me, first the kinglets and the gnatcatchers, then the white-throated and white-crowned sparrows, then the orioles and grosbeaks, then the warblers, the tiny neo-tropical butterflies of the bird world. Each species traces its unique ancestral migration route across three continents to find the same tree they nested in before. The birds stay here in the north only long enough to find each other and raise their young; then they return southward before the killing frosts and snows of fall and winter. I learned that every April, certain birds would come around, and that it was the same year after year after year, and all I had to do was learn, then wait. In pastures in Michigan and Ohio and Vermont and Massachusetts and Maine and Wisconsin, and all the other places where April has found me, so too have the woodcocks. The cycle repeats endlessly.

I began to notice birds, and then to seek them out.

And so it is summer when I write these words to you. The cardinals I've been watching brought their first batch of young to the feeder in the backyard two weeks ago, and yesterday the he-cardinal was seen tenderly, carefully feeding the she-cardinal sunflower seeds, and perhaps they'll grace us with another batch of anxious youngsters before fall comes again. My wife, Kim, the squirrel rehabilitator, has released the first bright-eyed young ones back into their native habitats, and now we wait for the inevitable August rain of squirrels to come. The chicory began to bloom this week, and I know from past years that the teasel will put forth its first belt of bluish flowers by mid-month. By mid-August, the sweet gums and sumacs will start to turn, and by mid-September the Cleveland skies will be swept clean of nighthawks. Fall color will be mostly gone by mid-October, and by Thanksgiving it will snow. Orion will return again to the winter skies, and days will grow short and cold. When the first bright blue days of January grace our lives, the days will be noticeably longer. The neighborhood red-tailed hawks will glide on their mating flights, and the great-horned owls will watch from their nests by February's end. March will be the month of buzzards again…and on it goes.

Ever changing, but never changing, the world of nature passes by each day. We have only to look, and see, and wait.

Robert D. Hinkle, Ph.D., is Chief of Outdoor Education for the Cleveland Metroparks. Proceeds from his contribution benefit the Emerald Necklace Endowment Fund.

WIND CHILL

Wind chill is a "feels-like" number that originated from research done by Ohioan Paul Siple in Antarctica in the 1940s. The formula is based on modern heat-transfer theories, and the wind speed is measured at five feet above ground. Wind chill temperatures of minus 19 and colder can cause frostbite in 15 minutes or less.

Wind chill applies to humans and animals, but not inanimate objects such as automobile radiators.

Temperature (°F)

Calm	40	35	30	25	20	15	10	5	0	-5	-10	-15	-20	-25	-30	-35	-40	-45
5	36	31	25	19	13	7	1	-5	-11	-16	-22	-28	-34	-40	-46	-52	-57	-63
10	34	27	21	15	9	3	-4	-10	-16	-22	-28	-35	-41	-47	-53	-59	-66	-72
15	32	25	19	13	6	0	-7	-13	-19	-26	-32	-39	-45	-51	-58	-64	-71	-77
20	30	24	17	11	4	-2	-9	-15	-22	-29	-35	-42	-48	-55	-61	-68	-74	-81
25	29	23	16	9	3	-4	-11	-17	-24	-31	-37	-44	-51	-58	-64	-71	-78	-84
30	28	22	15	8	1	-5	-12	-19	-26	-33	-39	-46	-53	-60	-67	-73	-80	-87
35	28	21	14	7	0	-7	-14	-21	-27	-34	-41	-48	-55	-62	-69	-76	-82	-89
40	27	20	13	6	-1	-8	-15	-22	-29	-36	-43	-50	-57	-64	-71	-78	-84	-91
45	26	19	12	5	-2	-9	-16	-23	-30	-37	-44	-51	-58	-65	-72	-79	-86	-93
50	26	19	12	4	-3	-10	-17	-24	-31	-38	-45	-52	-60	-67	-74	-81	-88	-95
55	25	18	11	4	-3	-11	-18	-25	-32	-39	-46	-54	-61	-68	-75	-82	-89	-97
60	25	17	10	3	-4	-11	-19	-26	-33	-40	-48	-55	-62	-69	-76	-84	-91	-98

(Wind (MPH))

Wind Chill (°F) = 35.74 + 0.6215T - 35.75($V^{0.16}$) + 0.4275T($V^{0.16}$)

T = Air Temperature (°F)   V = Wind Speed (mph)

Source: National Weather Service

Frostbite occurs in 15 minutes or less

JAN FEB MAR APR MAY JUN JUL AUG SEP OCT NOV DEC

Ohio's
Magnificent Seven
(Well, Sort Of)
Dick Goddard

In this Ohio bicentennial year it is appropriate that we take a close-up look (actually, cast a gimlet eye) at the seven United States presidents who have claimed Ohio as their birthplace. Don't be misled. The 1960 hit movie *The Magnificent Seven* was a classic shoot-'em-up western and not a tribute to the administrations of Ohio's national leaders.

All of Ohio's presidents took office under the banner of the Republican Party, and we had three in succession: Ulysses S. Grant, Rutherford B. Hayes, and James A. Garfield. Six native Ohio sons were elected president in only a 40-year time span. Ohio shone brightly in what was known as the Gilded Age, the time between the Civil War and World War I. Heroics and bravery in battle provided national fame and an entree into politics. Ohio was also a "must have" state at the polls.

In the year 2000 the C-SPAN cable network assigned 58 presidential historians the task of putting American presidents in their places. Ten criteria were used in the assessments, including quality of leadership, management of the economy, and moral authority. Of the 42 presidents who preceded George W. Bush, the highest ranked from Ohio was William McKinley, who came in at number 15. The ad hoc committee also concluded that the lowest ranked of Ohio's presidential septet was Warren G. Harding at 38 (the complete rankings are on page 38).

In the following brief stories of Ohio presidents I have not delved deeply into their political achievements or failures. I have attempted to uncover the personalities and foibles behind those always-solemn portraits that hang in official places.

It was gratifying to learn that the scandals and misdeeds that befell some of the Ohio presidents were usually the result of misplaced trust in their appointees rather than personal corruption on their part.

As we will see, Ohio has sent quite a cast of characters to the White House. From the legendary general who couldn't stand the sight of blood—and who was arrested in Washington for speeding in his carriage—to a president who could claim no legitimate children and a president who had to be rescued after becoming stuck in the White House bathtub.

Sic transit gloria!

Note: Some will argue that Ohio should claim our ninth chief executive, William Henry Harrison, as a Buckeye. While it is true that he spent most of his adult life in North Bend, Ohio (just west of Cincinnati), he was born (on February 9, 1773) at Berkeley Plantation in Charles City, County of Virginia. Both Virginia and Ohio call themselves the "Mother of Presidents," but it would be the ultimate political gerrymander—not to mention a major suspension of a law of physics—to claim Harrison as native to both states. Harrison served the shortest time as president: only 30 days. On March 4, 1841, at the age of 68, Harrison gave the longest presidential inauguration address: one hour and 40 minutes, and 8,445 words. He did this outdoors on a cold, windy, rainy day without wearing either a coat or hat. Harrison died of pneumonia on April 4, 1841.

WARREN G. HARDING
29TH PRESIDENT 1921–1923

Dick Goddard

Everyone agreed that when Harding was gone no one would be able to fill his shoes. That's because Harding wore a size 14 and only George Washington's size 15s were larger.

Harding was the last of Ohio's chief magistrates. He was born on November 2, 1865, at Blooming Grove, Ohio, in Morrow County. He was the oldest of six children who lived to maturity.

With gleaming white hair and black eyebrows, the handsome Harding was an even six feet tall and barrel-chested, with soft gray eyes and a classic Roman nose. The problem with our 29th president was that his eyes were even more roamin'.

Harding had a pleasing voice and was always fashionably dressed. His physical appearance and personality would have qualified him as a romantic leading man in the movies, and he took full advantage of the combination. According to his father, Warren was a kind and humble person who never learned how to say "No." His dad was quoted as saying, "If Warren had been born a girl he would have been in 'the family way' all the time."

JAN FEB MAR APR MAY JUN JUL AUG SEP OCT NOV DEC

Biographies acknowledge that the amorous Harding had no legitimate children. At the age of 24 Harding had a nervous breakdown, and throughout his life he was an occasional patient at a sanitarium in Battle Creek, Michigan.

In spite of his randy reputation, Harding was considered (especially by men . . . no surprise!) to be a good guy and a "people person." His kindness is shown by the fact that in 30 years as the publisher for the *Marion Star* newspaper he never fired an employee.

Without the benefit of military service, Harding made a deep impression on the public with his gift for oratory. In 1898 he was elected to the Ohio state senate, and in 1903 he became lieutenant governor. After a failed 1910 try for the governorship, he was elected a U.S. senator in 1914. He gained the Republican presidential nomination in 1920 because of a stalemate between two other candidates. Harding won the national election in a landslide.

Once in office he went out of his way not to antagonize anyone. That, perhaps, is the reason he has been called an ineffective leader by many politicians.

While president, Harding frequently played golf (low 100s) at the Chevy Chase Country Club. He attended baseball games and boxing matches. Occasionally, Harding would sneak out of the White House to view a Washington burlesque show. He was just "one of the boys," according to his male associates.

At least twice a week Harding hosted poker games in the White House, once betting (and losing) an entire set of White House china. While he felt it politically correct to support Prohibition, he kept the White House wet bar amply stocked with bootleg booze.

Harding enjoyed automobile excursions, yachting, and fishing, along with extramarital affairs.

The president was married to Florence DeWolfe of Marion. Because of her business savvy, she was given credit for making the *Marion Star* the great success it became. Obviously, she did not have a happy marriage. Florence was a big devotee of astrology.

One of Harding's extracurricular activities was Carrie Phillips, the wife of a longtime friend (this did not come into focus until the alliance was discovered—love letters were found in the 1960s). Harding met Phillips when both were patients at the sanitarium in Battle Creek. Carrie died a senile pauper in 1960 at a state home for the aged in Ohio.

While the president was cavorting with Mrs. Phillips for 15 years, he was also involved with Nan Britton, a groupie 30 years his junior, whom Harding called his niece when registering at hotels. This affair dated from 1917, when she applied for and was accepted as a stenographer in a corporation that was solicited by Harding.

After Harding became president their trysts continued in a closet near his office. A child, Elizabeth Ann Christian, was born on October 22, 1919. Thereafter, Harding never saw Elizabeth Ann except in photographs. Harding did provide generous child support payments, delivered by Secret Service agents.

After Harding died in 1923 Nan Britton tried, without success, to gain a trust fund for her daughter. Failing that, she wrote *The President's Daughter*. The best-selling book (90,000 copies sold) was "dedicated to all unwed mothers and to their innocent children whose fathers are usually not known to the world."

Considered an otherwise honest man, Harding had difficulty in his administration with mounting evidence of bribery and corruption by his government associates and friends. The infamous Teapot Dome scandal occurred on his watch. Oil reserves in Wyoming were illegally sold by his Secretary of the Interior, Albert Fall, for personal profit. Fall was jailed and fined $350,000. The Buckeye felons became known as the "Ohio Gang."

Harding complained that he had no problems with his enemies, it was his friends who brought him misery.

President Harding died in office on August 2, 1923, at the Palace Hotel in San Francisco. He was on an arduous cross-country tour he called the Voyage of Understanding, an attempt to regain lost favor and explain the curious politics of his administration. The death certificate listed stroke as the reason for Harding's demise, but the rumor that he was poisoned prompted a book, *The Strange Death of President Harding*.

Mrs. Harding refused permission for an autopsy. Florence Harding died less than 15 months after her husband and is buried next to him in Marion.

Of the 41 United States presidents rated in the recent C-SPAN survey, Harding is ranked 38th.

Flora & Fauna JANUARY

WEEK 1

BIRDS: The harshest time of winter has arrived. Keep bird feeders brimming full each day; birds will appreciate handouts at least through late March. High-energy suet at feeders will attract downy, hairy, red-bellied, and possibly pileated woodpeckers. **MAMMALS:** Although the pace of the rut has slackened, the breeding season for deer continues. Fawns conceived in January will still be born in late May, as these embryos will develop more quickly than those conceived in October.

WEEK 2

BIRDS: During the day red-tailed hawks and at night screech owls forage over open fields as their small furry prey disappears beneath the snows of winter. Woe be to the tiny brown mouse that ventures out for "one last look" and is spotted against the white background of snow
MAMMALS: Meadow voles and deer mice welcome the snowy white blanket as they stay safe in their snug tunnels beneath the snowpack until the coming of spring.

WEEK 3

BIRDS: Watch for small flocks of northern cardinals to appear at your feeder. Their normally tightly controlled territories break down as food becomes scarce. **MAMMALS:** Bucks begin to drop their antlers this week. Every year in late winter male deer shed their antlers and grow them back in the spring. Some may hold one or both antlers as late as March, however.

WEEK 4

BIRDS: Tree sparrows may scratc about under bird feeders this week. Watch for a sparrow-sized bird with a rusty cap and unstreaked breast with one central black spot. These birds come from northern Canada to winter in this area. Tufted titmice singing "Peter-Peter!," and the bright "cheer-cheer-cheer!" of cardinals announce their recognition of lengthening days and the first hints of spring. **MAMMALS:** Want to see a deer? CAREFULLY drive north from Rocky River Nature Center on Valley Pkwy. any evening before the snow melts. Best places to look include south of the I-480 bridge and near the river beneath the Lorain Road bridge. NEVER approach a wild deer. These powerful animals can be dangerous if frightened.

Adapted from the Nature Almanac by Robert Hinkle, with permission from Cleveland Metroparks.

FAHRENHEIT/CELSIUS CONVERSION

°F	°C	°F	°C	°F	°C	°F	°C	°F	°C	°F	°C	°F	°C
-20	-29	-2	-19	16	-9	34	1	52	11	70	21	88	31
-19	-28	-1	-18	17	-8	35	2	53	12	71	22	89	32
-18	-28	0	-18	18	-8	36	2	54	12	72	22	90	32
-17	-27	1	-17	19	-7	37	3	55	13	73	23	91	33
-16	-27	2	-17	20	-7	38	3	56	13	74	23	92	33
-15	-26	3	-16	21	-6	39	4	57	14	75	24	93	34
-14	-26	4	-16	22	-6	40	4	58	14	76	24	94	34
-13	-25	5	-15	23	-5	41	5	59	15	77	25	95	35
-12	-24	6	-14	24	-4	42	6	60	16	78	26	96	36
-11	-24	7	-14	25	-4	43	6	61	16	79	26	97	36
-10	-23	8	-13	26	-3	44	7	62	17	80	27	98	37
-9	-23	9	-13	27	-3	45	7	63	17	81	27	99	37
-8	-22	10	-12	28	-2	46	8	64	18	82	28	100	38
-7	-22	11	-12	29	-2	47	8	65	18	83	28	101	38
-6	-21	12	-11	30	-1	48	9	66	19	84	29	102	39
-5	-21	13	-11	31	-1	49	9	67	19	85	29	103	39
-4	-20	14	-10	32	0	50	10	68	20	86	30	104	40
-3	-19	15	-9	33	1	51	11	69	21	87	31		

JAN
FEB
MAR
APR
MAY
JUN
JUL
AUG
SEP
OCT
NOV
DEC

FIRST COUSINS OF
THE SNOWFLAKE

Snow Pellets are also known as soft hail or graupel. These small, white, opaque granules resemble tapioca and often shatter upon striking a hard surface. Snow pellets often precede snowflakes in the Northeast Ohio autumn.

Snow Grains are white, opaque, rice-like particles of ice that neither bounce nor shatter.

Ice Pellets are hard beads of clear or transparent ice (also called sleet). Ice pellets form when rain falls through cold air near the earth's surface; they rebound when hitting a hard surface.

SHOVEL TROUBLE

While some of us take the attitude that the nature that made snow will also take it away, we usually can't wait that long. Each year in the United States, nearly 500 people die from the effects of winter storms, many simply trying to remove snow from walks and driveways.

If snowflakes are more than 90 percent air, why do they weigh so much? That's because millions of snowflakes stack up on each other. If you shovel 15 inches of snow from a sidewalk that is 5 feet wide by 50 feet long, you will have lifted nearly one ton of snow. Shoveling snow is the equivalent of playing a singles tennis match or running at a speed of 9 mph.

Try to spread a light application of melting compound (salt or ice melt) PRIOR to the snowfall. This will help prevent the snow and ice from sticking and will make clearing much easier.

Do not shovel snow if you have high blood pressure, heart disease, or back problems. Do not use a shovel with too short a handle. Use both your arms and legs to lift the snow, and do not twist from the hips (this can injure your back). Do not shovel if you are angry since you are more likely to overexert yourself. Take frequent breaks: shovel 5 minutes, rest 5 minutes. Do not attempt to force snowblowers through difficult drifts.

FEBRUARY STATISTICS

SUNSHINE % 37

DRIEST MONTH . . . . 0.18"/1877

WARMEST MONTH . . . . 37.5°/1930

COLDEST MONTH . . . . 15.8°/1875

LIQUID PCPN AVG. . . . . 2.19"

RAINIEST DAY . . . . 2.33"/1959

RAINIEST MONTH . . . . 7.73"/1887

THUNDERY DAYS 1

SNOWIEST DAY . . . . 14.8"/1993

SNOWIEST MONTH . . . . 39.1"/1993

LEAST SNOWFALL . . . . 0.2"/1998

DAYS ONE INCH SNOW 4

The first two weeks of February are often the coldest of winter. King Winter is on his throne and Northeast Ohio is a still-life painting, a study in frozen motion. On the second day of the month, Ohio's official state groundhog, Buckeye Chuck (he lives in a heated burrow at a radio station in Marion), makes his end-of-winter forecast. No self-respecting meteorological marmot would be above ground at this time of the year; if it were, it would be an amorous boy groundhog looking for you-know-what. Ohio's lowest official temperature came on February 10, 1899, at Milligan, near Zanesville; the temperature may even have been under the observed -39°F reading, since the mercury probably froze (for temperatures that cold, alcohol thermometers are required).

Naturalists tell us that spring in the eastern United States begins during early February deep in the Florida Everglades, then moves northward at a rate of about 15 miles each day. As the frostline moves by, insects emerge from their winter hibernation places and migrant birds follow the movable feast northward. Each day the sun rides a little higher in the sky, and stays a little longer. Insects known as snow fleas (springtails) can be seen doing their circus act in the snow near the base of trees.

DAILY DATA FOR FEBRUARY

Date	Moon Phase	Day	Day of Year	Days Left in Year	Sunrise	Sunset	Length of Day	Avg. Hi	Avg. Lo
1	●	Sat	32	333	7:39	5:42	10:03	32	17
2		Sun	33	332	7:38	5:44	10:06	32	17
3		Mon	34	331	7:37	5:45	10:08	32	17
4		Tue	35	330	7:36	5:46	10:10	32	17
5		Wed	36	329	7:34	5:47	10:13	33	17
6		Thu	37	328	7:33	5:49	10:16	33	18
7		Fri	38	327	7:32	5:50	10:18	33	18
8		Sat	39	326	7:31	5:51	10:20	33	18
9	◑	Sun	40	325	7:30	5:52	10:22	33	18
10		Mon	41	324	7:29	5:54	10:25	34	18
11		Tue	42	323	7:27	5:55	10:28	34	18
12		Wed	43	322	7:26	5:56	10:30	34	18
13		Thu	44	321	7:25	5:57	10:32	34	19
14		Fri	45	320	7:24	5:59	10:35	34	19
15		Sat	46	319	7:22	6:00	10:38	35	19
16	○	Sun	47	318	7:21	6:01	10:40	35	19
17		Mon	48	317	7:19	6:02	10:43	35	20
18		Tue	49	316	7:18	6:04	10:46	36	20
19		Wed	50	315	7:17	6:05	10:48	36	20
20		Thu	51	314	7:15	6:06	10:51	36	20
21		Fri	52	313	7:14	6:07	10:53	37	21
22		Sat	53	312	7:12	6:09	10:57	37	21
23	◐	Sun	54	311	7:11	6:10	10:59	37	21
24		Mon	55	310	7:09	6:11	11:02	38	21
25		Tue	56	309	7:08	6:12	11:04	38	22
26		Wed	57	308	7:06	6:13	11:07	39	22
27		Thu	58	307	7:05	6:15	11:10	39	22
28		Fri	59	306	7:03	6:16	11:13	39	22

JAN FEB MAR APR MAY JUN JUL AUG SEP OCT NOV DEC

Rec. Hi°	Rec. Lo°	Avg. Lake°	On This Date …
59/1989	-6/1971	33	Actor William Clark Gable born in Cadiz (1901)
61/1903	-7/1971	33	Smallest crowd at Cleveland Arena, Cavs vs Golden State: 1,641 (1974)
57/1890	-8/1996	33	Charles Follis, 1st black US football player, born in Shelby, OH (1879)
65/1874	-10/1996	33	Woody Hayes born (1913)
61/1938	-13/1918	33	Cleveland Rockers guard Adrienne Johnson born (1974)
61/1938	-6/1895	33	NBA expands to include Cleveland Cavaliers (1970)
60/1925	-5/1988	33	Cleveland's WVIZ TV channel 25 (PBS) begins broadcasting (1965)
69/1937	-8/1977	33	Largest crowd at Cleve. Coliseum, Cavs vs Wash.: 21,130 (1976)
63/2001	-14/1899	33	47th NBA All-Star Game; East beats West 132–120 at Cleveland (1997)
66/1932	-16/1899	33	-39°F, Milligan, OH (state lowest temperature record) (1899)
73/1932	-15/1885	33	73°F highest temperature ever recorded in Cleveland in Feb. (1932)
68/1999	-9/1917	33	Actor Arsenio Hall born in Cleveland (1959)
68/1938	-9/1995	33	Stark County incorporated (1808)
62/1918	-11/1905	33	Broadcaster Hugh Downs born in Akron (1921)
67/1954	-4/1963	33	1st adhesive postage stamp in U.S. (1842)
72/1883	-8/1904	33	Cavs guard Mark Price born (1964)
62/1911	-7/1885	33	Cleveland Public Library established (1869)
62/1981	-5/1936	33	Author Toni Morrison born in Lorain (1931)
68/1939	-4/1936	33	Congress accepts Ohio's constitution (1856)
69/1930	-3/1968	33	Total eclipse of the Moon (1989)
68/1930	-3/1885	33	WHK-AM in Cleveland OH begins radio transmissions (1922)
72/1930	-8/1963	33	Cleveland Metroparks Zoo's Primate & Cat Building is dedicated (1979)
66/2000	-4/1873	33	Louis Stokes born (1925)
69/1961	-7/1889	33	Dick Goddard born in Akron (1931)
70/1930	-5/1993	33	Actor Jim Backus born in Cleveland (1913)
74/2000	-15/1963	33	Michael Owens of Toledo patents a glass-blowing machine (1895)
66/1996	-10/1863	33	People magazine begins sales (1974)
67/1939	0/1884	33	1st commercial railroad in U.S., Baltimore & Ohio, chartered (1827)

JAN
FEB
MAR
APR
MAY
JUN
JUL
AUG
SEP
OCT
NOV
DEC

Flora & Fauna FEBRUARY

WEEK 1

BIRDS: Chickadees begin to sing their spring songs in earnest this week. Goldfinches return to winter feeders in large flocks. Restock the thistle seed if you can. Great horned owls are already nesting in secret places high atop forest canopies. Imagine them incubating eggs in the winter's cold and snow! **MAMMALS:** First signs of spring bring skunks from their winter sleeping places. Most look quite trim after using much of their body fat reserve during the winter.

WEEK 2

BIRDS: Song sparrows, resplendent in their new brown coats with streaked breasts and a central chocolate spot, begin to reappear at area bird feeders. Most will not begin to sing in earnest for another few weeks. **MAMMALS:** Meadow voles' tunnels under the snow begin to appear as the warmer days "melt the roof off." Their exposed meandering trails in the snow look like snake tracks, giving rise to the old fable of "snow snakes." As temperatures rise above freezing, chipmunks may reappear in search of fresh food. Their underground storehouses of nuts and seeds may be running low! **WILDFLOWERS:** Skunk cabbage, one of the first harbingers of spring, should be blooming in the wetter lowlands of Brecksville, Hinckley, and Rocky River reservations this week.

WEEK 3

BIRDS: "Oka-reee!" Red-winged blackbirds begin to appear in large numbers, one of the first and surest signs of spring. Spring migrating ducks such as buffleheads, goldeneyes, and redheads begin to reappear at Cleveland Metroparks refuges. They are among the first of the waterfowl to follow spring northward as open water slowly becomes available. **MAMMALS:** Breeding seasons for squirrels, raccoons, and skunks begin. **INSECTS:** Mourning cloak butterflies, which overwinter as adults, may reappear on any warm day this month. Their velvety-brown wings tipped with yellow and small blue spots surprise the winter-weary hiker on Cleveland Metroparks trails.

WEEK 4

BIRDS: Forlorn-looking red-winged blackbirds huddle on snow-covered branches as the last of the month's snowstorms catch them by surprise. Look for the red and yellow shoulder patches that distinguish them from all other blackbirds. **TREES:** If days become warm enough and nights stay cold, the maple sugaring season should be in full swing. Watch for acrobatic squirrels licking tasty sap that drips from the ends of broken branches..

Adapted from the Nature Almanac by Robert Hinkle, with permission from Cleveland Metroparks.

SNOWFALL AVERAGES NORTHEAST OHIO

LAST WINTER'S SNOWFALL	
(2001–2002)	
Cleveland Hopkins	46.0"
Akron-Canton	25.6"
Mansfield	32.3"
Youngstown	43.1"
Toledo	19.0"
Chardon	125.0"
Thompson	104.0"
Hambden	77.0"
Erie, PA.	105.0"

BEST OF POLICE BLOTTER

FROM SUN NEWSPAPERS

Each year, *Sun Newspapers* editors round up the more unusual items from their police blotters. These are some of their favorites from Sept. 2001–Aug. 2002.

CHAGRIN FALLS—Mayor Lydia F. Champlin married a Cleveland Heights woman and her groom June 30 in Village Hall. But the $100 wedding fee check bounced the next week. Then it bounced again two weeks ago. The marriage is still legal, but Finance Director David B. Bloom turned the fee collection over to police after the bride's bank officials told him not to resubmit it for payment again because there were insufficient funds to cover it. The bride, 41, told police Friday she would be in Sunday with $100 cash or a bank check, but she never showed up.

BAINBRIDGE—On July 31, a plant caught fire in front of the K-Mart Garden Center, 17825 Chillicothe Road.

CHESTER—Two people, one dressed as a Ninja Turtle and one dressed as a Native American, were creating a disturbance outside Taco Bell–KFC, 8276 Mayfield Road, 7 p.m. May 21. They were asked to leave.

BENTLEYVILLE—Just after 5 p.m. Friday, a Munson man, 47, left the Eagles Aerie on South Main Street. A woman driving a burgundy Infiniti started following him. The Chagrin Falls woman, 58, followed him west on Miles Road so he pulled into Winding River Drive. When she pulled up behind him, he got out of his truck and asked her if there was anything she wanted. "No, I've got what I want," she said, and drove away.

BAINBRIDGE—A West View Drive woman has received hang-up calls for two weeks. When she yelled at the person, he called back and played a tape recording of her yelling at him.

JAN

FEB

MAR

APR

MAY

JUN

JUL

AUG

SEP

OCT

NOV

DEC

GATES MILLS—Stealing flags here and in Mayfield Heights Sept. 5 was not only a crime but unpatriotic. One judge applied the perfect punishment to one of the two thieves. On Sept. 24, an 18-year-old Mayfield High School senior was found guilty of petty theft in Lyndhurst Municipal Court. Judge Mary Kay Bozza sentenced him to wave the American flag in front of the Gates Mills Post Office from 10-11 a.m. every Saturday through Oct. 27. He and a Wickliffe boy, 17, were caught stealing an American flag from an Old Mill Road home. The boy will appear in Cuyahoga County Juvenile Court later this month.

CHAGRIN FALLS—Sunday evening two men visiting the Popcorn Shop, 53 N. Main St., brought their boa constrictors along for the trip. The men sat on a bench outside the shop, each with a 6-foot snake wrapped around his shoulders and body. Alarmed at the sight of the snakes, several passersby called police. The officers said neither the men nor the snakes were violating any laws. The men were spotted earlier outside the Baskin-Robbins ice cream store in the Shopping Plaza. It is not known what ice cream flavors, if any, the snakes consumed at either shop.

PARMA HEIGHTS—A Parma Heights resident called police to report a suspicious man in a blue sweatshirt walking down the street. Police quickly tracked down the suspect—a postal carrier delivering mail. Expect an all-points-bulletin when the Girl Scouts hit the cookie trail.

NORTH RIDGEVILLE—North Ridgeville police were called by employees of the Beckett Group of companies after someone "screwed" and "bolted" with a batch of chili made for a United Way luncheon—literally—by adding screws, bolts, and even a few nuts (the metal kind that hold parts on) in the recipe. Naturally, employees weren't pleased with the secret ingredients, so they canceled the luncheon. Police were investigating and no further reports were found.

FAIRVIEW PARK—A drunken, 30-year-old Fairview Park man confused himself for an ashtray when police asked him to put out his cigarette. In a matter of seconds, the man literally was lit up. Fairview Park police officers came across the plastered pedestrian as he stepped leg over leg along a Lorain Road sidewalk near West 215th Street. Police were about to arrest him for disorderly conduct while intoxicated. Before handcuffing him, they asked him to extinguish his cigarette. He did so—by putting the lit end against his sleeve, and he set his shirt on fire. Officers jumped on him, padding down his arm before he was injured. The pyrotechnic person was carted off to the pokey before he self-combusted.

NORTHFIELD—Having the wrong book in the house caused trouble for a Northfield couple. Police were sent to the residence after someone called 911 and hung up. When they arrived they found the couple fighting. She said she became angry at him after finding a book called *How to Get Rid of Your Girlfriend in 30 Days.*

NORTHFIELD—It all started with chickens. A Northfield woman called police about a neighborhood feud that had been escalating for several days. First, she complained that the neighbor's chickens wandered into her yard. When her daughter tried to return them, the neighbor yelled at the girl, which brought the mother to her aid. The mother and neighbor exchanged words, and the neighbor threw coffee on the mother. The mother's adult son, who witnessed the java toss, threatened to shoot the neighbor between the eyes. A few days later, the neighbor's young son rammed the mother's son with his bike, causing the boy to fall into a ditch. The adult son confronted the neighbor's son. Then the neighbor's husband got in on the action, shoving the adult son and demanding an apology for his wife and son. Police warned both families that such behavior would not be tolerated and the neighbors were told to keep their chickens locked up.

INDEPENDENCE—A St. Louis, MO, man in town to work at a local church borrowed the pastor's car to sample the nightlife in Cleveland's Flats. He invited two women to his Independence hotel room, where he said they stole his wallet, keys, and the pastor's car. The red-faced man was at a loss to explain the situation to the pastor. (Fortunately, the car was recovered the next day.)

The first transcontinental highway that stretched from Times Square in New York City to Lincoln Park in San Francisco was due in large part to two Ohio men who helped develop the plan for the road: Frank Seiberling, president of Goodyear in Akron, and Henry Joy, president of the Packard Motor Car Company, which started in Warren. The Ohio section of the first coast-to-coast highway passed through 11 Ohio counties and seven county seats. Only three original highway markers remain. They can be seen along U.S. Route 30 in East Canton, Mifflin, and near Dalton.

JAN FEB MAR APR MAY JUN JUL AUG SEP OCT NOV DEC

NORTHEAST OHIO
2001 WEATHER YEAR IN REVIEW

AT CLEVELAND HOPKINS AIRPORT:

Average high: 59.7°, which is 1.3° above normal

Average low: 43.3°, 2.8° above normal

Average temperature: 51.5°, 1.7° above normal

Warmest day: 94° on August 8

Coldest day: 7° on January 2 and 9

Record highs: 63° on Feb 9, 80° on April 8, 82° on April 12, 71° on Dec 5

Record lows: none

Precipitation: 34.36", 2.27" below normal

Peak wind: 53 MPH from the west on Feb 9 and 53 MPH from the west on Oct 25

HIGHLIGHTS:

Second warmest November on record with an average temperature of 48.8°. The warmest is 51.2° in 1931.

Driest July on record with 0.68".

Eighth wettest October on record with 5.56". The wettest is 9.50" in 1954.

Snowiest March on record with 26.7".

Tenth snowiest October on record with 1.0". The snowiest is 8.0" in 1962.

AT AKRON/CANTON AIRPORT:

Average high: 59.9°, which is 0.8° above normal

Average low: 41.9°, 1.6° above normal

Average temperature: 50.9°, 1.2° above normal

Warmest day: 95° on Aug 8 and 9

Coldest day: 3° on Jan 9

Record highs: 80° on April 8, 69° on Dec 5

Record lows: none

Precipitation: total 32.90", 3.92" below normal

Peak wind: 56 MPH from the west on Feb 9

HIGHLIGHTS:

Second warmest November on record with an average temperature of 48.8°. The warmest is 51.2° in 1931.

Third driest July on record with 1.18". The driest is 0.67" in 1991.

Second least snowiest November on record with a trace of snow. The least snowy is 0.0" in 1946.

Ninth least snowy December on record with 1.6". The least snowy is 0.0" in 1931.

AT MANSFIELD AIRPORT:

Average high: 59.6°, which is 0.9° above normal

Average low: 41.7°, 1.3° above normal

Average temperature: 50.7°, 1.2° above normal

Warmest day: 92° on July 24

Coldest day: 2° on Jan 9

Record highs: 57° on Feb 8, 61° on Feb 9, 80° on April 8, 80° on April 9, 80° on May 2, 82° on May 3, 81° on May 4, 91° on July 23, 91° on Aug 1, 63° on Nov 24, 68° on Dec 5

Record lows: none

Precipitation: total 33.99", 5.66" below normal

Peak wind: 54 MPH from the southwest on Feb 25

HIGHLIGHTS:

Sixth coldest March on record at 33.3°. The coldest is 23.9° in 1960.

Fourth warmest April on record at 52.3°. The warmest is 54.4° in 1985.

Warmest November on record at 47.6°.

Sixth warmest December on record at 34.0°. The warmest is 39.4° in 1982.

Eighth warmest year on record at 50.7°. The warmest is 53.0° in 1973.

Seventh driest March on record with 1.72". The driest is 1.16" in 1960.

Third driest July on record with 1.05". The driest is 0.65" in 1960.

Second least snowy February on record with 2.2". The least snowy is 0.2" in 1998.

Eighth snowiest March on record with 12.3". The snowiest is 17.1" in 1993.

Least snowy November on record with 0.0".

AT YOUNGSTOWN AIRPORT:

Average high: 60.1°, which is 2.4° above normal

Average low: 40.9°, 2.0° above normal

Average temperature: 50.5°, 2.2° above normal

Warmest day: 95° on Aug 8

Coldest day: 8° on Jan 3 and 9

Record highs: 57° on Feb 8, 62° on Feb 9, 81 on April 7, 81° on April 8, 83° on April 12, 84° on May 3, 90° on Aug 6, 93° on Aug 7, 95° on Aug 8, 65° on Nov 24, 71° on Dec 5

Record lows: 34° on May 31, 40° on July 2, 50° on July 14

Precipitation: total 29.40", 7.92" below normal. Fourth driest year on record.

Peak wind: 54 MPH from the southwest on April 12.

HIGHLIGHTS:

Seventh warmest April on record at 51.2°. The warmest is 53.6° in 1955.

Warmest November on record at 47.7°.

Eighth warmest December

on record at 34.6°. The warmest is 40.3° in 1982.

Seventh warmest year on record at 50.5°. The warmest is 52.1° in 1998.

Sixth driest June on record with 1.89". The driest is 0.71" in 1988.

Fourth driest year on record with 29.40". The driest is 23.79" in 1963.

Tenth least snowy February on record with 6.2". The least snowy is a trace in 1998.

Seventh snowiest October on record with 1.6". The snowiest is 7.7" in 1993.

Fifth least snowy November on record with 0.3". The least snowy is a trace in 1985.

Second least snowy December on record with 2.4". The least snowy is 1.4" in 1943.

The first successful blood transfusion was performed in Cleveland in 1905 by Dr. George Crile, co-founder Cleveland Clinic Foundation.

JAN FEB MAR APR MAY JUN JUL AUG SEP OCT NOV DEC

OHIO'S MAGNIFICENT SEVEN

WILLIAM HOWARD TAFT
27th PRESIDENT 1909-1913

Dick Goddard

William Howard Taft was born not only with a silver spoon in his mouth, but with a fork and knife as well. At 332 pounds he was our heaviest president.

Taft was born at the family home in the affluent Mount Auburn section of Cincinnati. His close friends called him Will, but because of his dimensions he also went by the nickname Big Lub.

At six feet, two inches, Taft weighed 243 pounds in college, before his avoirdupois ballooned while in the White House. Taft lived in an age when being overweight was viewed as a symbol of success—and he was an exemplar of achievement. Taft's motto must have been "Hail to the Chef." He endured national embarrassment when his girth caused him to become stuck in the White House bathtub. A larger vessel was quickly ordered.

In his relatively svelte youth, Taft was very athletic and was an avid baseball player, playing second base. All agreed that he was not a good runner, but he was a good fielder who hit with power. Taft was the first president to take up golf, and he was the first chief executive to throw out the first pitch on major league baseball's opening day. As the president stood up to leave during the middle of the seventh inning, the entire crowd took notice and also stood in respect. That, say some baseball historians, was the beginning of the traditional seventh-inning stretch.

When Big Lub wasn't playing sports, his main task was acting as referee in fights between his brothers. (His siblings were two half-brothers, two brothers, and one sister.)

Taft was affable and friendly, and with his sunny disposition he accumulated many friends and was extremely popular. He loved jokes, and his soft, high-pitched voice frequently gave way to chuckles and bursts of laughter.

At the age of 28, Taft married 25-year-old Helen (Nellie) Herron of Cincinnati. She was the first First Lady to ride with her husband down Pennsylvania Avenue (a role previously taken by the outgoing president). Suffering a stroke just two months after entering the White House in 1909, she was thereafter speech-impaired. Nellie's most lasting contribution was overseeing the planting of 3,000 Japanese cherry trees around the Washington Tidal Basin.

The President and the First Lady were divided about Prohibition. Taft was a "Dry," Nellie a "Wet."

Taft was a Unitarian, believing in God and the humane tenets of the Christian creed, but not in the divinity of Christ. He was a staunch advocate for the rights of African-Americans.

Taft saw no military service. Our 27th president graduated from law school at the University of Cincinnati, and was second in his graduating class at Yale. He practiced law in Cincinnati.

Taft said that politics made him sick, and his main interest was in the judiciary. He served on the Ohio Superior Court in 1887 before becoming the first civil governor of the Philippines.

President Theodore Roosevelt and Taft became great friends and "TR" encouraged him to run for the presidency in 1908. Ironically, six years earlier Taft had made the statement "I have no ambition to be president and any party that would nominate me would make a great mistake."

Taft, who had served as secretary of war under Roosevelt, reluctantly ran for president against perennial candidate William Jennings Bryan. For the third time Bryan lost the national election to an Ohioan.

JAN FEB MAR APR MAY JUN JUL AUG SEP OCT NOV DEC

Taft's only term as president was turbulent and he lamented his election to the job, complaining that being chief executive was "the most lonesome job in the world." Taft had few intimates, and he faced each crisis alone.

After Taft's four-year presidency he and Roosevelt became estranged over economic and environmental policies. (Roosevelt was a puzzle: he seemed bent on shooting every wild animal that ever lived, yet would not allow a Christmas tree in the White House.) It was the split between Taft and Roosevelt that allowed the Democrats to elect Woodrow Wilson in 1912.

Eight years after leaving the presidency, Taft reached his lifetime goal by becoming the first and only chief executive to also be appointed Chief Justice of the Supreme Court. Taft regained his former good spirits and happily served until his death in 1930 of congestive heart failure.

Nellie Taft died in 1943 and is buried next to her husband at Arlington National Cemetery. The grave is near the final resting place of Robert Todd Lincoln, the son of Abraham Lincoln.

Taft and John F. Kennedy are the only United States presidents buried at Arlington.

Of the 41 United States presidents rated in the recent C-SPAN survey, William Howard Taft is ranked 24th.

POPULARITY RANKING OF U.S. PRESIDENTS

1. Abraham Lincoln (1861–65)
2. Franklin Roosevelt (1933–45)
3. George Washington (1789–97)
4. Theodore Roosevelt (1901–09)
5. Harry Truman (1945–53)
6. Woodrow Wilson (1913–21)
7. Thomas Jefferson (1801–09)
8. John Kennedy (1961–63)
9. Dwight Eisenhower (1953–61)
10. Lyndon Johnson (1963–69)
11. Ronald Reagan (1981–89)
12. James Polk (1845–49)
13. Andrew Jackson (1829–37)
14. James Monroe (1817–25)
15. William McKinley (1897–1901)
16. John Adams (1797–1801)
17. Grover Cleveland (1885–89, 1893–97)
18. James Madison (1809–17)
19. John Quincy Adams (1825–29)
20. George Bush (1989–93)
21. Bill Clinton (1993–2001)
22. Jimmy Carter (1977–81)
23. Gerald Ford (1974–77)
24. William Howard Taft (1909–13)
25. Richard Nixon (1969–74)
26. Rutherford B. Hayes (1877–81)
27. Calvin Coolidge (1923–29)
28. Zachary Taylor (1849–50)
29. James Garfield (1881)
30. Martin Van Buren (1837–41)
31. Benjamin Harrison (1889–93)
32. Chester Arthur (1881–85)
33. Ulysses S. Grant (1869–77)
34. Herbert Hoover (1929–33)
35. Millard Fillmore (1850–53)
36. John Tyler (1841–45)
37. William Henry Harrison (1841)
38. Warren Harding (1921–23)
39. Franklin Pierce (1853–57)
40. Andrew Johnson (1865–69)
41. James Buchanan (1857–61)

Rated by 58 historians in a C-SPAN survey.

POOP PATROL

by Big Chuck Schodowski

The year was 1960. I was married, with two sons, and living in a three-family home in Cleveland. This was the year I left the foundry and began working at (WJW) TV8 as an engineer. Two years later, the famed "booth announcer," Ernie Anderson, came over from (then) KYW-TV Channel 3 . . . and we became very good friends.

In October of 1962, now with a baby daughter added to my family, I bought my first home. It was a typical small six-room bungalow on a tiny lot in Parma. But it was home, and for me, no home is complete without a dog. So, I let it be known at TV8 that I was looking for a puppy—one that wouldn't get too large, since I had a small yard.

JAN FEB MAR APR MAY JUN JUL AUG SEP OCT NOV DEC

In a few weeks, Ernie called me and said, "I have a puppy for you."

"Oh great," I said. "What kind is it?"

"It's a Rhodesian ridgeback," he said.

"I never heard of them," I said.

"No one has," he said. "They're a very rare and beautiful breed of dog. They're reddish-brown hounds with very short hair, much like my Weimaraners."

"Whoa," I said. "Wait a minute. Your Weimaraners are big dogs. How big will this puppy get?"

Ernie paused, and said, "They're a very sound dog."

Now, I had never heard the word "sound" used to describe anything before. Ernie being from the East Coast, I thought perhaps this was some kind of nautical New England expression. But to me, the word "sound" sounded like it could mean "big." So I reminded him my home was a small Parma bungalow on a tiny lot, and I asked him, "How big is a 'sound' dog?"

He got a little upset and said, "Don't worry about it . . . trust me!"

When our puppy was five months old, he weighed 85 pounds. His name was "Rowdy." When Rowdy matured, about two years later, he was the most handsome 120-pound dog you ever saw, and we loved him dearly.

Our home was near State Road Park in Parma, and at least once every day I faithfully walked him to the park and let him run through the woods to get his exercise and "do his business." When I wasn't home, my wife, June, would let Rowdy out into our backyard to "do his business." Now, for this "backyard business" I assigned my sons Mike and Mark a responsibility that I gave an exciting name to: Poop Patrol. Each day they would patrol the backyard for poop, pick it up, and put it in a bucket, and each day when I took Rowdy to run in the park, I took the bucket and emptied it into the woods, where it would "biodegrade" along with all the other wild animal poop there. Life was good—it was possible to have a big dog and live in a small home in Parma. My family and I were in total harmony with nature.

He was the most handsome 120-pound dog you ever saw.

In 1963, Ernie Anderson began his legendary Ghoulardi show, and he started using me in a lot of his skits—usually in a hero-type role. I became very recognizable and somewhat of an idol to kids. Ernie dubbed me "Big Chuck." Even though I played Big Chuck on TV, I was still a full-time engineer at TV8, and being relatively low on the seniority list, I was still rotating all three work shifts.

Early one winter night, I was working the 4 to midnight shift, "switching" the 6 and 11 p.m. news shows. That night our newfound weatherman, Dick Goddard, predicted that we were in for frequent snow for quite a while, and, as usual, he was right. It snowed every day for a week. Then I started working the midnight to 8 a.m. shift. At suppertime one evening my sons informed me that poop patrol had been postponed for several days; because of all the snow, they could not locate Rowdy's daily deposits. I said, "Don't worry about it, this is just a temporary problem." However, the snow continued to fall almost every day for five or six weeks. It was never enough to cause problems—but it was enough to keep us shoveling our walks, building snowmen on the front lawn, and sledding in State Road Park. Poop patrol had become a thing of the past.

About this time Dick Goddard gave us a new "weather term" to add to our vocabulary—the "February Thaw." He predicted unusually high temperatures for perhaps a week. But he also warned us not to think spring was here, because we would return to our cold Cleveland winter after the thaw.

That morning, as I drove home from the station at about 8:30 a.m., the air was noticeably warm, the sun was out, and birds were singing. Once again, Dick was right on target.

When I got home, I ate breakfast and went to bed. When I got up about suppertime, my sons told me that the snow in the street had melted and asked if we could throw the football around after supper, before it got dark. So we did. It was a pleasant preview of things to come. Then, my sons did their homework, watched a little TV, and went to bed. I took Rowdy for his walk, watched a little TV with my wife, made my lunch, and went to work.

As I drove home from TV8 the next morning, it was even warmer, almost 70 degrees. The birds were really singing, the Parma streets were filled with the sounds of running water in the sewers, I thought "more football in the street after school," and I went to sleep with a smile on my face.

At about 2:30 p.m. my wife woke me up. I knew something was wrong. She said, "We have a big problem—you won't believe our backyard!" I looked out the back window, and what to my wondering

JAN FEB MAR APR MAY JUN JUL AUG SEP OCT NOV DEC

eyes should appear? At least one big pile of poop in every square foot of our backyard. The snow had just about all melted, and it was still getting warmer. My wife was in a panic. "You'd better get that cleaned up before the neighbors see it," she said. "Hurry! Before it starts to smell!"

I hurried to get dressed—in just minutes I was in the backyard, shovel in hand, surveying the monumental task I had to do A.S.A.P.

I got a big, sturdy cardboard box I was saving in the garage and began filling it with poop. When my kids came home from school, I said, "Hurry and change your clothes, get out here and help me! No one eats supper until we're done." About two hours later, we finished the gruesome job, and the big cardboard box was filled to the top.

My sons went in to clean up for supper, and I stood there, looking at the box and wondering, "What the hell am I going to do with this?" I couldn't leave it for the rubbish men; they'd kill me. I thought of flushing it down the street sewer with a hose, but there was too much for that. So I decided to put the box, a shovel, and a flashlight in the trunk of my car. (I could barely lift the box into my trunk.) Later that night, I would leave for work an hour early, take the box into the woods of State Road Park, scatter the poop over a large area, chop up the box with the shovel, go to work, and no one would be any the wiser.

About 10 p.m., my family went to bed, and I set out on my mission. The sky was overcast and the park was unusually dark. It was perfect. Or so I thought. As I drove slowly through the park, I passed a squad car with two of "Parma's finest" eyeing me suspiciously. They turned around and began to follow me. "Damn," I thought. "No way can I do it now."

I left the park. The police car stayed at the park entrance. I decided not to risk another pass through the park, and I went to work an hour early.

Late that night, it got very cold and started to snow. Goddard was right again. As I was leaving the station at 8 a.m., our morning news bulletins were warning people of the hazardous driving conditions for that morning's rush hour. It took me a while to get home. It snowed all day and all evening. I had to shovel the drive that night to get out to go to work. It snowed frequently for the next three weeks or so, and you got it—I forgot about the box of poop in my trunk.

Then spring had sprung. The weather really warmed up, and the snow was rapidly melting. It was a Saturday morning, and I had the day off. June asked me to do the grocery shopping. I drove to the shopping center at Snow and Broadview roads, went to Food Town, and bought four bags of groceries.

The bag boy recognized me. I never saw such a look of admiration on anyone's face in my life. He couldn't tell me enough about how much he enjoyed watching me on TV, and how he and his friends never missed the Friday-night show. He helped me carry the bags to my car and asked me for my autograph. I said, "Okay. Let me put the bags in my trunk first." I fumbled with the two bags I was carrying and got my car keys out of my pocket. Stooping and hunched over, I opened the

Confronting me was the Mother of all Poop Piles.

trunk. As the trunk lid opened fully, a piercing odor stung my nose. I jerked back, my head hit the trunk lid, my eyes began to water—I couldn't believe what I saw. Confronting me was the Mother of all Poop Piles. The cardboard box had disintegrated, every square inch of the bottom of the trunk was covered with dog poop, and there, in the middle, was a shovel handle sticking out.

The bag boy tried to muffle a gagging cough. His look of admiration for his hero, Big Chuck, had turned to the frightened stare of someone looking at Hannibal Lecter! He put the bags on the ground and quickly stepped backwards.

"Wait!" I shouted. "I can explain."

"Ugh—that's . . . that's all right," he said, still walking backwards.

I started walking towards him. "Wait," I said again. "Uh, here's your tip."

"No, that's okay," he said, breaking into a sideways run.

At first I wanted to run after him, but I thought that would really freak him out. As I stood there watching him run back into the store I knew that somehow I must explain this incident to him or it would always trouble me, as I wondered what he must think of his hero, Big Chuck, who has a poop fetish.

I went back to the store a few times over the next couple weeks hoping to run into him, but I never did. To this day I sometimes think of this incident. And I wonder if when he sees me on TV he thinks of it too.

I've been living in Hinckley for over 30 years now. I have an acre of lawn now, and I still have a big ridgeback—Buddy, my fifth one. I still pick up dog poop, but I don't throw it into the woods anymore—I have a "Doggie Septic System." I figure the bag boy must be about 50 years old now. I sure hope that somehow he reads this essay, or hears about it, and will no longer wonder if Big Chuck is riding around Parma with a trunk full.

You see—I'm okay; you're okay.

Sleep well, my friend, and I will too.

"Big Chuck" Schodowski is the popular co-host of the Emmy Award-winning *Big Chuck & Lil John Show* seen Fridays at 11:30 p.m. and Saturday afternoons on FOX 8. For more than 35 years, he has written, produced, and starred in hundreds of comedy skits that remain local television favorites.

STORM SAFETY — *Ice*

Be wary of a lake or pond with heavy snow cover, as the ice underneath could be weak. New ice is stronger than old, and ice that turns to a darker shade of gray is thinning. Always test before you step onto ice. Toss a large rock onto the ice surface to determine support. Eskimos carry ice chisels and thump the ice frequently, remembering that "when ice cracks it will bear, when ice bends it will break."

ICE SAFETY TIPS:

1. Pond ice one or two inches thick is not considered safe for skating or winter sports. A three-inch layer of clear, firm ice is safe for one person.

2. Four inches will support a small group of people placed several feet apart. This thickness will also support snowmobiles, if spaced at 33-foot intervals.

JAN FEB MAR APR MAY JUN JUL AUG SEP OCT NOV DEC

Spring

In Ohio, the first day of spring is one thing, the first spring day another. Buckeye folklore says that spring doesn't really arrive until you can step on five dandelions with one foot (without using a snowshoe).

NORTHEAST OHIO'S WARMEST AND COLDEST SPRINGS
(by Median Temp)

....

WARMEST

Cleveland: 53.4° / 1991

Akron/Canton: 55.1° / 1991

....

COLDEST

Cleveland: 41.3° / 1885

Akron/Canton: 43.5° / 1926

Spring in Ohio comes in fits and starts, and true spring does not embrace most of the state until mid to late April. A late spring is not always undesirable at our latitude, because it retards any premature burgeoning of buds and tender plants that then succumb to frosty nights in May.

During March, the Ohio soil begins to warm under the lengthening, strengthening sunshine, and by month's end the first real signs of nature's rebirth are evident.

April has been called the cruelest month, the month of fools, and we all know what Ohio's April showers bring. That's right—doubleheaders in August!

While the month of May will have some meteorological disappointments for us—gutsy thunderstorms and some unseasonably chilly days—the fragrance of lilacs and apple blossoms assures us of the fruitful season just ahead.

Mid-spring produces Ohio's most fitful and chaotic weather of the year. There is a continual parade of weather fronts through the state. Onrushing warm and humid air from the Gulf of Mexico often collides with cool Pacific Ocean air directly over our state, resulting in frequent severe thunderstorm and tornado watches. Nearly 70 percent of all Ohio tornadoes have occurred during the spring season.

IN THE
✴ Northeast Ohio Sky ✴
THIS SEASON

URSA MINOR   POLARIS

BOOTES   URSA MAJOR

ARCTURUS

REGULUS ✴

Spring

In spring that childhood favorite, the Big Dipper (Ursa Major, the Great Bear), is almost directly overhead in the Northeast Ohio sky.

Rising in the east is the constellation Bootes (boo-OO-tees), called the Herdsman for no obvious reason. The lowest star in Bootes is the orange-yellow Arcturus (arc-TO-russ), the second-brightest star in the Ohio sky (do not confuse stars with the bright planets Venus, Mars, Jupiter, or Saturn that masquerade as stars).

To the lower right is the blue-white royal star, Regulus (REG-you-luss), the Little King.

On a late-spring night try to find Zubenelgenubi (zoo-BEN-el-je-NEW-be) low in the southern sky. Nothing special, I just like the name.

MARCH STATISTICS

SUNSHINE %	45
DRIEST MONTH	0.41"/1910
WARMEST MONTH	49.5°/1946
COLDEST MONTH	24.0°/1960
LIQUID PCPN AVG.	2.91"
RAINIEST DAY	2.76"/1848
RAINIEST MONTH	8.31"/1913
THUNDERY DAYS	2
SNOWIEST DAY	16.4"/1987
SNOWIEST MONTH	26.3"/1954
LEAST SNOWFALL	Trace/1927
DAYS ONE INCH SNOW	3

The winds of March that make your heart a dancer have occasionally brought record amounts of snow with them. On March 30–31, 1987, Cleveland received its second-heaviest 24-hour snowfall, 16.4 inches. Several days later the Akron/Canton area was buried under a record 20.6 inches. Curiously, many of Northeast Ohio's monumental snowfalls have come in November and March, on either side of what is officially winter. Snows in March are usually very wet and hard to shovel, but the crystals melt quickly. March is the month of reawakening, and on mild nights the tiny tree frogs known as spring peepers begin their vernal concerts.

Spring, the vernal equinox, arrives on the 20th of the month; this is one of only two times each year that our sun rises due east and sets due west. We now enjoy three more hours of daylight than we did in dark December, and we'll gain another three hours by the summer solstice in June.

DAILY DATA FOR MARCH

Date	Moon Phase	Day	Day of Year	Days Left in Year	Sunrise	Sunset	Length of Day	Avg. Hi	Avg. Lo
1		Sat	60	305	7:02	6:17	11:15	46	23
2	●	Sun	61	304	7:00	6:18	11:18	40	24
3		Mon	62	303	6:59	6:19	11:20	41	24
4		Tue	63	302	6:57	6:20	11:23	41	24
5		Wed	64	301	6:55	6:22	11:27	42	25
6		Thu	65	300	6:54	6:23	11:29	42	25
7		Fri	66	299	6:52	6:24	11:32	43	25
8		Sat	67	298	6:51	6:25	11:34	43	26
9		Sun	68	297	6:49	6:26	11:37	43	26
10		Mon	69	296	6:47	6:27	11:40	44	26
11	◐	Tue	70	295	6:46	6:28	11:42	44	27
12		Wed	71	294	6:44	6:30	11:46	45	27
13		Thu	72	293	6:42	6:31	11:49	45	27
14		Fri	73	292	6:41	6:32	11:51	46	28
15		Sat	74	291	6:39	6:33	11:54	46	28
16		Sun	75	290	6:37	6:34	11:57	46	28
17		Mon	76	289	6:36	6:35	11:59	47	29
18	○	Tue	77	288	6:34	6:36	12:02	47	29
19		Wed	78	287	6:32	6:37	12:05	48	29
20		Thu	79	286	6:31	6:38	12:07	48	30
21		Fri	80	285	6:29	6:40	12:11	48	30
22		Sat	81	284	6:27	6:41	12:14	49	30
23		Sun	82	283	6:26	6:42	12:16	49	30
24	◑	Mon	83	282	6:24	6:43	12:19	50	31
25		Tue	84	281	6:22	6:44	12:22	50	31
26		Wed	85	280	6:20	6:45	12:25	50	31
27		Thu	86	279	6:19	6:46	12:27	51	32
28		Fri	87	278	6:17	6:47	12:30	51	32
29		Sat	88	277	6:15	6:48	12:33	52	32
30		Sun	89	276	6:14	6:49	12:35	52	32
31		Mon	90	275	6:12	6:50	12:38	52	33

JAN FEB MAR APR MAY JUN JUL AUG SEP OCT NOV DEC

Rec. Hi °	Rec. Lo °	Avg. Lake °	On This Date ...
69/1912	-2/1984	34	Ohio becomes 17th state (1803)
64/1991	-4/1978	34	Cavaliers win 22nd straight home game (1989)
74/1974	2/1984	34	Summit County incorporated (1840)
76/1983	2/1943	34	Collinwood School fire (1908)
81/1983	-2/1873	34	U.S. rocket flies record 4800 KPH to 126k height (1948)
74/1973	-2/1960	34	Lake County incorporated (1840)
76/2000	3/1960	34	Huron County incorporated (1809)
79/2000	-1/1960	34	WFMJ TV 21 in Youngstown OH (NBC) begins broadcasting (1953)
73/1878	-5/1984	34	Cleveland Spiders sign Louis Sockalexis (1897)
72/1973	5/1983	34	Harry Gammeter of Cleve. patents multigraph duplicating machine (1903)
73/1973	-3/1983	34	President & Chief Justice William Taft buried in Arlington (1930)
75/1990	-5/1948	34	1st branch of Cleveland Public Library system opens on Pearl St. (1892)
76/1990	3/1960	34	Band leader Sammy Kaye born in Cleveland (1913)
79/1990	6/1993	34	1st American town meeting (1743)
80/1990	3/1993	35	Buzzards first appear at Hinckley (1881)
78/1945	7/1885	35	Erie County incorporated (1838)
72/1945	0/1900	35	It is announced there is no smoking in Jacobs Field (1994)
75/1903	0/1877	35	WGSF TV channel 31 in Newark OH (PBS) begins broadcasting (1963)
76/1903	7/1885	35	Indians reject Boston's offer of $1 million for Herb Score (1957)
76/1995	0/1885	35	Harriet Beecher Stowe's *Uncle Tom's Cabin* published (1852)
76/1938	-4/1885	35	Moon Dog Coronation Ball (1st rock and roll concert) (1952)
83/1938	0/1885	36	Indians players Steve Olin and Tim Crews killed in accident (1993)
77/1966	5/1885	36	Draper takes 1st successful photo of the Moon (daguerrotype) (1840)
83/1910	8/1888	36	83°F highest temperature ever recorded in Cleveland in March (1910)
83/1945	8/1888	36	Musician Michael Stanley born (1948)
80/1967	14/2001	36	Dayton almost destroyed by flood stage simultaneously (1913)
80/1989	12/1982	36	Morman temple at Kirtland dedicated (1836)
80/1945	9/1982	36	Ohio passed law restricting movement of Blacks (1804)
81/1910	11/1887	36	Notorious gangster Alex "Shondor" Birns blown up in his car (1975)
82/1986	16/1987	37	15th Amendment passes, guarantees right to vote regardless of race (1870)
77/1943	11/1923	37	Cavaliers clinch their 1st ever NBA playoff berth (1976)

JAN FEB MAR APR MAY JUN JUL AUG SEP OCT NOV DEC

JAN FEB MAR APR MAY JUN JUL AUG SEP OCT NOV DEC

Flora & Fauna — MARCH

WEEK 1

BIRDS: Bluebirds may have returned to Hinckley Reservation by now if the winter has not been too harsh and cold. Early migrating robins feed among the holly berries and crab apples.
MAMMALS: All but a few of the bucks in Cleveland Metroparks have lost their antlers. It becomes hard to tell male from female deer until the bucks begin to regrow their antlers in early May.
WILDFLOWERS: Pungent skunk cabbage begins to bloom in low wet places in Cleveland Metroparks valleys. The hooded flower pokes its head up through ice to attract early spring insects.

WEEK 2

BIRDS: Great blue herons reappear as soon as open water makes fish available for them to eat. They first reappear along Cleveland Metroparks rivers, but quickly move to lakes and ponds as soon as the shore ice melts. The song sparrow, one of the first and most vocal of the spring sparrows, should have arrived by now. The male's calls begin with three sharp notes, then blur into a melodious trill. **WILDFLOWERS:** Colorful wildflowers at last! The dandelion-like blossoms of the coltsfoot may even poke their determined heads through the snow to bloom. They prefer recently disturbed soils as blooming places. Watch for them along road cuts and construction sites.

WEEK 3

BIRDS: The first of the migrating woodcocks may begin their spring mating flights in certain secret places this week. Watch the nature centers' program listings and join a naturalist in April to view this spectacle. The buzzards are back! On March 15, the buzzards (turkey vultures) return to Hinckley. Visit the famous "buzzard roost" on the first Sunday after March 15 and watch for the newly arrived migrants. **MAMMALS:** Female woodchucks have awakened to greet the males who awakened in February. Spring comes quickly and summer is only a few weeks away! The rapid changes of April give way to a slower and more stately procession of nature as May begins.

WEEK 4

BIRDS: The phoebe's raspy "fee-bree" call reassures forest hikers that spring is truly here. Male goldfinches grow progressively more brilliant yellow each week. Set out fresh thistle seed for them. Golden-crowned kinglets return to Cleveland Metroparks on their way northward to Canada. Only half the size of chickadees, they flit continuously from branch to branch in search of food. **AMPHIBIANS:** Spring peepers "peep" and wood frogs "quack" as their spring mating cycle begins. Shallow temporary ponds in Big Creek, Brecksville, Mill Stream Run, and North Chagrin reservations are home to these small frogs for only a few days each spring as mates are found and eggs are laid.

Adapted from the Nature Almanac by Robert Hinkle, with permission from Cleveland Metroparks.

24-HOUR RAINFALL RECORDS

CITY	AMOUNT	DATE
Toledo	5.98"	September 4, 1918
Akron/Canton	5.96"	July 7, 1943
Cincinnati	5.22"	March 12, 1907
Mansfield	5.06"	July 4, 1969
Cleveland	4.97"	September 1, 1901
Columbus	4.81"	January 20, 1959
Dayton	4.75"	April 12, 1886
Youngstown	4.31"	October 15, 1954

NORTHEAST OHIO'S WETTEST AND DRIEST SPRINGS

(Rainfall)

WETTEST

Cleveland: 16.33" / 1989

Akron/Canton: 18.18" / 1964

DRIEST

Cleveland: 4.45" / 1895

Akron/Canton: 4.19" / 1915

THOU KNOWEST THOU CAN TRUST OUR KING ARTHUR ACCOUNTANTS!

The Ohio Country Myth

Dick Goddard

No one knows how the Ohio Country Myth was born, but flowing tankards of ale on cruel, frigid winter nights in New England no doubt played a large part in fueling the wild speculation.

It was the late 1700s, and the intriguing story was that just over the snow-covered mountains west of New England lay a bountiful land of milk and honey whose weather was so mild and benevolent that ice and frost were almost total strangers. This 18th-century version of

Camelot was known as Ohio Country, and the land was there for those who were ambitious and adventurous enough to pack up and claim it for a modest fee. The goal of those who decided to take on the challenge was, basically, quick wealth. How could they go wrong in an uncharted land where, it was rumored, "plants yielded ready-made candles and trees spontaneously produced sugar."

One brochure describing the Ohio Country read as follows: "A climate wholesome and delightful with frost even in winter almost entirely unknown, and a river called, by way of eminence, the beautiful, and abounding in excellent fish of vast size. Venison in plenty, the pursuit of which is uninterrupted by wolves, foxes, lions, or tigers. A couple of swine will multiply themselves a hundred-fold in two years without taking any care of them."

Unfortunately, it didn't take long for those who crossed the Appalachian Mountains to the Ohio Country to be disabused of their optimism.

Somehow overlooked in the glowing prospectus was the imminent danger of attack by Indians along with the threat of injury or death from an assortment of crawling and leaping indigenous creatures (I will grant that—to my knowledge—free-roaming lions have never been a problem in Ohio).

The plentiful wildlife included the much-feared cougar, plus deer, bear, elk, beaver, muskrat, and turkey. The raccoon was a favored hunting target and food source for both the Indians and settlers. This clever animal with its bandit's mask is still abundant in Ohio, as our tipped-over garbage cans demonstrate. Ohio's Geauga County was named for this mammal (the Indian name for raccoon being "sheauga").

Other creatures the Ohio Country pioneers faced were poisonous serpents. Copperhead snakes abounded, with their nasty penchant for living near human dwellings.

Rattlesnakes pervaded the Lake Erie islands north of Sandusky, basking on lily pads in the shimmering summer sunshine. Trappers warned others not to set foot on the islands.

To the early settlers' dismay, Ohio winters were just as harsh and snowy as those in New England. Often, more so. But, there certainly was an abundance of flora and fauna. The Ohio Country in the 1700s was 95 percent forest. It would have been possible for an imaginative and agile squirrel to climb a tree along the Lake Erie shore and travel all the way to the Ohio River without touching the ground.

Since trees return a tremendous amount of water to the air via a process called transpiration (a large oak tree can contribute 50 gallons each day), Ohio summers in those days must have been incredibly humid. The rising moisture in the atmosphere would have also fomented rain and thunderstorms

> **TO THE EARLY SETTLERS' DISMAY, OHIO WINTERS WERE JUST AS HARSH AND SNOWY AS THOSE IN NEW ENGLAND. OFTEN, MORE SO.**

(the legendary Burlington tornado of 1825 wiped out whole forests and may have been the strongest twister ever to strike Ohio).

Add malaria, yellow fever, cholera, and dysentery to the litany of problems, and you can understand why the Ohio Country Myth was called by one early naturalist "a vulgar error."

In the 1700s the Ohio Country was home to a number of Indian tribes, and most were hostile to the invaders from the east. The Shawnee of southern Ohio, led by their great chief, Tecumseh, were particularly forceful in delaying the settlers' advance. The northeast portion of the Ohio territory was part of an Indian no-man's-land; the Erie tribe had been all but annihilated in 1655 by their cousins to the east, the five-nation confederation known as the Iroquois.

Defying the prospect of Indian attacks, the first permanent settlement in Ohio was established in Marietta, in the extreme southeastern portion of the state, in April of 1788. These pioneers were primarily from Massachusetts, and they called their organization the Ohio Land Company. Concurrently, the state of Connecticut had domain over a large portion of Ohio territory that it named the Western Reserve—in essence, New Connecticut. The extreme portion of the claimed land was designated the Firelands (it now comprises Erie and Huron counties). In 1775, 35 investors had subscribed to form the Connecticut Land Company, and three million acres of the Western Reserve was purchased for about 40 cents an acre. The person chosen to lead entrepreneurs to the Promised Land was a prominent attorney from Canterbury, Connecticut, named Moses Cleaveland. Cleaveland, a Yale graduate, had served in the Revolutionary War and at the time was general of the Connecticut militia.

Described as swarthy and robust, Cleaveland led a 50-man surveying and plotting party along the Lake Erie shore in July of 1796, searching for the mouth of the river the Indians called "crooked water"—the Cuyahoga. On the steamy 22nd day of the month, Cleaveland and his crew reached their goal, then spent the next three months chopping and hacking, carving out townships that were five miles square.

Moses Cleaveland and his surveyors never intended to settle in the Western Reserve, and they yearned to return to the comforts of New England. After a few months they returned to Connecticut, and Cleaveland died at the village of Wyndham in 1806 (three years after Ohio became a state). He never saw the success of the town that was named after him. (The story goes that the letter a was dropped from

Cleaveland's name in a newspaper story of the time—and that, too, never returned.)

In retrospect, the name Carterland would have been more fitting for the settlement, since it was Lorenzo Carter and his wife who decided to stay and tough it out on the shores of Lake Erie. The Carter home became the town meeting place, and Carter welcomed new arrivals while imposing a modicum of law.

In 1800, Cleveland's population was 7; by 1810 it had reached 57. By 1820, with the Ohio and Erie Canal open and access gained to Lake Erie, the population had grown to 606, with 50 houses. In 1826, with 9,000 denizens, Cleveland was incorporated as a city.

Cleveland's population peaked in 1940 at over 900,000, while the 2000 census put our citizenry at 478,403.

OHIO SYMBOLS

Flower—scarlet carnation, adopted in 1904
Wild flower—white trillium, adopted in 1987
Animal—white-tailed deer, adopted in 1853
Bird—cardinal, adopted in 1933
Insect—ladybug, adopted in 1975
Tree—buckeye, adopted in 1953

Mineral—flint, adopted in 1965
Fossil—trilobite, adopted in 1985
Beverage—tomato juice, adopted in 1965
Song—Beautiful Ohio, adopted in 1969
Rock Song—Hang on Sloopy, adopted in 1985
Reptile—black racer, adopted in 1995

OUR TALE OF CASSANDRA:

Mythology Comes to Our Lives

WILMA SMITH

Well, she has been with us now for more than a year.
There are days it seems so much longer, but then there are days
that would be much more boring without her in the mix.

Where do you start in the story of our Cassandra? Certainly her personality came from her heritage and experiences before she came to our home. But she has learned so much from us and from her brothers, Clifford, Clarence, and Romeo. If the guys could speak for themselves, they would certainly say she is a handful! The pure love she gives to us more than pays her bill. What a character!

My friends at the Animal Protective League knew that we were looking for another puppy. We wanted another male beagle. They are very good about keeping their eyes and ears open to help you find the breed of your choice, and they let you know if one becomes available.

One day the call came that they had a beautiful, tricolored beagle—a female! Well, this was half a match. It's just that we wanted another male beagle because the "boys" have been so good. We even had a name chosen for the new little guy, Clyde! He would fit right in namewise. But you should always be open to changing your mind—even if you think you know exactly what you want. So, with my initial "No, we're looking for another male beagle," Cassandra's story had just begun.

Some wonderful friends of ours decided to go see her at the APL. Well, after their meeting it looked like a done deal. You see, the little eight-week-old puppy had her "wrap you around her paw" technique in full form. She kissed constantly, wagged her tail like you were her long-lost friend, and made you feel like she had never looked at another human. They were smitten and thought they had a simply wonderful, wonderful idea. What they didn't know was that I had already said "No" because of gender.

Our good pals told us they made the decision to bring her home to Tom and me as a surprise. They said they whispered to her, "Little girl, you just won the doggy lottery!"

So . . . there we all were on that eventful, surprising night. Tom and I thought our friends were just stopping over to say hello. But as they got out of their car, they were carrying a little package. "What's that?" one of us said. "Well . . . ," they replied, with a very pregnant pause, a skittish little smile, and then the hand-off. Cassandra, as we named her, had arrived! We chose the name Cassandra because in mythology she was a heroine, a princess, a prophetess, and ultimately a controller of men, which we thought she would have to be to live with all the male animals who already ruled our home. Little did we know that she would come by her name ever so naturally!

How can I really describe a little dab of love like her? Would it be the freckles on her nose? Would it be those sad, soulful eyes she can use so well? Would it be the way she tilts her chin down and looks up at you as if to say, "Don't you love me? I would never do anything wrong." Then again, maybe it's her ability to charm—and not just the other dogs and cat in our household, she's pretty good with the real man of our house, her master and my beloved husband, Tom.

Tom has labeled me "the human vending machine." He says I have all the animals loving me and following me around like a modern-day pied piper because I'm always giving them treats. Actually he is partially right: I am very often attentive to those sad little looks of hunger, and I love my animals to be happy, so if it's a treat they seek I do sometimes relent. All right, maybe I do it "most" of the time, but I love them and they deserve to be spoiled. Needless to say, they do follow me around and proclaim that I'm on the way into a room before I get there. Usually they are only a few steps away.

> *Tom has labeled me "the human vending machine."*

Now, when Tom was a little boy he found a stray and brought it home. He named his new best friend "Tag Along," and that is exactly what the little guy did. Wherever Tom went as a child, his little best friend went with him. If you're a dog or cat owner you know the feeling of always having a little buddy with you. As if they understand what you're doing and even thinking, they are at your side or just a few steps behind looking up at you with wisdom.

I do believe Tom missed that feeling from his wonderful "Tag Along" days. But, not to worry—as I said, Cassandra is a "controller" of men—all men, it seems! Whatever she may lack, she is a charmer.

Whenever she sees Tom, she stops whatever she is doing and runs to him, seemingly powered by a motorized wagging tail. The girl knows, I'll tell you!

Every day she and Tom go to get the paper. Whatever fun or food she might be enjoying, everything grinds to a halt so she can accompany Tom to get the paper, her tail wagging the whole time, and a playful mode to her proud stride. She loves her dad.

Tom, on the other hand, professes that she loves anyone who is around. What was that song about loving the one you're with? That might be her theme song.

It has now been almost two years since she was "delivered" to our home. I must say the way she has blended in with Clifford, Clarence, and Romeo has been terrific. She adds a new dimension and fullness to our home. She and the others are such a joy. Whenever they go to the groomer or the vet, there is a real void in the house. Even for that brief time, it seems lonely.

JAN FEB MAR APR MAY JUN JUL AUG SEP OCT NOV DEC

You may remember from Greek mythology that one of the heroine Cassandra's most memorable roles was that of prophetess. Our canine Cassandra does always seem to know ahead of time what she's about to get—usually in the form of toys, food, or attention that one of the other animals is enjoying. Once she sets her sights on something she wants (and it's usually what someone else already has), through flirting, staring, or sheer persistence, she gets it.

The name Cassandra itself means "shining upon man."

But then there are the oh-so-frequent tender moments with the "boys," as we call our other pets. In spite of the slights, they love her, too. In fact, they seem to vie for her attention. When one of them is resting on the floor or in their bed, she often goes up to him, lays her head down level with his, looks right in his eyes, and kisses him on the face. As our little family saga continues and we turn the daily page of memories, we thank God for our little pals Clifford, Clarence, and Romeo, and their sister, Cassandra.

Aside from its meaning in mythology, the name Cassandra itself means "shining upon man." Indeed, she does shine in our lives.

As for Romeo and his role in our daily travels? That's for next time, when I'll share with you the story of our little "cover boy."

Wilma Smith is anchor of the 6 and 10 p.m. editions of FOX 8 NEWS. She is the recipient of 10 Emmy nominations and 9 Emmy Awards for excellence in her television work. She was voted "Anchor of Excellence" by the National Association of Career Women, "Newscaster of the Year," a Cleveland Pacesetter, and "Best Anchorperson" by *Cleveland Magazine*, and is a member of the Ohio Television/Radio Hall of Fame. She is also one of the few women to be named to the NATAS prestigious "Silver Circle."

JAN FEB MAR APR MAY JUN JUL AUG SEP OCT NOV DEC

APRIL STATISTICS

SUNSHINE % 51

DRIEST MONTH . . . . 0.65"/1915

WARMEST MONTH . . . . 55.9°/1955

COLDEST MONTH . . . . 39.6°/1874

LIQUID PCPN AVG. . . . . 3.14"

RAINIEST DAY . . . . 2.24"/1961

RAINIEST MONTH . . . . 6.61"/1961

THUNDERY DAYS 4

SNOWIEST DAY . . . . 11.6"/1982

SNOWIEST MONTH . . . . 14.3"/1943

LEAST SNOWFALL . . . . Trace
(most recently in 1991)

DAYS ONE INCH SNOW 1

April is also known as the month of fools. It's foolish, indeed, to set out any tender plants during this fourth month of the year. April marks the beginning of the tornado season in Northeast Ohio, and April tornadoes are often strong, accounting for the highest monthly death toll from twisters in the United States. The April 11, 1965, Palm Sunday tornado killed 19 at Pittsfield in Lorain County. The massive F5 twister that struck Xenia, Ohio, on the 3rd of April in 1974 killed 35. (That tornado was part of the greatest "family outbreak" of tornadoes in American weather history.) Thanks to Ben Franklin, who came up with the idea, we revert to Daylight Savings Time on the first Sunday of April. At 2 a.m. we'll lose an hour's sleep by setting our clocks ahead to 3 a.m. Raucous and cunning crows are returning from the depths of the winter woods. Juncos (snow birds) have returned and bluebirds often arrive by the third week in April.

Woollybear caterpillars, who spent all winter in their larval stage, will be munching on dandelion and plantain weed before spinning cocoons out of their body hair. In a few weeks a beige, purple-spotted tiger moth will emerge and flit away in the spring sunshine. Each moth lays thousands of eggs, which will become the woollybears of autumn. If snow should cover your flowers, don't bother to brush it away; snow acts as a protective, insulating blanket.

DAILY DATA FOR APRIL

Date	Moon Phase	Day	Day of Year	Days Left in Year	Sunrise	Sunset	Length of Day	Avg. Hi	Avg. Lo
1	●	Tue	91	274	7:10	7:52	12:42	53	33
2		Wed	92	273	7:09	7:53	12:44	53	33
3		Thu	93	272	7:07	7:54	12:47	53	34
4		Fri	94	271	7:05	7:55	12:50	54	34
5		Sat	95	270	7:04	7:56	12:52	54	34
6		Sun	96	269	7:02	7:57	12:55	55	34
7		Mon	97	268	7:00	7:58	12:58	55	35
8		Tue	98	267	6:59	7:59	13:00	55	35
9	◐	Wed	99	266	6:57	8:00	13:03	56	35
10		Thu	100	265	6:55	8:01	13:06	56	36
11		Fri	101	264	6:54	8:02	13:08	56	36
12		Sat	102	263	6:52	8:03	13:11	57	36
13		Sun	103	262	6:51	8:05	13:14	57	36
14		Mon	104	261	6:49	8:06	13:17	57	37
15		Tue	105	260	6:47	8:07	13:20	58	37
16	○	Wed	106	259	6:46	8:08	13:22	58	37
17		Thu	107	258	6:44	8:09	13:25	58	38
18		Fri	108	257	6:43	8:10	13:27	59	38
19		Sat	109	256	6:41	8:11	13:30	59	38
20		Sun	110	255	6:39	8:12	13:33	60	39
21		Mon	111	254	6:38	8:13	13:35	60	39
22		Tue	112	253	6:37	8:14	13:37	60	39
23	◑	Wed	113	252	6:35	8:15	13:40	61	40
24		Thu	114	251	6:34	8:16	13:42	61	40
25		Fri	115	250	6:32	8:18	13:46	61	40
26		Sat	116	249	6:31	8:19	13:48	62	41
27		Sun	117	248	6:30	8:20	13:50	62	41
28		Mon	118	247	6:28	8:21	13:53	62	41
29		Tue	119	246	6:27	8:22	13:55	63	41
30		Wed	120	245	6:25	8:23	13:58	63	42

Rec. Hi°	Rec. Lo°	Avg. Lake°	On This Date ...
80/1986	10/1964	37	Baseball Hall of Fame opens in Cooperstown, NY (1938)
81/1963	19/1883	37	Record wind speed 450 kph in tornado, Wichita Falls, TX (1958)
78/1999	19/1954	38	ICC transfers Ohio to Eastern time zone (1927)
77/1882	19/1971	38	Cleveland Society for Prevention of Cruelty to Animals founded (1873)
81/1988	17/1881	38	World Trade Center opens in NYC (1974)
84/1929	21/1982	38	George D. Forbes elected 1st black pres. of Cleve. City Council (1973)
83/1929	17/1982	39	1st settlement in Ohio, at Marietta (1788)
80/2001	11/1982	39	House of Representives 1st meeting (1789)
81/1931	17/1972	39	General Lee surrenders to General Grant (1865)
83/1978	20/1997	39	Cleve Cavaliers win their 1st NBA Central Division title (1976)
82/1945	22/1982	40	Actor Joel Gray born in Cleveland (1932)
82/2001	21/1874	40	Highest wind velocity recorded—231 mph, Mt Washington, NH (1934)
85/1941	20/1950	40	Best view of Halley's Comet in 2000 years (837)
85/1883	20/1950	41	John Wilkes Booth shoots Abraham Lincoln (1865)
81/2002	22/1935	41	Titanic snks (1912)
85/2002	18/1875	41	Bob Feller pitches opening-day no-hitter (1940)
84/1896	15/1875	41	Benjamin Franklin dies at 84 (1790)
85/1896	17/1875	42	Paul Revere's famous ride (1775)
84/1941	22/1887	42	Eliot Ness born (1903)
83/1985	23/1904	42	86% of black students boycott Cleveland schools (1964)
86/1942	24/1875	42	Fire at Ohio State Penitentiary kills 320 (1930)
84/1985	23/1875	43	Actor Ralph Byrd born in Dayton (1909)
86/1985	27/1994	43	Hank Aaron hits 1st of his 755 homers (1954)
88/1925	28/1930	44	1st AL game, White Sox beat Indians 8-2 (1901)
87/1990	27/1888	44	US declares war on Spain (1898)
87/1948	26/1972	44	Charles Richter, earthquakes seismologist born in Ohio (1900)
86/1990	27/1971	45	NFL officially recognizes Hall of Fame in Canton (1961)
88/1986	25/1947	45	Chernobyl nuclear power plant disaster (1986)
84/1899	25/1977	45	Cleve Indian Wes Ferrell no-hits St Louis Browns, 9-0 (1931)
88/1942	28/1969	46	Brightest supernova in recorded history is observed (1006)

JAN FEB MAR APR MAY JUN JUL AUG SEP OCT NOV DEC

OHIO'S MAGNIFICENT SEVEN

WILLIAM McKINLEY
25TH PRESIDENT 1897–1901

Dick Goddard

William McKinley was born in a small frame house at Niles, Ohio, on January 28, 1843. He was the seventh of eight children who lived to maturity.

McKinley grew to be five feet, seven inches in height and weighed nearly 200 pounds, gradually developing a bit of a paunch in his later years. A handsome man, he had penetrating blue-gray eyes, fair skin, bushy eyebrows, a strong jaw, and a substantial nose and was the only clean-shaven president between Andrew Johnson and Woodrow Wilson. McKinley spoke in a clear, stentorian voice. Not considered vain, he dressed impeccably and conservatively, usually wearing a white vest. He avoided exercise, but walked at a brisk pace and had good posture. While favored by general good health, the young McKinley did experience a physical breakdown due to overwork while in college.

McKinley had a dry wit, and while not a great yarn spinner, he appreciated a good joke. Described as energetic and optimistic, McKinley was friendly, even-tempered, cheerful, and well liked.

McKinley attended public schools in Niles and Poland, Ohio, before enrolling at a Methodist seminary in Poland. His favorite subject was speech, and he became a smooth and persuasive orator.

After moving to Canton, he joined the First Methodist Church and became superintendent of its Sunday school. The devout McKinley kissed the Bible at his inauguration and as president he invited friends over to the White House Blue Room where they would sing hymns on Sunday evenings.

In 1871, at the age of 27, McKinley married 23-year-old Ida Saxton, the daughter of a Canton banker whose father had founded the *Canton Repository* newspaper. Ida was very attractive, but had a nervous disposition. They enjoyed opera and the theater and frequently played euchre and cribbage with friends. McKinley smoked cigars and had the distracting habit of biting the stogies in two and then munching on them. The cigar chomping was occasionally accompanied with a glass of wine or scotch.

McKinley had a pet parrot that would finish singing "Yankee Doodle Dandy" once the president got it started by whistling.

Ida suffered a mental breakdown and developed epilepsy soon after the death of her mother and her infant daughters, becoming totally dependent on her faithful and loving husband. Ida became an invalid and spent countless hours crocheting hundreds of slippers for friends and family. McKinley was such a devoted husband that his friend and benefactor, Cleveland Republican senator Mark Hanna, remarked, "The President has made it pretty hard for the rest of us husbands in Washington."

It was Hanna who pushed McKinley toward the presidency, even though the modest McKinley frequently acknowledged that he knew one day he would become president.

McKinley volunteered as a private in the Civil War after one year at Allegheny College and served with Ohio's Twenty-third Volunteer Infantry. He rose to the rank of major (and was forever called "The Major" by his friends). At Antietam he was cited for valor for transporting much-needed rations to the front lines under Confederate fire. He was never wounded in battle.

McKinley cast his first presidential vote for Abraham Lincoln in 1864. After being admitted to the bar in 1867, McKinley joined the local Republican Party. He steadily climbed the political ladder, serving many years in Congress before becoming governor of Ohio in 1892. In 1896 McKinley defeated the firebrand orator William Jennings Bryan for the presidency. Bryan had toured the nation like a fire-and-brimstone evangelist, traveling 18,000 miles in only three months. McKinley, however, conducted a stay-at-home strategy that became known as the "front porch campaign." It worked. McKinley solidly defeated Bryan, getting 51 percent of the popular vote to Bryan's 47 percent. Both Democrats and Republicans admired McKinley's fairness and courtesy.

JAN FEB MAR APR MAY JUN JUL AUG SEP OCT NOV DEC

President McKinley's successful conclusion of the Spanish-American War in 1898 made him even more popular, and, using the slogan "Four More Years of the Full Dinner Pail," he easily won election to a second term.

McKinley's lucky charm was a scarlet carnation that was developed by Dr. Levi Lamborn of Alliance. On September 6, 1901, the president attended the Pan-American Exposition in Buffalo, New York. He was shaking hands with well-wishers and admirers when he removed his lucky carnation and gave it to a little girl. He then reached out to shake the hand of a man who had his other hand wrapped in a bandage. The bandage contained a .32 Iver Johnson pistol. McKinley was shot twice, the first bullet harmlessly striking a coat button with no penetration. The second bullet entered his abdomen and lodged in his pancreas. McKinley doubled over and fell backward into the arms of Secret Service agents.

As his assailant was taken to the floor McKinley cried out, "Don't hurt him!" He then told an assistant, "My wife . . . be careful how you tell her!"

McKinley was rushed to the hospital, and two operations were performed, but the bullet was not found.

Doctors became optimistic five days later when the president's fever subsided and he asked for a cigar—which was denied. McKinley ate well, but the following day he relapsed. He died the next morning, eight days after being shot, with the cause of death listed as gangrene.

Public funeral services were held at Canton's Methodist Church. After temporary burial at Westlawn Cemetery in Canton, his remains were transferred to the McKinley National Memorial in Canton in 1907.

With her husband's death, Ida's health continued to worsen, and she spent the next few years in seclusion, passing away in May of 1907. She is buried next to her husband, along with their infant daughters. Mount McKinley in Alaska, the highest peak in North America, is named after the Ohio president.

The presidential assassin was Leon Czolgosz, a self-proclaimed anarchist, and on October 29, 1901, the demented man was electrocuted at Auburn State Prison. His last words: "I killed the President because he was the enemy of the people—the good working people. I am not sorry for my crime."

Sulfuric acid was poured on the body to accelerate decomposition.

Of the 41 United States presidents rated in the recent C-SPAN survey, McKinley was ranked 15th.

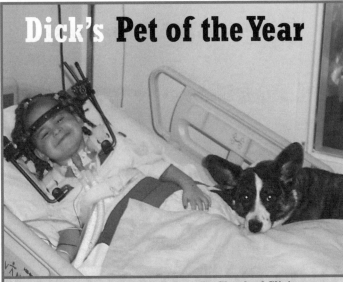

Dick's Pet of the Year

Josie and her friend Carmen DeLeon at the Cleveland Clinic Rehabilitation Center for Children

Name: Conifer Royal Majestic Josie CGC TDI/AOV. Conifer Royal is our kennel name, and I guess my human mom and dad thought I was "majestic." Then the name "Josie" was just the right size to fill in the rest of the blanks on the AKC registration form.

Birthdate: March 5, 1997

Breed: Cardigan Welsh Corgi

Height/weight/length: I'm about 12 inches tall, maybe 18 inches long (not including my tail), and weight—well, what lady likes to discuss that?

Favorite snack: lettuce, bananas, and the usual dog biscuits.

Favorite toy: big, plush squeaky toys

Turn-ons: When mom says "time to get in the bathroom for your bath and teeth brushing," because I know we're getting ready for a therapy visit to spend time with the kids.

Turn-offs: When mom and dad leave without us.

Why I'm Pet of the Year: I would like to think it is because of the therapy work I do. My brother Sherman and I are regular pets at home, but our therapy work is really very important to us.

When we enter a room and see a child hooked up to all kinds of monitors with needles, bandages, breathing tubes, feeding tubes and bags, and anything else needed to either help them or heal them, and watch that child smile and listen to the laughter, that makes us feel good.

We don't care what is wrong with them, what they look like, who they are, or where they are from—we give unconditional love to all of them. I show them that I have overcome a handicap and learned to walk, run, and play on three legs instead of four, and hopefully they'll be inspired to overcome whatever their handicap is, too. Therapy Dog "Work" is what some people say we do, but Sherman and I know that we do Therapy Dog "Love."

{ DICK'S INSECT OF THE YEAR }

WHAT'S BUGGING YOU

· DICK GODDARD ·

When you see a tiny orange bug with black spots climb into your companion's nose this autumn, you can impress your friends by shouting out, "You've just inhaled *Harmonia axyridis*, the multicolored Asian lady beetle!"

Make sure that you don't mix up Harmonia with the official Ohio state ladybug, *Hippodamia converaens*, the Convergent lady beetle! It's easy to get confused, since there are about 400 kinds of ladybugs in North America, and nearly 5,000 different types worldwide.

For the last several autumns there has been a steadily increasing population of ladybugs that insist on taking up winter headquarters in Northeast Ohio homes. Returning from the Woollybear Festival in Vermilion early last October, I saw veritable clouds of these insects swarming through the sky.

There was urgency to the air show, since the ladybug, which beats its wings 85 times each second, will not fly if the temperature is below 55 degrees Fahrenheit. The air speed of a ladybug is around 15 mph (with gusts to 18).

Ladybugs are known in Europe as ladybirds. Whatever you call them, these are the most commonly known of all the beneficial insects. Both the adults and larvae munch on a host of soft-bodied insects, with the destructive, minute aphid being their favorite meal. Aphids are basically plant lice, so eating them is a lousy job but somebody has to do it. A ladybug will devour some 75 aphids every 24 hours and up to 5,000 in its lifetime.

It was because of the help the ladybug provides to Ohio gardeners and farmers that this beetle was named the official (accept no substitutes) state insect in 1975. Four other states have also honored the ladybug: Delaware, New Hampshire, Massachusetts, and Tennessee.

Ladybugs range in color from orange through reddish-orange and pale yellow. The number of black spots varies widely, with Ohio's Convergent characteristically sporting seven. The widespread lady beetle that has become an autumn nuisance in Ohio—the Asian, or Halloween ladybug—shows off with nearly 20 (some of which may be faint and some missing). At the other extreme you have the modest twice-stabbed and two-spotted lady-bugs (as the beetle ages the spots become less obvious).

While Ohio's favorite ladybug usually behaves like a lady should, last autumn many viewers reported that the Asian beetles were pinching their skin (they do not "sting" and are not venomous, nor do they

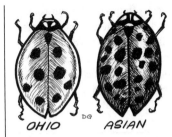

OHIO   DG   ASIAN

transmit disease). If you squish a ladybug it can eject a slimy, yellow liquid with a distinct odor (you could stain surfaces by doing this). Spraying your home with insecticide will do little good. Your only indoor weapon is a vacuum cleaner.

You will be pleased to know that the overwintering ladybugs will not cause damage to your furniture or carpets by chewing or boring holes.

The Asian lady beetle was imported in 1916 in order to help control the aphid problem in the United States. It was around 1994 that the little flying spheres began to bug housewives in the eastern U.S.

In autumn ladybugs go into hibernation, often at the base of a tree or fence, or under a rock or log—or in your home (they love warmth). They fly away in early spring.

Ladybugs thrive because their colors tell birds that they are not a tasty snack. The tiny ovals with six legs will also, like a possum, "play dead" when threatened. Most predators won't eat an insect that doesn't move.

While sealing your doors and

windows from a ladybug invasion is very difficult, there is one rather expensive thing you can do to make your home less attractive to the critters: paint it a dark color (ladybugs prefer light-colored dwellings).

If all else fails, you might consider turning your ladybug infestation into a cottage industry. Greenhouses will pay $7.50 for two thousand ladybugs.

Flora & Fauna APRIL

WEEK 1

BIRDS: White-throated sparrows, singing their plaintive "old Sam Peabody-Peabody-Peabody" calls continue to pour through Ohio on their way to northern Canada. Rufous-sided towhees return this week. Killdeer return to the Cleveland area in large numbers. If you approach a nest, watch the female perform the "broken wing" act to draw you away. ❧ **WILDFLOWERS:** Spring beauty and hepatica begin to bloom throughout most of Cleveland Metroparks. Some years North Chagrin Reservation's wildflowers bloom almost a week later due to the "lake effect." Trout lily or "yellow adder's tongue" begins to bloom in Cleveland Metroparks southern reservations. Watch for them a week or so later in Rocky River, Mill Stream Run, and Garfield Park reservations..

WEEK 2

BIRDS: Male woodcocks perform their spectacular "sky dance" in morning and evening twilight each day through mid-May in hopes of attracting a female. Watch open fields with some shrub cover and discover the spectacle for yourself. Canada geese are incubating eggs at Lake Isaac in Big Creek Reservation and Sunset Pond in North Chagrin Reservation. ❧ **WILDFLOWERS:** Violets, bloodroot, rue anemone, and cut-leaf toothwort should be in bloom this week along most of Cleveland Metroparks nature trails. ❧ **AMPHIBIANS:** On warm, wet rainy evenings in Brecksville, North Chagrin, and Mill Stream Run reservations hundreds of salamanders may trudge to their ancestral breeding ponds. Valley Parkway in Brecksville is occasionally closed to protect them as they cross the road. American toads' long trilling calls can be heard in wet spots throughout Cleveland Metroparks as their short breeding cycle begins.

WEEK 3

BIRDS: If south winds prevail this week, a major bird migration should be underway. Look for Swainson's and hermit thrushes, sandpipers, and some of these warblers: yellow-throated, yellow-rumped, black-throated, green, and (especially in North Chagrin Reservation) hooded warblers. ❧ **WILDFLOWERS:** Three-petaled, three-leafed white trilliums should be up but not quite yet blooming in most Cleveland Metroparks forests. Marsh marigolds add their yellow beauty to low wet places this week. ❧ **SHRUBS:** Spicebush and shadbush (serviceberry) are blooming throughout Rocky River Valley. Their soft whites and pinks still provide a contrast with the emerging forest canopy overhead. ❧ **REPTILES:** Garter snakes should be seen frequently as they leave their winter dens and soak up the warm spring sunshine.

WEEK 4

BIRDS: Bluebirds should be back in force this week. Is your bluebird house cleaned out and ready for this year's visitors? More birds of the deep forest such as the rose-breasted grosbeak and the northern oriole should have returned from their winter haunts in tropical rain-forests. ❧ **WILDFLOWERS:** Grassy open places are carpeted with tiny four-petaled bluets. So many may bloom that they resemble a pale blue snowdrift in the spring woods. Snowy white trilliums now dot most of Cleveland Metroparks deep woodlands. Look around them for Virginia bluebell, Dutchman's breeches, and squirrel corn.

Adapted from the Nature Almanac by Robert Hinkle, with permission from Cleveland Metroparks.

THE MAKING OF
A WEATHERMAN

A. J. COLBY

I'm not sure when my interest in the weather first began. My earliest memories of Mother Nature are of warm, sunny afternoons sharing a picnic lunch with my mom and younger siblings. I recall looking up at the clouds and trying to match the amorphous shapes to something more familiar to a four-year-old: Mickey Mouse, Winnie the Pooh, Goofy, and simpler dog and cat shapes.

My interest in weather grew into full-blown fascination when, on May 31, 1985, a tornado outbreak struck Northeast Ohio and Northwest Pennsylvania. One town in particular, Albion, PA, was hit extremely hard. More than a dozen perished in the F4 twister, and millions of dollars in damage resulted from the fury. My aunt and uncle took me to Albion to see the devastation firsthand. I was shocked to witness the raw power of weather. That was it. I was hooked.

JAN FEB MAR **APR** MAY JUN JUL AUG SEP OCT NOV DEC

Looking back, I realize now that it's rare to know what you want to do in life at such a young age. The vast majority of students didn't declare a major until they were absolutely forced to by the university hierarchy. I was incredibly fortunate to discover the wonderful people who cultivated my interest in

> *My desire was to talk to the "King of Cleveland Weather."*

meteorology. One afternoon while home from school (I was sick . . . not playing hooky), I placed a phone call to Channel 8. I did not know what to expect, but my desire was to talk to the "King of Cleveland Weather." Much to my surprise, this other guy answered, saying, "Weather, this is Andre." I was speechless for a moment. I had no idea who this person on the other end of the line was, but I was determined to tell someone about my love affair with the weather even if it wasn't Dick Goddard! I stammered through my slightly rehearsed speech, and Andre Bernier immediately put me at ease. This was the start of my long association with WJW television.

Andre began broadcasting my weather reports from Conneaut, Ohio, that very afternoon. I was his very first "Weather Spy." What an honor, since that network grew from one to a hardy 50 "Web Weather Spies." The Weather Spy Network has become a Cleveland morning television tradition. I remember the first time Andre said my name on TV. I was not expecting it. You are never supposed to hear a personal message on TV, especially your name, but that all changed that afternoon. Andre said, " . . . and A.J. Colby from Conneaut called in a temperature at 32 degrees." I was flabbergasted. My jaw dropped, my heart skipped a beat, and I began to run around the house furiously despite my physical malady. My grandma, my aunt, and a cousin almost instantaneously called the house to inquire as to why they had just heard my name on Channel 8. I said, "Andre and I are like this," crossing my fingers. Countless mornings and afternoons I reported Conneaut weather from my thermometer at my parents' house, and countless mornings Andre mentioned my name on the air. It resulted in encouragement beyond measure and was a kind of salve to my already troubled self-esteem. I was, and still am, very grateful.

With Andre's guidance, I began to plot a course to ready myself for the rigors of a higher education in meteorology. What a ride! I had not anticipated the intense math and science requirements. The earth's atmosphere is a complex mechanism and can best be described using a special kind of math called differential equations. Andre alerted me to the fact that a strong background in mathematics, specifically calculus and physics, would be a prerequisite to entering college courses with some degree of confidence.

Andre's insights were a blessing.

My sophomore year in high school was a whirlwind. I was 16, and raging with passion for weather—and nothing else. I made it my mission to get experience in the field. I had not anticipated that it would come so quickly. I was made aware of a part-time position, as an on-air weather person, that had recently opened up at a station in Erie, PA. Andre encouraged me to apply for the job, having helped me make a demo tape at Channel 8 a few weeks before. He wrote a glowing letter of recommendation, saying, "Despite A.J.'s age, he has a real affinity for weather and a competent on-air presentation." I felt so honored that he felt that way about me, and that he felt strongly about my work. Although I was just 16, the station management guessed my age at 23, and when they found out I was so young, they were rightfully hesitant about putting me on the air. After some heavy-duty convincing and pleading by the chief meteorologist, Mr. Tim Earl, management decided to give me a shot. Within about a year, I was filling in during the prime-time shows. It was a dream come true.

I thought things couldn't get any better, but the unthinkable was about to happen.

The year I turned 19, Andre called me on a warm summer morning and asked me to send him a tape of my recent shows and live shots. He explained that there was a position open at Channel 8, and he wanted to submit my work to the news director. I never believed that lightning could possibly strike twice. Well, it did. I remember bursting into tears after Grant Zalba, then the news director at Channel 8, called me to offer me the job. I recall that the first person I called to tell the good news to was my dad. He was, as one might imagine, quite proud. I'll never forget what he said: "Wow, A.J., what you've managed to accomplish in just a few short years is amazing. Congratulations." I was elated. My first day on the air at Channel 8, sitting in the same chair that Andre Bernier and Dick Goddard sat in, made the whole experience surreal. Life was good. But Murphy's Law dictated that a good, healthy dose of reality must be imminent. That reality was pumping some neurons and getting educated in my field of choice.

Trying to find a college that offered a degree in meteorology was a challenge, to put it mildly. After an exhaustive search through various college catalogues, I discovered that the curriculum in Ohio colleges was devoid of upper-level meteorology courses. To my chagrin, the closest school that offered them was Penn State University, and that came with a hefty price tag. Meanwhile, I developed a friendship with a gentleman by the name of Jeff Halblaub. He wrote me a letter (which I kept) explaining that Ohio State University offered an undergraduate degree in meteorology, but that it was hidden under the guise of "B.S. in geography." As it turns out, this meteorology degree is conferred by the College of Arts and Sciences. Due to inadequate descriptions in university course listings and the general scarcity of university-level programs in meteorology, it is not surprising that I did not discover the information on my own. I credit Mr. Halblaub with steering me in the right direction—one that led to the experience of a lifetime at Ohio State. I was to become a Buckeye.

I focused on getting the tough prerequisites out of the way first by tackling physics and calculus, while sharpening my communication skills with a couple of speech classes. I also belonged to an organization called Toastmasters, which offered a series of excellent exercises to strengthen off-the-cuff repartee. I was never a prolific writer, but the whole ad-lib "speech thing"— well, I could do that. I continued filling in at WSEE in Erie during my summer breaks, and also at what came to be known as "Fox 8 is News."

To wannabe meteorologists, I have this advice: Get involved early. Use any opportunity you have to practice your craft. Perhaps most importantly, get connected with someone already working and successful in your profession of choice. These people know the road to success and, more importantly, some of the bumps you may encounter on it. Their sagacity can never be captured in the classroom or duplicated in a textbook. It is the real-life experience so many prospective employers seek that is the backbone of any successful endeavor.

A.J.Colby serves as meteorologist for the 6 p.m. and 10 p.m. weekend editions of FOX 8 NEWS.

fun facts OHIO

Ten largest cities (according to population in 2000): Columbus, 711,470; Cleveland, 478,403; Cincinnati, 331,285; Toledo, 313,619; Akron, 217,074; Dayton, 166,179; Parma, 85,655; Youngstown, 82,026; Canton, 80,806; Lorain, 68,652

Land area: 40,953 sq mi. (106,067 sq km)

Geographic center: In Delaware Co., 25 mi. NNE of Columbus

Number of counties: 88

Largest county by population and area: Cuyahoga, 1,393,978 (2000 census); Ashtabula, 703 sq mi.

State forests: 20 (more than 183,000 acres)

State parks: 73 (more than 204,000 acres)

The state of Ohio encompasses 41,330 square miles. Ohio owns 2,097,000 acres of Lake Erie, and 320 miles of its shoreline.

MAY STATISTICS

SUNSHINE % 58

DRIEST MONTH . . . . 0.58"/1934

WARMEST MONTH . . . . 66.9°/1991

COLDEST MONTH . . . . 51.1°/1907

LIQUID PCPN AVG. . . . . 3.49"

RAINIEST DAY . . . . 3.37"/1995

RAINIEST MONTH . . . . 9.14"/1989

THUNDERY DAYS 5

SNOWIEST DAY . . . . 2.1"/1974

SNOWIEST MONTH . . . . 2.1"/1974

LEAST SNOWFALL . . . . Trace
(most recently in 1986)

DAYS ONE INCH SNOW 0

The emerald month can be a cool and sometimes cruel jewel. This month is notorious for claiming prematurely planted flowers and vegetables. May 20 is a safe date for most plantings, but some veteran Northeast Ohio gardeners wait until the Memorial Day weekend before digging in. A tip: When you slip on the gardening gloves that have spent all winter in the dark recesses of your garage, be sure to squeeze each finger vigorously. That's because spiders (the brown recluse and black widow are especially venomous) often use the fingers of gloves for cozy winter headquarters. Colorful woodland wildflowers dominate the month of May in Northeast Ohio before the spreading canopy of leaves shuts off the springtime sunlight. Ohio's only hummingbird—the ruby-throated—usually makes its first darting appearance about midmonth. Towards the end of May and into early June, those pesky non-stinging insects called muckleheads (also known as midges) move inland from Lake Erie, joined by mayflies (a.k.a. Canadian soldiers).

On Memorial Day Northeast Ohioans are often reminded that the reason three-day weekends were created is because it's impossible to cram all the bad weather into only two days. Beware during those early-season picnics—strong thunderstorms that can spawn deadly tornadoes can happen at any time during May.

DAILY DATA FOR MAY

Date	Moon Phase	Day	Day of Year	Days Left in Year	Sunrise	Sunset	Length of Day	Avg. Hi	Avg. Lo
1	●	Thu	121	244	6:24	8:24	14:00	63	42
2		Fri	122	243	6:23	8:25	14:02	64	42
3		Sat	123	242	6:22	8:26	14:04	64	43
4		Sun	124	241	6:20	8:27	14:07	64	43
5		Mon	125	240	6:19	8:28	14:09	65	44
6		Tue	126	239	6:18	8:29	14:11	65	44
7		Wed	127	238	6:17	8:30	14:13	65	44
8		Thu	128	237	6:15	8:32	14:17	66	45
9	◐	Fri	129	236	6:14	8:33	14:19	66	45
10		Sat	130	235	6:13	8:34	14:21	67	45
11		Sun	131	234	6:12	8:35	14:23	67	46
12		Mon	132	233	6:11	8:36	14:25	67	46
13		Tue	133	232	6:10	8:37	14:27	68	46
14		Wed	134	231	6:09	8:38	14:29	68	47
15	○	Thu	135	230	6:08	8:39	14:31	68	47
16		Fri	136	229	6:07	8:40	14:33	69	47
17		Sat	137	228	6:06	8:41	14:35	69	48
18		Sun	138	227	6:05	8:42	14:37	69	48
19		Mon	139	226	6:04	8:43	14:39	70	48
20		Tue	140	225	6:03	8:44	14:41	70	48
21		Wed	141	224	6:02	8:44	14:42	70	49
22	◑	Thu	142	223	6:02	8:45	14:43	71	49
23		Fri	143	222	6:01	8:46	14:45	71	50
24		Sat	144	221	6:00	8:47	14:47	71	50
25		Sun	145	220	5:59	8:48	14:49	72	50
26		Mon	146	219	5:59	8:49	14:50	72	51
27		Tue	147	218	5:58	8:50	14:52	72	51
28		Wed	148	217	5:58	8:51	14:53	73	51
29		Thu	149	216	5:57	8:51	14:54	73	52
30		Fri	150	215	5:56	8:52	14:56	74	52
31	●	Sat	151	214	5:56	8:53	14:57	74	52

Rec. Hi°	Rec. Lo°	Avg. Lake°	On This Date ...
88/1942	28/1876	46	TV host Jack Paar born in Canton (1918)
86/1951	26/1963	47	Olympic baseball pitcher Mark Johnson born in Dayton (1975)
85/1949	27/1986	47	David Bell debuts for the Indians; 3rd generation player, Gus & Buddy (1995)
89/1949	23/1971	47	Four killed in antiwar protest at Kent State University (1970)
89/1949	30/1968	48	Charles Nagy born in Fairfield CT (1967)
92/1959	26/1968	48	Representative Eric D Fingerhut born (1959)
87/1936	28/1970	48	Actress Tracy Lords born in Steubenville (1968)
88/1889	30/1976	49	Representative James A Traficant Jr born (1941)
88/1979	29/1983	49	WJW-AM in Cleveland OH begins radio transmissions (1929)
90/1953	25/1966	49	25ºF lowest temperature ever recorded in Cleveland in May (1966)
87/1881	33/1977	50	BF Goodrich manufactures 1st tubeless tire, Akron (1947)
89/1881	32/1976	50	Philadelphia A's Chief Bender no-hits Cleveland Indians, 4-0 (1910)
86/1991	32/1895	50	Pachyderm Building at Cleveland Metroparks Zoo opens (1956)
91/1962	33/1994	51	Indians' Stan Coveleski sets club record for most innings pitched–19 (1918)
89/1962	35/1977	51	Cleveland Clinic fire kills 129 people (1929)
89/1991	29/1984	52	Actress Debra Winger born in Cleveland (1955)
90/1962	33/1979	52	Cleveland Indian Tris Speaker gets his 3,000th hit (1925)
91/1962	36/1985	52	Tropical Butterfly Garden at Cleveland Metroparks Zoo opens (1994)
89/1911	33/1976	53	George II grants charter to Ohio Company to settle Ohio Valley (1749)
91/1962	34/1981	53	Cleveland Indians tie AL record of 18 walks (beat Red Sox 13-4) (1948)
90/1941	32/1895	53	Humphrey Bogart and Lauren Bacall married in Mansfield (1959)
90/1941	35/2002	53	Indians' pitcher Jose Mesa born (1966)
90/1991	34/1961	54	Actor/Comedian Drew Carey born (1958)
89/1950	32/1963	54	Astronaut Ronald A Parise born in Warren (1951)
89/1914	35/1956	54	Actress Ann Heche born in Aurora (1969)
89/1914	34/1969	54	Actor Philip Michael Thomas born in Columbus (1949)
90/1967	35/1969	54	Golden Gate Bridge is completed and open to pedestrian traffic (1937)
91/1941	37/1971	54	White Sox beat Indians, 6-3, in 21 innings; game started 5/26 (1973)
91/1991	38/1949	55	Patriot Patrick Henry born in Studley, VA (1736)
92/1879	32/1961	55	92º F highest temperature ever recorded in Cleveland OH in May (1972)
92/1944	39/1984	56	Arcade opens (1917)

JAN FEB MAR APR MAY JUN JUL AUG SEP OCT NOV DEC

{ DICK'S **FLOWER** OF THE YEAR }

CORONATION OF THE CARNATION

· DICK GODDARD ·

While we live in a democracy, we have established a monarchy of national and state symbols. The national flower is the rose, while Ohio's is the scarlet carnation. How the blood-red carnation was crowned the official state flower illustrates the affection the citizens of Ohio had for the 25th president of the United States, William McKinley of Niles.

The history of the carnation centers around Alliance, Ohio, in Stark County. Alliance is known as the Carnation City, since it was an Alliance doctor, Levi L. Lamborn, who cultivated the flower in his greenhouse at the northwest corner of Main Street and Union Avenue.

Dr. Lamborn first purchased six of the then rare carnations in 1866 from a botanist overseas. Aside from his medical practice and flower growing, the good doctor was also very interested in politics. In 1872, he ran unsuccessfully against

William McKinley for the Alliance district's congressional seat. Before each debate, Dr. Lamborn would present McKinley with a red carnation, and, in spite of their political differences, they became good friends.

McKinley admired the carnation so much that it soon became his trademark "lucky charm." He wore it throughout his campaigns as he became governor of Ohio and, eventually, president of the United States.

In 1901, near the beginning of his second term, President McKinley made a goodwill stop at the Pan-American Exposition in Buffalo, New York. He had been greeting and shaking hands with well-wishers, and when a child approached, he took the lucky carnation from his lapel and gave it to her. Moments later, McKinley was shot twice by an anarchist who had concealed a gun in his bandaged right hand.

President McKinley died eight days later. His last words were: "It is God's way. His will, not ours, will be done."

In 1904, the Ohio General Assembly proclaimed the scarlet carnation the official state flower "as a token of love and reverence for the memory of William McKinley."

On each anniversary of McKinley's birth, January 29, students from Canton McKinley High School travel to Canton's McKinley Monument and place carnations in the curved hands of the McKinley statue.

An annual Carnation Festival is held in Alliance.

⚡ STORM SAFETY — *Tornado*

It is estimated that 75 percent of all tornadoes occur in the conterminous U.S. and nearly all the F5 super twisters strike within our borders. Most tornadoes develop during the months of April, May, and June, but when conditions are right, they can drop from the sky in any month at any time. In the U.S. an average of 818 tornadoes are reported each year, with Ohio averaging about one dozen annually.

TORNADO SAFETY RULES:

1. When a tornado watch has been issued, conditions are right for a tornado. Be prepared to take shelter and keep informed of the latest storm conditions. A tornado warning means that a tornado has been sighted and confirmed in the area. When a warning is issued, take cover immediately.

2. Take a flashlight and transistor radio with you to the area that will provide the most shelter.

3. Go to the center of the basement, taking cover under heavy tables or a workbench, if possible. If no basement is available, take shelter under heavy furniture or in a closet, near the center of the house. In any case, stay clear of large windows or any other glass.

4. If caught in the open, lie flat in the nearest ditch or depression. A culvert offers good protection. Abandon your car for a ditch if you cannot outrun the storm.

JAN FEB MAR APR MAY JUN JUL AUG SEP OCT NOV DEC

Dog and cat fur is used to cover these stuffed animals.

The Dog and Cat Protection Act

Dick Goddard

Some people are appalled when they learn that I share my bed with a German shepherd and two (mostly) Siberian huskies. "How can you sleep with something that has body odor, bad breath, and is continually shedding?" My standard response is that I share their concern. I know some dogs that have those problems, too.

Most humans believe that we are special creatures on earth, and many are surprised and offended when they are told that we carbon-based bipedal mammals are also animals. Humans are special in at least one sense: Man is the only animal that blushes—or needs to.

In my four-plus decades on television the greatest response to any feature I've done is when I showed video from the Humane Society of the United States that exposed the production-line strangling of dogs and cats in Asia. It is estimated that more than two million dogs and cats are slaughtered each year in China, Thailand, Korea, and the Philippines. Their fur is used to cover figurines, other "art" objects, and apparel. The prime market for these items is the United States, and the retail markup is 100 percent.

This utter inhumanity raised such a furor in this country that President Clinton signed the Dog and Cat Protection Act into law in November of 2000. It is now illegal to import and sell items that are made from the pelts of domestic dogs and cats.

It is sometimes difficult to tell real hair from synthetic, but if it looks like a duck and quacks like a duck you can bet that it is a duck. Many of the items are labeled "rabbit," which implies that rabbits have no central nervous system and cannot feel pain.

When I aired this terrible story on television I received more than 300 letters and e-mails from people asking what they could do to help stop this profiting from pain. Three responses told me to mind my own business and one was a definite threat.

I have been told by the United States Customs Service in Washington that they are actively enforcing the Dog and Cat Protection Act of 2000 and that the importation of products made from dog or cat fur has been stopped. DNA testing is used by customs officials who have been specially trained in identifying suspect shipments. Items that have been seized range from dolls and animal figurines to full-length coats. The Customs Service promises to fulfill its responsibility, and this can result in a $10,000 fine as well as criminal prosecution.

A great number of businesses in Northeast Ohio and throughout the country continue to illegally sell products made from dog and cat fur, with gift, craft, and flower shops the main providers.

What can you do if you are aware of businesses that continue to sell such items? First, tell the seller about the law. The Customs Service recommends that you report violators by calling 1-800-BE-ALERT. Be direct and concise.

All the defenseless animals thank you.

JAN FEB MAR APR MAY JUN JUL AUG SEP OCT NOV DEC

JAN
FEB
MAR
APR
MAY
JUN
JUL
AUG
SEP
OCT
NOV
DEC

Brandy at her new home with Lucy and Dan McDonald

Animal Adoptions Success Stories

KATE MALARNEY

Patches

Jan Ward wanted an all-around good family dog. "My main requirement was that it be good with kids," says this Avon Lake mother of three, who was waiting until her children were past toddlerhood before taking on the task of raising a dog. When her youngest turned four, she and her husband decided they were ready, and they called a friend connected with the Oasis Animal Shelter in Oberlin.

The very next day they were told about a possible match. So the whole family went to the shelter—Jan thinks it was as much for the shelter to check them out as for them to check out the dog. Enter Patches, who has quickly become the Wards' newest family member. "I can't imagine life without her now," says Jan. "She's as much a part of the family as the kids."

An Australian shepherd mix who was about a year old when they adopted her in April, Patches lives up to her name: She's brown with black-and-white spots and has one eye that's blue and one that's brown and blue. A little skittish at first, she took a few weeks to get settled in her new home. Now, according to Jan, "She's high energy, but pleasant and just great with the kids." The Wards' seven-year-old twin boys love throwing a toy for her to fetch in the yard—her speed makes her fun to watch. She's quick in other ways, too, picking up basic obedience commands and being trained on the invisible fence.

Jan was amazed at how good Patches was during a recent weekend when they had a houseful of guests. "She'd sit and wait to be petted instead of jumping all over people like she did when she first came home with us. She's come such a long way in a short time. I look at her now, and it's so hard to think of her languishing in a shelter." Seems like it would be just as hard for Patches to imagine life without the Wards.

Brandy

When Lucy McDonald asked the Lake County Humane Society to let her know if a golden retriever ever came up for adoption, she didn't expect to hear from them anytime soon. She had heard it was such a nice breed, and wonderful with kids (she's got five grandchildren), so she was surprised when she got a call in March 2002 to stop by the shelter and meet Brandy. "She came right to us in the little waiting room," says Lucy. "I get goose bumps just thinking of it!"

She and her husband, Dan, felt like Brandy had been sent to them from above. Dan had just lost his mother, and Lucy was struggling with back problems; Brandy was their comfort. "She'd come and put her head on my lap when I was down about not being able to get around," says Lucy, who attributes some of her recent recovery to Brandy, for giving her something to focus on besides her back pain.

At first, the McDonalds were a little worried about the six-year-old retriever, who weighed in at a whopping 144 pounds and panted all the time. "The vet said it was going to be a lot of work dealing with her obesity, but instead of work it's been a joy," says Lucy. Brandy dropped 20 pounds by midsummer thanks to a special diet and twice-daily walks with Dan around their Mentor-on-the-Lake home.

"We had dogs when our children were younger, and it was more like a chore, cleaning up the hair and taking care of them when we both worked. But not with Brandy! I'm home now and Dan's retired, and our children and grandchildren come over to take care of her when we're away. We hope and pray she lives a long time because we just love her."

Rebound

Rebound's name pretty much says it all. Rebound the cat had been resting on a car engine when the driver unknowingly started the car. The feline was brought in to Berea Animal Rescue in very bad shape. Due to the extent of his injuries, no one was able to check his gender, and the unknown cat was named Lydia at first.

Leah Kubiak was working as a volunteer at the shelter when the cat arrived. She was there when they discovered that the "she" cat was really a "he" cat and renamed him Lyndon. "He went through heck," Leah says. "He had multiple surgeries on his neck and hind legs. And he was always such a gentleman!" He let the workers give him antibiotics, which he was on for weeks, let them apply hot compresses and Neosporin to his wounds, and even let Leah cut off his casts after his many surgeries.

"He was so patient, so kind—of course I had to take him home. Apparently everyone else knew I was taking him home before I did, but I'll never forget when I finally decided—it changed my life!" It was Leah who started calling him Rebound.

"Rebound is so grateful. He just loves life. He talks to me and follows me around the house like a dog. I have four cats, all rescued, and they all seem to know, but Rebound really seems to know he was rescued." Leah says she was a little skeptical about bringing another cat home, but never regrets her decision—except when the cats keep her up at night!

Pandora and Thor Started it All

Word seems to have gotten around the animal kingdom that Sharon and Joe French's house in Edinburgh Township is the place to be. The couple owns 11 happy pooches and cares for neighborhood cats out of their garage-turned-kennel. And it all started with a sweet little pair of pups named Pandora and Thor.

The Frenches visited the Portage County Animal Protective League in Ravenna, where a litter of puppies—a Labrador-collie-hound mix—had come in. "I knew I had to have the one that looked up at me with these big brown eyes, and Joe knew he had to have the one that practically waddled up to him," says Sharon, so the sister and brother came home to join the two dogs Sharon already had.

Pandora and Thor brought new life to the older dogs, and started a ball rolling. Sharon started volunteering at the Portage APL, and it was on one of

Pandora and Thor brought new life to the French household

her trips taking supplies to the shelter that she ran across Jasmine, a sweet Sheltie-husky mix with bright blue eyes. "Even Joe, when he saw those eyes, knew she was ours," Sharon says, so home she went.

And then came Kowia and Banjo, two Plott hounds the Frenches waited over a year to take home, while an APL court case kept them housed at the shelter. They love having another set of siblings like Pandora and Thor, who will turn three in December. "They grow up together, they grow old together," says Sharon, who used to raise dogs and teach obedience. Joe once worked at a veterinarian's office, so together the couple has a lot to offer their brood. The last four dogs the Frenches took in were injured or lost pets Sharon thinks were just abandoned out in the country where they live. And the cats have come from all over. The Frenches adopted Sheba from the APL and keep her indoors with four other feline friends. The others are neighbor cats for whom they provide food and shelter whenever the kitties come looking for it.

"People say the animals are so lucky, but really, we're the lucky ones," says Sharon. "And it was Pandora and Thor who started it all. They opened our eyes to the need, the want, the love that's returned to you when you adopt these animals."

JAN FEB MAR APR MAY JUN JUL AUG SEP OCT NOV DEC

NORTHEAST OHIO ANIMAL SHELTERS

ASHLAND COUNTY

Ashland County Animal Shelter
1710 Garfield Ave., Ashland, (419)
289-1455

ASHTABULA COUNTY

Animal Protective League
5970 Green Rd., Ashtabula, (216)
224-1222

Ashtabula County Dog Warden
25 W. Jefferson, Jefferson,
(440) 576-3750

CARROLL COUNTY

Carroll County Dog Pound/Dog Warden
2185 Kennsington Rd. NE,
Carrollton, (330) 627-4244

COLUMBIANA COUNTY

Columbiana County Dog Pound
131 1/2 North Jefferson St.,
Lisbon, (330) 424-6663

COSHOCTON COUNTY

Coshocton County Dog Warden
349 1/2 Main St., Coshocton, (740)
622-9741

CUYAHOGA COUNTY

Animal Protective League
1729 Willey Ave., Cleveland, (216)
771-4616

Berea Animal Rescue Shelter
400 Barrett Rd., Berea,
(440) 234-2034

Bide-A-Wee Cat Shelter
8800 Akins Rd., North Royalton,
(440) 582-4990

Cleveland City Kennel
2690 W. 7th St., Cleveland,
(216) 664-3069

Cuyahoga County Animal Shelter
9500 Sweet Valley Dr.,
Valley View, (216) 525-7877

Euclid Animal Shelter
25100 Lakeland Blvd., Euclid, (216)
289-2057

Greyhound Adoption of Ohio
7122 Country Ln., Chagrin Falls,
(440) 543-6256

Parma Animal Shelter
6260 State Rd., Parma,
(440) 885-8014

Sanctuary for Senior Dogs
P.O. Box 609054, Cleveland, (216)
485-9233

Valley Save-A-Pet
715 Broadway Ave., Bedford, (440)
232-9124

ERIE COUNTY

Erie County Dog Shelter
2900 Columbus Ave., Sandusky,
(419) 627-7607

Erie County Humane Society
1911 Superior St., Sandusky, (419)
626-6220

GEAUGA COUNTY

Geauga Dog Warden
12513 Merritt Rd., Chardon, (440)
286-8135

Rescue Village (Geauga County Humane Society)
15463 Chillicothe Rd., Novelty, (440)
338-4819

HARRISON COUNTY

Harrison County Dog Pound
100 West Market Street, Cadiz, (740)
942-4080

HOLMES COUNTY

Holmes County Dog Shelter
5387 County Rd. 349,
Millersburg, (330) 674-6301

HURON COUNTY

Huron County Dog Pound
258 Benedict Avc., Norwalk, (419)
668-9773

JEFFERSON COUNTY

Jefferson County Dog Pound
Fernwood Rd., Wintersville, (740)
264-6888

LAKE COUNTY

Lake County Dog Pound
49 Fairdale Rd., Painesville,
(440) 350-2640

Lake County Humane Society
7564 Tyler Blvd., Suite E, Mentor,
(440) 951-6122

North Coast Humane Society
269 Shoregate Mall, Willowick,
(440) 585-5155

LORAIN COUNTY

Animal Protective League
8303 Murray Ridge Rd., Elyria, (440)
322-4321

Lorain County Dog Pound
301 Hadaway, Elyria,
(440) 329-5599

Oasis Dog Shelter
P.O. Box 11, Oberlin,
(440) 775-4101

MAHONING COUNTY

Mahoning County Kennel
589 Industrial Rd., Youngstown,
(330) 740-2205

MEDINA COUNTY

Forgotten Animal Shelter
P.O. Box 46, Medina,
(330) 769-1321

Medina County Animal Shelter
6334 Deerview Ln., Medina, (330)
725-9121

Medina County S.P.C.A.
P.O. Box 135, Medina,
(330) 723-7722

PORTAGE COUNTY

Happy Trails Farm Animal Sanctuary
5623 New Milford Rd., Ravenna,
(330) 733-1478

Portage County Animal Protective League
903 E. Lake St., Ravenna,
(330) 296-4022

RICHLAND COUNTY

Richland County Dog Warden
50 Park Avenue, East, Mansfield,
(419) 774-5893

Richland County Humane Soc.
395 Lantz Rd., Mansfield,
(440) 774-4795

STARK COUNTY

Stark County Humane Society
5100 Peach St., Louisville,
(330) 453-5529

SUMMIT COUNTY

Friends of Pets
2780 Fallen Log Ln., Akron, (330) 864-7387

Greater Akron Humane Society
4904 Quick Rd., Peninsula, (330) 657-2010

Hearts and Paws Adoption
P.O. Box 313, Canal Fulton, (330) 668-9706

Pet Guards Shelters
730 Portage Trail Ext., Akron, (216) 920-1522

Precious Lives Animal Sanctuary
147 Brittain Rd., Akron, (330) 633-5959

South Summit Kitten/Puppy Rescue
3700 Massillon Rd., Uniontown, (330) 882-6007

Summit County Animal Shelter
460 E. North St., Akron, (330) 643-2845

Tri-County Animal Protective League
1611 Amherst Rd. NE, Massillon, (330) 833-8479

TRUMBULL COUNTY

Trumbull County Kennel
7501 Anderson, Warren, (330) 675-2787

TUSCAWARAS COUNTY

Tuscawaras County Shelter
441 University Dr., New Philadelphia, (330) 339-2616

ℱlora & ℱauna MAY

WEEK 1
BIRDS: —Newly hatched goslings follow their parents in fuzzy yellow armadas at Cleveland Metroparks refuges. House wrens start to breed next week. Are your wren houses ready? 🐾 **MAMMALS:** Woodchucks seem to be everywhere along parkways and all-purpose trail edges, already stuffing themselves with tender young grasses. Young woodchucks will venture forth with their mothers next month. 🐾 **WILDFLOWERS:** Mayapple flowers should be blooming under their umbrella-like leaves by this weekend. 🐾 **SHRUBS:** Redbud is in bloom.

WEEK 2
BIRDS: Hummingbirds, rose-breasted grosbeaks, nighthawks, and chimney swifts should all be arriving this week or next. The peak of warbler migration is likely to occur this week. Bird walks in the forests and fields of Cleveland Metroparks are likely to turn up more birds than you ever knew existed! Many will soon be gone as they continue migration, while others "disappear" in the newly unfolding leaves of the treetops. 🐾 **SHRUBS:** Flowering dogwood is blooming. A drive down Valley Parkway or Hawthorn Parkway is a breathtaking sight in the early morning sun.

WEEK 3
BIRDS: Wood thrushes and veeries return to fill Cleveland Metroparks forests with their haunting flute-like calls each evening. Northern orioles begin to look for elms to build their hanging nests. 🐾 **TREES:** Tall, white flowers of Ohio buckeye stand in sharp contrast to the new green leaves in many places along the parkways. Apple trees and wild lilacs are now in bloom and mark old farmsteads long abandoned in the Rocky River Valley. 🐾 **AMPHIBIANS:** Green frogs call at midday. Their banjo-like "gunk-gunk" calls are easy to tell from the "jug-o-rum" calls of the lookalike bullfrog.

WEEK 4
BIRDS: Many birds are in courtship and some have begun building nests and incubating eggs. Get up early this weekend and listen to the early morning chorus in Cleveland Metroparks forests. Bluebird houses are sometimes appropriated by tree swallows, house wrens, or chickadees. Though they're not bluebirds, each species is a beautiful addition to the world. 🐾 **WILDFLOWERS:** Daisy fleabane, first of the summer daisies, may begin to open its white blossoms this week. It was rumored to be used as an insect repellent when crushed or burned.

Adapted from the Nature Almanac by Robert Hinkle, with permission from Cleveland Metroparks.

JAN FEB MAR APR MAY JUN JUL AUG SEP OCT NOV DEC

Happy Trails To Me!

JANICE THE PIG

(as told to Annette Fisher)

This is the story of how I started the rescue organization
called Happy Trails Farm Animal Sanctuary.

My name's Janice, and I'm a pot-bellied pig. I used to live in a cramped, dark dungeon in a barn, with barely enough room to move around. I never really got to see the sunshine, which I've come to love so much, because my door was always kept closed. It wouldn't have mattered though: I couldn't walk well enough to get out of my prison anyway. I shared my tiny area with some scary-looking spiders who lived in the thick, dusty cobwebs that hung down all around me. I know there was another pig in a stall near me, but that's just because I could hear him and smell him—I couldn't really see him through the slats in the wall. It was pretty lonely, actually, not being able to see anyone or anything. I was really sad, not to mention pretty miserable.

Though I'm really a very clean animal, I had no choice but to lay in my own waste, because my area was so small and no one ever really cleaned it up for me. The wet ground sure didn't help matters any—my legs and shoulders hurt so badly, and my arthritis got worse with the damp conditions. My owner thought my legs were broken when she got me—they dropped me when they took me out of the truck—but she didn't find out for sure.

And my skin was dry, cracked, and peeling because of the unhealthy living conditions and because of my diet—I was fed sweet feed for horses. Because of that I was also very overweight, but at the same time undernourished when it came to the dietary needs of a pot-bellied pig. My legs just got worse and worse, and my knees, shoulders, and feet hurt. I gave up trying to move around and mostly just lay in the back corner. I wasn't given anything for pain.

It seemed like an eternity went by, six years to be exact, and then my owner prepared to go on vacation. This other lady came over to learn what all the animals ate so she could take care of us while my owner was gone, and she opened the door to my box and met me, Janice.

She asked all kinds of questions about me and tried to find out what was wrong with me and why I was kept in my little cubicle. The lady was probably pretty nice, but I didn't really trust anyone at the time, so I tried to bite her anyway. I just didn't want to be bothered, and up to this point people hadn't been very kind to me.

So my owner went on vacation, and the nice lady would come talk to me every day when she'd feed me, and leave my door open on purpose so I could get some light and air in my room. She even held my bowl for me while I ate so it wouldn't tip over (I couldn't stand up well enough to eat a whole meal standing up over a bowl, so I lay down to eat). She gave me dry hay to lie on and tried to pet me, but I wouldn't hear of it. I was sure she would be like everyone else—just up to something.

So my owner came back after about a week and asked this new person what she owed her for feeding us animals. Imagine my surprise when the lady said, "Instead of paying me, how about letting me take your pig?" My ears perked up—they were talking about me! Her offer was accepted, and the next day a big van showed up to move me. But moving again! I hated new situations—things always seemed to go from bad to worse.

This nice man came along with the lady and helped me onto a sling, and though I protested quite loudly, they hoisted me up into the back of the van. They set me on soft blankets, and the lady actually crawled into the back of the van and held me on the ride home! What? People trying to be nice to me? Amazing! Yet I was still nervous about the whole situation.

I later went to the animal hospital. They gave me anesthesia so I wouldn't feel anything, and the nice doctors took x-rays of my legs, cleaned out my eyes and ears, filed my tusks, and trimmed my long hooves. I later heard them say that my legs weren't broken, but had atrophied due to lack of use. They gave me pain medication for my arthritis, and put healing salves on my skin.

Back at my new home, I saw a beautiful log cabin being built. Imagine my happiness when I learned that it was for me! A house all my own! How lucky can a pig get? It was filled with clean, dry straw,

A house all my own! How lucky can a pig get?

and a ramp was built so I could go in or out as I pleased. My new family brought out tiny pieces of low-fat bagels and made a line of them on the ground. I would have to get up and walk to eat the pieces of bagels, and so I started to get some exercise for my legs (and enjoyed some scrumptious healthy treats along the way!). I slowly learned to walk better, and though I'll never fully recover, I sure have made great progress. The nice people still massage my legs and shoulders daily, which helps me feel a lot better.

When winter came they installed a heat lamp for me and would bring me clean, warm sleeping bags to help keep me nice and toasty. I had finally found people who cared!

And then in the spring they brought me a little obnoxious baby pig for a friend. His name was George. George was a little pain in the neck at first—he had no manners and really annoyed me. But as he grew up, he started to be a true friend. I've heard them say that his job is to take care of me, and he sure does take his job seriously! When they bring us out fresh, sweet hay, George takes mouthful after mouthful, makes a wonderful, snuggly nest around me, and makes sure that I'm comfortable. I still have to keep him in line sometimes, though, but I truly enjoy having a companion. I don't feel lonely or miserable anymore.

Since I've moved here I've watched more farm animals come in one at a time. They all seem to be sad or injured at first. I've watched them get better and recover, and sometimes they leave to go to a new home. I've heard that they've been chosen by families who will love them and take excellent care of them. I can't believe the number of animals that have come through here in the past three years—there have been dozens, including horses, ponies, goats, chickens, geese, ducks, other pigs, hogs, a cow, and much more.

I've been told that I'll get to live here for the rest of my life, and that the log cabin will always belong to me and George. What a relief—I don't think I'd like to go through a move again!

I never realized how important my job in life was going to be or what a great responsibility I would have—a single pig who would start an entire farm animal rescue group. I now know that my purpose in life was to start the organization called Happy Trails Farm Animal Sanctuary. It would help other animals like me who had been neglected, abused, or abandoned. And since I have suffered so much and had such a huge responsibility, I now get to enjoy just being a pig for the rest of my life. I occasionally visit with guests who come to Happy Trails, but mostly like to nap with George under my warm heat lamp in the soft hay. They love me so much here—they tell me a million times a day, and I think they understand me when I say it back to them! I'm very proud to have been the first farm animal rescued here, and to have encouraged people to help more of us. And it all just started with me . . . Janice.

Annette Fisher is the director of the Happy Trails Farm Animal Sanctuary in Ravenna. Proceeds from her contribution benefit the Happy Trails Farm Animal Sanctuary.

JAN FEB MAR APR **MAY** JUN JUL AUG SEP OCT NOV DEC

JAN FEB MAR APR MAY JUN JUL AUG SEP OCT NOV DEC

Almanac Puzzler
NORTHEAST OHIO CITY NAMES

TERRY OBLANDER

Find all the names of Northeast Ohio cities below. They're listed forwards, backwards, and diagonally. Then arrange the unused letters to spell out a special message from Dick Goddard.

```
O L M S T E D F A L L S H D R O F D E B
E G A L L I V Y A B E U B E R E A N T R
L T B E N D G K N V N N P A R M A S A E
L S K I I R E O E T O A V O N V R V G A
I A L L A W B N I T H E I L A E E A N K
V E C F O S H N R B N I O R H N L I E O
S U T O I I G U N E R D R M N L D N W B
E O D L L V B D G B I E A A I E T N P E
N S L L A F N I R G A H C V M L W O H R
I D S L T A R O R U A L E K O L O R I L
A L L A L E O L A L E G A K S I L T L I
P E N I I K A L H V N E E R G V L H A N
Y I M R L K U I E A U T N A M Y I O D A
K F E Y R B N L R C N W O T S E W L E V
S Y N O A C A O A Y A E A S L L N M L R
U A N T K N O L O S L R T R S T E S P E
D M H L D N O T N A C E R A R N L T H N
N S E R E V I R Y K C O R O R E G E I I
A Y S T R O N G S V I L L E L B N D A M
S W E S T H G I E H G R U B E L D D I M
```

Akron, Amherst, Ashtabula, Aurora, Avon, Bay Village, Bedford, Bentleyville, Berea, Bratenahl, Brecksville, Brooklyn, Burton, Canton, Carroll, Chagrin Falls, Cleveland, East, Elyria, Erie, Euclid, Geneva, Glenwillow, Grafton, Green, Hinckley, Hiram, Hunting Valley, Kent, Lakewood, Lisbon, Lodi, Mantua, Mayfield, Medina, Middleburg Heights, Minerva, Navarre, New Philadelphia, Niles, North Olmsted, Oberlin, Olmsted Falls, Orange Village, Painesville, Parma, Ravenna, Rocky River, Sandusky, Seven Hills, Solon, Stark, Stow, Strongsville, Warren, West

SPECIAL MESSAGE: __ __   __ __ __ __ __   __ __   __ __ __   __ __ __ __ __ __ __

Summer

Ah, summer in Northeast Ohio. We can't wait until it arrives, we complain when it's here, and we are sorry to see it end...

<table>
<tr><td colspan="2">NORTHEAST OHIO'S WARMEST AND COLDEST SUMMERS
(by Median Temp)</td></tr>
<tr><td colspan="2">WARMEST</td></tr>
<tr><td>Cleveland:</td><td>75.0° / 1949</td></tr>
<tr><td>Akron/Canton:</td><td>73.9° / 1931</td></tr>
<tr><td colspan="2">COLDEST</td></tr>
<tr><td>Cleveland:</td><td>66.7° / 1927</td></tr>
<tr><td>Akron/Canton:</td><td>67.3° / 1992</td></tr>
</table>

By June the struggle between the warm inroads of spring and the cold remnants of winter has been decided. While June supplies Ohio with its share of thunderstorm squall lines and tornado activity, the approach of the lazy, hazy days of summer brings on a more stable weather regime.

Ohio is no stranger to periods of withering heat in summertime, especially during the traditional 40-day Dog Day sizzle from July 3 through August 11. Post-frontal winds across the waters of Lake Erie can provide several days of welcome air-conditioned relief for the northeast corner of the state, while the remainder of Ohio is still in the sauna

On the first day of summer we receive an average of 15 hours and 11 minutes of daylight. Sunshine is a steady companion in the Ohio sky during June, July, and August. Even the northeast counties, so heavily clouded from November into March, are bathed in more sunshine during this three-month period than are such fabled Sunbelt cities as Tampa-St. Petersburg, New Orleans, and San Diego.

A melancholy paradox is that the moment summer begins the sun also begins it gradual journey southward. The days shorten, and by the end of August we notice lengthening shadows, shadows that were not there as recently as June and July.

IN THE
✶ Northeast Ohio Sky ✶
THIS SEASON

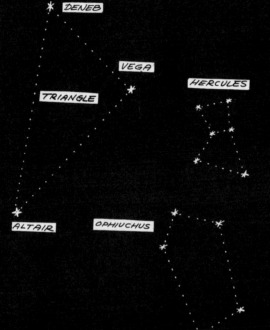

Summer

The featured stars of the summer are Deneb, Vega (VEE-gah), and Altair and together they form the Summer Triangle. Nearly overhead, Vega is the brightest star in our summer sky.

Near the southern horizon you can find the Mars-red star called Antares (an-TAIR-ese). Indeed, the name means "rival of Mars."

Two prominent constellations are Ophiuchous (OFF-ih-YOU-kus) (which means "snake-holder"), and Hercules (in Greek mythology, the strongest man on earth).

Under the darkest of skies (clear, moonless nights), the Milky Way paints a ghostly river across the heavens.

JUNE STATISTICS

SUNSHINE %	65
DRIEST MONTH	0.39"/1933
WARMEST MONTH	73.9°/1949
COLDEST MONTH	62.2°/1903
LIQUID PCPN AVG.	3.70"
RAINIEST DAY	4.00"/1972
RAINIEST MONTH	9.77"/1902
THUNDERY DAYS	7
SNOWIEST DAY	Trace/1907
DAYS ONE INCH SNOW	0

As the song says, "June is bustin' out all over." The first consistently warm—even hot—weather often delays until this month. Mid- to late June can sometimes be a blazer here. At 4:37 p.m. on June 25, 1988, Cleveland's temperature rocketed to an all-time high of 104° F. (Bone-dry and very windy thunderstorms added a meteorological exclamation point that evening.)

Thunderstorms are common here in June and tornadoes are not strangers. The great Sandusky-Lorain tornado hit on June 28, 1924. The tornado that killed 9 in Cuyahoga County (20 in Ohio) on June 8, 1953, passed very close to Cleveland's Public Square before exiting over Lake Erie around East 40th Street. In 1959, heavy rains caused severe flooding on Cleveland's East Side, submerging many vehicles; passengers on a transit bus in University Circle were rescued by motorboats. The latest Cleveland snow—only a trace—fell on June 5, 1907. Summer arrives with the solstice occurring around the 21st (leap year can make it vary).

Sun worshipers should be aware of the strengthening sunshine, especially powerful between the hours of 10 a.m. and 2 p.m. On warm, moist evenings fireflies (glowworms) will jet across the grass, eternally followed by small children carrying glass mason-jar prisons.

JAN FEB MAR APR MAY JUN JUL AUG SEP OCT NOV DEC

DAILY DATA FOR JUNE

Side tabs: JAN FEB MAR APR MAY JUN JUL AUG SEP OCT NOV DEC

Date	Moon Phase	Day	Day of Year	Days Left in Year	Sunrise	Sunset	Length of Day	Avg. Hi	Avg. Lo
1		Sun	152	213	5:55	8:54	14:59	74	53
2		Mon	153	212	5:55	8:55	15:00	75	53
3		Tue	154	211	5:55	8:55	15:00	75	53
4		Wed	155	210	5:54	8:56	15:02	75	54
5		Thu	156	209	5:54	8:57	15:03	76	54
6		Fri	157	208	5:54	8:57	15:03	76	54
7	◑	Sat	158	207	5:53	8:58	15:05	76	55
8		Sun	159	206	5:53	8:59	15:06	77	55
9		Mon	160	205	5:53	8:59	15:06	77	55
10		Tue	161	204	5:53	9:00	15:07	77	56
11		Wed	162	203	5:53	9:00	15:07	77	56
12		Thu	163	202	5:52	9:01	15:09	78	56
13		Fri	164	201	5:52	9:01	15:09	78	56
14	○	Sat	165	200	5:52	9:02	15:10	78	57
15		Sun	166	199	5:52	9:02	15:10	78	57
16		Mon	167	198	5:52	9:02	15:10	79	57
17		Tue	168	197	5:52	9:03	15:11	79	57
18		Wed	169	196	5:52	9:03	15:11	79	58
19		Thu	170	195	5:53	9:03	15:10	79	58
20		Fri	171	194	5:53	9:04	15:11	79	58
21	◐	Sat	172	193	5:53	9:04	15:11	80	58
22		Sun	173	192	5:53	9:04	15:11	80	59
23		Mon	174	191	5:53	9:04	15:11	80	59
24		Tue	175	190	5:54	9:04	15:10	80	59
25		Wed	176	189	5:54	9:04	15:10	81	59
26		Thu	177	188	5:54	9:04	15:10	81	59
27		Fri	178	187	5:55	9:04	15:09	81	59
28		Sat	179	186	5:55	9:04	15:09	81	60
29	●	Sun	180	185	5:56	9:04	15:08	81	60
30		Mon	181	184	5:56	9:04	15:08	81	60

Rec. Hi °	Rec. Lo °	Avg. Lake °	On This Date ...
95/1934	40/1981	57	Superman Comics launched (1938)
94/1934	39/1966	57	Congress grants citizenship to Native Americans (1924)
91/1925	35/1977	58	Alexander Graham Bell transmits first wireless message (1880)
93/1925	40/1947	58	10-cent beer night riot at Municipal Stadium (1974)
93/1925	38/1990	59	Browns' Marion Motley born (1920)
92/1988	38/1945	59	Cleveland Museum of Art opens (1916)
91/1999	39/1977	59	Actor Dean Martin born in Steubenville (1917)
98/1933	39/1977	60	Tornadoes kill 110 in Mich. & Ohio (1953)
92/1914	41/1949	60	Donald Duck debuts (1934)
92/1999	31/1972	60	Rocky Colavito homers in 4 consecutive at-bats for Indians (1959)
93/1933	31/1972	61	WJW-AM/TV in Cleveland Ohio change call letters to WRMR (1985)
92/1954	42/1980	61	Race riot in Cincinnati Ohio (300 arrested) (1967)
93/1954	43/1979	62	Comedian Paul Lynde born in Mt Vernon, OH (1926)
95/1988	43/1978	62	U.S. Army founded (1775)
97/1954	43/1997	62	1 inch of snow falls in northern Pennsylvania (1918)
96/1952	39/1961	62	1st Father's Day celebrated in Spokane, WA (1010)
93/1994	38/1980	63	Final edition of *Cleveland Press* published (1982)
96/1944	41/1950	63	Challenger launched; Sally Ride 1st U.S. woman in space (1983)
95/1995	46/1965	63	KYW-AM in Cleveland Ohio returns call letters to Philadelphia (1965)
96/1988	46/1962	64	Joe Dimaggio's 2,000th hit, Yanks beat Indians 8-2 (1950)
95/1941	45/1897	64	Carl Stokes, first black mayor of major U.S. city, born in Cleve. (1927)
98/1988	39/1992	64	Last (?) of the Cuyahoga River fires rages (1969)
94/1948	41/1963	65	U.S. Secret Service created (1860)
96/1952	44/1915	65	Picasso's first exhibit (1901)
104/1988	41/1979	65	Custer's last stand (1876)
99/1952	47/1984	65	U.N. Charter signed (1945)
98/1944	44/1981	65	Browns' Don Rogers dies of cocaine poisoning (1986)
101/1944	49/1988	66	Lorain-Sandusky tornado kills 72 (1924)
94/1952	51/1985	66	Statesman Henry Clay dies at age 72 (1852)
95/1941	41/1988	66	Battle of Fort Recovery, Ohio (1794)

JAN FEB MAR APR MAY JUN JUL AUG SEP OCT NOV DEC

BENJAMIN HARRISON
23rd PRESIDENT 1889–1893

Dick Goddard

Descended from a distinguished family, Benjamin Harrison was the grandson of our ninth president, William Henry Harrison, who held office only briefly in 1841.

Along with eight brothers and sisters, Harrison was "to the manor born," growing up on a 2,000-acre estate at North Bend, Ohio. He was born on August 20, 1833. At five feet, six inches tall he was one of our most diminutive presidents. (James Madison, at five feet, four inches was our shortest, while Abraham Lincoln at six feet, four inches was our tallest.)

Weighing around 165 pounds, and known as "Little Ben," Harrison was stocky, with blue eyes and light brown hair that was as flaxen as corn silk in his youth. He was not athletic but did enjoy brisk walks and carriage rides. Harrison was a fashionable dresser and was one of the last 19th-century statesmen to sport a full beard.

Disdaining small talk, Harrison was stiff and formal when meeting the public and frequently put on gloves when required to shake hands (this move—whose wisdom has been verified by modern medicine—kept him generally free of colds and infections). On the campaign trail, journalists found him cold and remote and added another nickname: "The Human Iceberg."

While faulted for lacking the common touch, Harrison was praised for his integrity, intellect, and political decency. Dedicated to detail, he was a perfectionist and could not tolerate inefficiency or incompetence.

Harrison was tutored at home and in a nearby one-room log schoolhouse. His teacher called him the brightest in his family, although "terribly stubborn." Very religious, Harrison was a devout Presbyterian (taught by his strict, churchgoing mother). He became a church deacon and Sunday school teacher. As president he held a special pew at the Presbyterian Church of the Covenant in Washington. He supported legislation that denounced the influence and power of the Mormon Church, and conducted no state business on Sunday.

As with some other Ohio presidents, it was Harrison's military service during the Civil War that gave him an entree to high political office. He served with the 70th Indiana Infantry Regiment from July of 1862 to June of 1865, rising from second lieutenant to brigadier general. Harrison disliked the military life, but he performed bravely on the battlefield and marched with Ohio's General William Sherman into Georgia.

While a student at Miami University in Oxford, Ohio, Harrison became engaged at the age of 20 to Caroline (Carrie) Scott, who was 21. Harrison spent so much time courting Carrie that he became known as "the pious moonlight dude." (Cowabunga!)

They were married in 1853, but it was to be 36 years before they resided in the White House. Carrie was credited with putting up the first Christmas tree in the White House, and also purged the residence of its rather large rodent population. Harrison was the first president to have a telephone in the chief executive's mansion, and the first electric lights were also installed while he lived there (until then only candles and gaslights were used for illumination). However, the First Family was afraid of using them. The fearful Harrisons didn't turn the lights off or on for weeks. They would sleep with the lights glowing until an engineer arrived to turn them off in the morning.

Harrison followed a circuitous route to the presidency. He had moved to Indianapolis to practice law and in 1881 was elected to the United States Senate from Indiana. In 1881 Harrison backed into the Republican nomination for president when the favorite refused to run. While he lost the popular vote against Grover Cleveland in the national election, Harrison won the electoral vote, 233 to 168.

During Harrison's administration the Monroe Doctrine was changed, setting the stage for territorial expansion. He was a dedicated women's rights advocate, stating that "the manner by which women are treated is a good criterion to judge the state of society. If we knew but this one feature of the character of a nation, we may easily judge the rest, for as society advances, the true character of woman is discovered."

JAN FEB MAR APR MAY JUN JUL AUG SEP OCT NOV DEC

Harrison's term in office is often overlooked, since many called him an "inactive" president whose term in office was a fluke, claiming that he did not possess the temperament required of the office.

Harrison ran for a second term as president in 1892. His wife suddenly passed away during the campaign and he lost the strength and stamina to continue.

Much to the shock and dismay of family members, Harrison remarried four years after Carrie's death. His new wife was 25 years his junior. None of the former president's family attended the wedding.

Harrison died on March 13, 1901, of pneumonia in Indianapolis. He was buried alongside his first wife at Crown Hill Cemetery in Indianapolis. Renowned Hoosier poet James Whitcomb Riley delivered the eulogy.

Harrison's second wife outlived him by 48 years, passing away in 1948.

Flora & Fauna JUNE

WEEK 1
BIRDS: Adult chickadees and titmice grow scarce at bird feeders as they busily hatch and fledge their young. June evenings bring the flute-like calls of wood thrushes and veeries as twilight settles on the land. **WILDFLOWERS:** Summer flowers begin to dot the open meadows of Cleveland Metroparks with oranges and yellows of hawkweed and yellows of cinquefoil

WEEK 2
BIRDS: Nighthawks (not true hawks but relatives of whippoorwills) grace the evening skies throughout the region as they hunt for their insect prey. Listen for the "b-z-z-z-t" made by their wings as they power-dive for food. **MAMMALS:** Young woodchucks emerge to learn the ways of the woodchuck world with their mothers. **WILDFLOWERS:** Yellow iris adds a touch of bright color to the green of marsh edges. Cow parsnip as tall as a person appears with umbrella-shaped white blossoms along stream banks and marsh edges. **TREES:** Snow in June? No, just uncountable millions of seeds of the cottonwood tree drifting about in the summer breeze.

WEEK 3
BIRDS: Fledgling chickadees begin to appear at bird feeders with their tired parents. **WILDFLOWERS:** By tradition, St. John's wort blooms on June 21 to ward away evil spirits on a midsummer's night eve. Wild strawberries ripen in this third week of the "strawberry moon." Watch open fields and roadsides for the first of the pale blue flowers of chicory, sometimes called blue sailors. **FISHES:** Carp begin to thrash along shorelines of Lake Isaac and the lower reaches of the Rocky River as they spawn and lay eggs in warm shallow water.

WEEK 4
WILDFLOWERS: Common milkweed unfolds fragrant purple flowers beginning this week and continuing through July. The flowers turn into green dill-pickle-sized pods and are a prized "wild edible" in some parts of the country. Queen Anne's lace begins to bloom. Yellow and orange spotted jewelweed is blooming on moist sites throughout Cleveland Metroparks. Later in summer, their "exploding" seed pods delight hikers brave enough to touch! **REPTILES:** Snapping turtles may travel great distances from their native waters to lay eggs in warm sandy hillsides.

Adapted from the Nature Almanac by Robert Hinkle, with permission from Cleveland Metroparks.

JAN FEB MAR APR MAY JUN JUL AUG SEP OCT NOV DEC

AP Wide World / photo illustration by Newbomb Design

Dick & Mick

MICHAEL STANLEY

For most, fame is a fleeting thing. Hardly a week passes where someone doesn't stop me to ask, "Hey, didn't you used to be Michael Stanley?" And, although this query usually is delivered with a smile and what seem like the best of intentions, it still tends to throw a hitch in the old self-image stride. I guarantee you that Madonna and/or Mark Koontz will not handle this type of situation well!

Early on in my musical career Cleveland radio legend Kid Leo stuck me with the tag of "Cleveland's Favorite Son." Now for a long time this was quite flattering but, as I move through my fourth year as a card-carrying AARP member, it seems to me that the moniker might just be a bit "youthful" for my present circumstances. A few years ago, at a charity event, I even tried to pass the title on to Drew Carey but he decided to pass, citing contractual problems and a previous obligation to help one of the cocktail waitresses study for her SAT test. See . . . fame isn't always what it's cracked up to be!

And that brings me to Dick & Mick. Dick Goddard and Mick Jagger: the two most famous individuals I've ever met. As of this writing Mick's band, The Rolling Stones, have just announced their plans for their World Tour 2002/2003 (coming nearly 40 years after their first public performance) and

Dick Goddard is halfway through his 36th year as Channel 8's chief meteorologist. And although these two milestones may seem totally unrelated and these two cultural icons may seem to have traveled quite different paths, I would tend to disagree.

Sure there were rock 'n' roll bands before The Rolling Stones and there were probably even folks who forecast the weather before Dick Goddard, but with the arrival of Dick & Mick (Mick in a tour bus filled with groupies and Dick in a Nash Metropolitan filled with Neil Zurcher) the bar had been raised for all those who would try and follow in their footsteps. They had big shoes to fill and you know what they say about big shoes . . . yes, that's right: big socks.

I first met Mick in a club in New York City. He was quite gracious, bought me a drink, and a good time was had by all. I first met Dick near the vending machines at Channel 8. He didn't offer to buy me anything but did give me a Woollybear sticker. Advantage, Mick? I think not. Dick could have easily sprung for a cool refreshing beverage just like Mick did, but no way Mr. Jagger was going to hook me up with the coat of arms for our furry little friend. Result? Advantage, Dick!

Now we all know rock stars are supposed to be real skinny and wear colorful clothes. And it's safe to say that Mr. Jagger has that part of the routine down. But let's be honest here (and since you probably haven't met Mick you're going to have to take my word for this): Dick has got him beat again!

The man is a rail! Possibly negative % body fat (and don't forget about that old TV adding ten pounds to you thing!). Plus, if you put up some of Dick's legendary mid-'70s sport coats against Mick's stage attire, well, it's just not even a contest. There's colorful and then there's colorful!

But what about all those trappings of fame? Mick's got a private jet. Mick's got more cars than Del Spitzer. Mick's got so many houses he's not even sure where to have his mail sent. He seems to have it all, right? Wrong again! Dick could have the jet and the cars and the houses if he wanted to (and maybe even more houses since we all know that one's housing dollar goes a lot further here on the North Coast than in musty old London). But Mr. G has gone the J-man one better. He went and got himself one of those quadruple-storm chasing-Doppler radar thingamajigs! Do you know anybody else who has one of those babies? And you thought it was Channel 8's. No way! Dick just lets them use it. How cool is that?

And now we're getting down to the nitty gritty. With the possible exception of Bruce Willis, Yul Brynner, Michael Jordan, and Mr. Clean, famous people are supposed to have good hair (and forget about Donald Trump: nobody around him has the guts to tell him). Now, sure, Mick has quite a mane but just think about it. He's been changing his look for years! One tour it's long and shaggy, the next tour it's layered, and the next tour, well, you get the picture. He's on a continual search for the answers to his ongoing tonsorial questions. And Dick? Focused like a laser beam. He found his look and he's ridden it like the favorite in the third at Thistledown! The man is locked and loaded and his hair hasn't moved in over 30 years. And speaking as someone who has spent the better part of his own life searching for the right hair spray, I can only bow in sincere reverence.

Now we all know that the really famous guys get all the good-looking women. It was like that in high school and, with the exception of study hall and 50-cent lunches, not much has changed. And no question about it, Mick has always been a chick-magnet! He's got more supermodels than you could shake Kate Moss at! But not to worry because, when all is said and done, Dick wins again. The man knows the ultimate secret that every bachelor or divorced guy should know. If you want to meet women, always have a cute puppy around. It makes you irresistible. And he not only has the cute puppies around, he lets the women take them home. That, my friend, is genius! Plus, does Mick have Robin, Wilma, and Denise's home numbers? I rest my case.

So there you have it. Dick & Mick. Two giants who have each stomped on the terra firma in unique ways. And while Mick may belong to the world, Dick belongs to us. Advantage? Definitely us!

And I haven't even begun to address the rumor that the song was originally called "(I Can't Get No) Cumulonimbus."

Maybe next time …

Michael Stanley, longtime Cleveland musician, was the founding member of The Michael Stanley Band and continues to record music and perform live with Michael Stanley and The Resonators. Formerly a co-host of WJW TV 8's *PM Magazine*, he can currently be heard weekdays from 3–7 p.m. on 98.5 FM WNCX, Cleveland's Classic Rock Station.

JAN FEB MAR APR MAY JUN JUL AUG SEP OCT NOV DEC

First of three tornadoes that struck Ohio on June 8, 1953. Rated an F4, the twister ripped across southern Wood County, south of Bowling Green, and killed eight on its 60-mile journey.

Cleveland's Killer Twister

Dick Goddard

Many in Ohio have the date of a certain weather event fixed indelibly in their minds and on their calendars. In Cleveland that date of meteorological infamy is June 8, 1953, and this coming year marks the 50th anniversary of the evening when the gates of "weather hell" swung open here.

The weather on that Monday 50 years ago began cool and quiet with the early-morning temperature around 50 degrees. A big change was ahead. A warm front that was connected to a deep storm center over Iowa (29.29 inches of mercury) was moving northward in Ohio. After the front passed Cleveland early in the afternoon the temperature soared to 86 degrees, with oppressive humidity.

Everyone yearned for a refreshing breeze. The "breeze" that came later that evening blew in at over 200 miles per hour as one of three tornadoes that formed over Ohio ripped and ravaged its way into our meteorological memory. The twister, which first caused damage near the hamlet of Birmingham in Erie County, 40 miles southwest of Cleveland, took dead aim at the city's west side and headed for the heart of downtown Cleveland.

Tornado watches and warnings, with which we are so familiar today, did not exist in 1953. The tornado forecast techniques of the United States Weather Bureau (now the National Weather Service) were rudimentary at best; as recently as 1938, it had been illegal to even mention the word tornado in a forecast. At the time it was felt that this type of needle-in-a-haystack forecast would only result in panic.

The tornado outbreak that occurred on June 8–9 in 1953 was the third-deadliest in United States weather history. A total of 19 twisters killed 247 in Ohio, Michigan, and Massachusetts (at 8:30 p.m. on June 8—about a half hour before the Birmingham touchdown—a savage F5 tornado with 300-mile-per-hour winds struck the area around Flint, Michigan, killing 115 and becoming the last tornado in the U.S. to kill 100 or more people).

The first of Ohio's three twister sisters struck in the western part of the state at 7 p.m. Touching down in Wood County, the twister killed eight along its lengthy 60-mile path. The resultant damage gave this storm a Fujita scale rating of F4, with winds up to 260 miles per hour.

At about 7:30 a second tornado, later rated an F3 with winds up to 206 miles per hour, touched down on the ground in Erie County, killed one person, and then traveled a 10-mile path before lifting near Vermilion.

The Toledo weather bureau alerted the Cleveland Hopkins airport weather office at 7:40 that tornadic weather was headed their way. At 8:55, as the sky to the west turned black, Hopkins forecasters issued a rare tornado warning—the warning was almost as surprising as a tornado itself.

In Northeast Ohio homes that sultry evening nearly all the small-screen black-and-white television sets were tuned to *I Love Lucy*, with *The Red Buttons Show* coming up. Programming was interrupted twice with weather bulletins. The following day the Cleveland *Plain Dealer* reported that with the tornado warning on television "the city felt a panic as never felt before." The excitement was warranted.

At 9:08 a cumulonimbus cloud spawned a tornado over the northeastern corner of Erie County. Without the benefit of today's invaluable Skywarn ham radio operators, the Ohio funnel continued unannounced on a general east-north-east path. The tornado, which would eventually qualify as an F3, moved at a leisurely pace. At 9:45 a startled forecaster at Hopkins shouted, "There it is!" The vortex was indeed passing over the northern edge of the airport. Witnesses said the funnel looked like "a gray sheet of rain," alternately appearing and disappearing amid vivid flashes of lightning.

"We didn't hear anything until it got close," recalled one observer. "It was giving off a soft purr with a sort of blaze across the bottom."

The Weather Bureau anemometer recorded a wind gust of 65 miles per hour. Leaving Hopkins airport, the tornado became more energized as it moved across Linndale parallel to Bellaire Road, and by 9:55 it was just south of Lakewood, pummeling the area with baseball-sized hailstones.

The first major damage came northeast of Hopkins from West 130th to West 117th and Bellaire, where 100 homes were leveled. A three-month-old baby was carried from its home and flung against a garage. One house was picked up intact and dropped more than 30 yards from where it had stood. On Summerland and St. Johns avenues more than 20 homes were demolished.

Art Zimmerman was 10 when he lived through the nightmare. His family lived just off West 117th Street, near Linndale. He recalls how incredibly humid and sticky the air had become. After a cold bath he and his brother attempted to go to sleep in their stifling hot upstairs bedroom.

Art's father was looking out the front door as the torrential rain began. The rain soon stopped, followed by a brief silence before the wind began to pick up and golf-ball-size hail arrived. This was followed by a terrific, deafening roar "like a thousand freight trains." It was at that point that Art's dad rushed into the boys' bedroom and dragged the brothers out of bed (Art figured he was about to be punished for something he had done wrong). With the electricity out, the family stumbled downstairs and into the basement where they spent the entire night.

The early-morning light revealed not only the surrealistic devastation around the Zimmermans' house, but also what a close call the brothers had had. The window to the boys' bedroom was smashed, and embedded in the middle of their mattress was a large boulder.

The tornado grew wider (about half a mile) at West 45th Street and stronger as it reached Dennison and Lorain avenues by 10:05 p.m. From West 28th to West 25th and Detroit the damage was especially severe. Five were killed in one home at Franklin Circle. Thousands of trees were felled, and the tree roots brought the natural gas lines up with them. Stone and cement walks were torn from the ground, and the jumble of trees and downed power lines made streets impassable.

At about 10:08 the weakening and now skipping tornado vortex crossed the Cuyahoga River valley and headed for Public Square, where a charity street carnival—Fun for Funds—was in full force on Short Vincent Avenue.

On the bandstand Mrs. Al Rosen, the wife of the Cleveland Indians' star third baseman, had just finished singing the words "they're not painting the skies as blue this year" when the thunder, heavy rain, and wind began. After a few bars of "Singin' in the Rain" the event organizers told the guy sitting on a flagpole and everyone else who valued their lives to immediately take cover—somewhere.

Around 10:12 the whirling tornado funnel passed almost directly over the 52-story Terminal Tower, causing negligible damage. At 10:16 the tornado moved out over Lake Erie at East 40th Street and disintegrated as it passed over the cool lake

JAN FEB MAR APR MAY JUN JUL AUG SEP OCT NOV DEC

waters.

More than a few dazed citizens headed for the nearest bar. At a West 25th Street saloon an inebriated customer was denied further service. He broke a bottle over the bartender's head and was promptly shot. He survived his wounds. As the post-tornado turmoil continued, beleaguered Cleveland police chief Frank Story declared a state of emergency and the Ohio National Guard was called out. Nature's twisted revenge left seven dead in Greater Cleveland, with two contingent fatalities, one by heart attack and one by electrocution from touching a live wire. This was an amazingly low total considering the voracity of the storm and the damage that resulted. Property damage was estimated at $5 million, which would equate to well over $100 million today.

In addition to the 18 deaths registered across Ohio on June 8, 1953, a total of 229 other fatalities were attributed to the tornado outbreak over a two-day period. Congressman James Zandt (not from Ohio) made national news on June 10 when he blamed the massive tornado outbreak in the United States on the recent atomic testing in the Nevada desert. He called for a congressional investigation, but his request was denied.

Photo courtesy Tom Stepwith

The F3 tornado that would kill nine in Cuyahoga County as it appeared over the northern portion of Cleveland Hopkins Airport on the evening of June 8, 1953. Many reported that prior to the twister's appearance, the sky took on a strange yellow color.

NORTHEAST OHIO'S WETTEST AND DRIEST SUMMERS
(Rainfall)

. . . .

WETTEST
Cleveland: 19.88" / 1972
Akron/Canton: 20.28" / 1892

. . . .

DRIEST
Cleveland: 3.63" / 1933
Akron/Canton: 3.18" / 1991

JULY STATISTICS

SUNSHINE % 67

DRIEST MONTH . . . . 0.74"/1930

WARMEST MONTH . . . . 79.1°/1955

COLDEST MONTH . . . . 67.6°/1960

LIQUID PCPN AVG. . . . . 3.52"

RAINIEST DAY . . . . 2.87"/1969

RAINIEST MONTH . . . . 9.12"/1992

THUNDERY DAYS 6

SNOWIEST DAY . . . . None

DAYS ONE INCH SNOW 0

July can be a meteorological firecracker in Northeast Ohio. Lightning laces the sky more in this month than any other. The legendary dog days begin on July 3 and continue for 40 days. The ancient Egyptians came up with the canine idea because they believed that the dog star, Sirius (the brightest star in our skies), lent its heat to that of the sun. Sirius is unseen in our summer sky because of the brightness of our sun; indeed, Sirius comes over the eastern horizon each summer morning just ahead of the star we call our sun.

Our July atmosphere is often humid, and torrential rains can fall. On July 12, 1966, a state record 10.51 inches of rain fell in 24 hours at Sandusky. Even on a blistering July day, the raindrops will feel cold. That's because nearly all rainfall at Ohio's latitude begins as ice crystals and snow high above. On July 4, 1969, 12 hours of nearly continuous thunderstorms resulted in 42 deaths, most by drowning. Just northwest of Wooster, 14 inches of rain fell from the storms. On warm and sultry July nights heat lightning can be seen. The lightning is unaccompanied by thunder, since it is coming from a thunderstorm that may be a thousand miles away, in Oklahoma or southern Canada.

In this lush and verdant festival month the ubiquitous Queen Anne's lace will proliferate in unmowed fields. Katydids are fiddling away the nights.

JAN FEB MAR APR MAY JUN JUL AUG SEP OCT NOV DEC

DAILY DATA FOR JULY

Date	Moon Phase	Day	Day of Year	Days Left in Year	Sunrise	Sunset	Length of Day	Avg. Hi	Avg. Lo
1		Tue	182	183	5:56	9:04	15:08	81	60
2		Wed	183	182	5:57	9:04	15:07	82	60
3		Thu	184	181	5:58	9:04	15:06	82	60
4		Fri	185	180	5:58	9:04	15:06	82	60
5		Sat	186	179	5:59	9:03	15:04	82	61
6	◑	Sun	187	178	5:59	9:03	15:04	82	61
7		Mon	188	177	6:00	9:03	15:03	82	61
8		Tue	189	176	6:01	9:02	15:01	82	61
9		Wed	190	175	6:01	9:02	15:01	82	61
10		Thu	191	174	6:02	9:02	15:00	82	61
11		Fri	192	173	6:03	9:01	14:58	82	61
12		Sat	193	172	6:03	9:01	14:58	82	61
13	○	Sun	194	171	6:04	9:00	14:56	82	61
14		Mon	195	170	6:05	9:00	14:55	82	61
15		Tue	196	169	6:06	8:59	14:53	82	61
16		Wed	197	168	6:06	8:58	14:52	82	62
17		Thu	198	167	6:07	8:58	14:51	83	62
18		Fri	199	166	6:08	8:57	14:49	83	62
19		Sat	200	165	6:09	8:56	14:47	83	62
20		Sun	201	164	6:10	8:56	14:46	83	62
21	◑	Mon	202	163	6:11	8:55	14:44	83	62
22		Tue	203	162	6:12	8:54	14:42	83	62
23		Wed	204	161	6:13	8:53	14:40	83	62
24		Thu	205	160	6:13	8:52	14:39	83	62
25		Fri	206	159	6:14	8:51	14:37	83	62
26		Sat	207	158	6:15	8:50	14:35	83	62
27		Sun	208	157	6:16	8:49	14:33	83	62
28		Mon	209	156	6:17	8:48	14:31	82	62
29	●	Tue	210	155	6:18	8:47	14:29	82	62
30		Wed	211	154	6:19	8:46	14:27	82	62
31		Thu	212	153	6:20	8:45	14:25	82	62

JAN FEB MAR APR MAY JUN JUL AUG SEP OCT NOV DEC

Rec. Hi°	Rec. Lo°	Avg. Lake°	On This Date ...
95/2002	45/1988	67	Cleveland Municipal Airport opened (1925)
97/1954	47/1943	67	James A. Garfield shot in Washington, D.C. by Charles J. Guiteau (1881)
98/1949	46/1907	67	U.S. Veterans Administration created (1930)
98/1990	41/1968	67	Marilyn Shephard murdered in Bay Village (1954)
96/1911	48/1979	67	Larry Doby signs with Indians-1st black player in AL (1947)
97/1988	45/1979	67	Congress resolves to name U.S. currency the "dollar" (1785)
99/1988	45/1968	67	Cleveland Indians sign Leroy Satchel Paige (1948)
99/1988	45/1984	68	Architect Philip Johnson born in Cleveland (1906)
97/1936	43/1961	68	Football coach Paul Brown born in Norwalk (1908)
97/1936	46/1963	69	Trumbull County incorporated (1800)
99/1936	48/1996	69	Actress Beverly Todd born in Ohio (1946)
95/1936	48/1978	70	10.51 inches of rainfall, Sandusky, (state record) (1966)
95/1952	51/1976	70	Live Aid concert (1985)
99/1954	51/1888	70	Sportscaster Steve Stone born in Cleveland (1947)
97/1980	48/1960	71	Senator George Voinovich born in Cleveland (1936)
100/1988	50/1954	71	15 drown in Old Riverbed when commuter boat overturns (1896)
96/1942	49/1946	71	Comedienne Phyllis Diller born in Lima (1917)
96/1878	51/1971	71	Hough riots begin (1966)
95/1930	50/1979	72	Gov. Rhodes declares state of emergency in Cleveland race riot (1966)
98/1930	46/1965	72	Actress Lola Albright born in Akron (1924)
97/1952	46/1966	72	Poet Hart Crane born in Garretsville (1899)
99/1952	47/1966	72	Moses Cleaveland arrives at mouth of Cuyahoga River (1796)
96/1933	49/1981	72	National Inventors Hall of Fame opens in Akron (1995)
99/1934	50/2000	72	Writer Ambrose Bierce born in Ohio (1842)
99/1941	47/1953	72	Cavaliers' Nate Thurmond born in Ohio (1941)
99/1941	46/1946	73	1st electric streetcar in U.S. operates in Cleveland (1884)
103/1941	47/1946	73	Singer Maureen McGovern born in Youngstown (1949)
96/1993	52/1977	73	14th Amendment ratified (1968)
95/1941	50/1948	73	Jefferson County incorporated (1797)
96/1941	50/1981	73	U.S. motto "In God We Trust" authorized (1956)
97/1955	52/1960	73	1st Indians game at Municipal Stadium (1932)

JAN FEB MAR APR MAY JUN JUL AUG SEP OCT NOV DEC

JAN FEB MAR APR MAY JUN JUL AUG SEP OCT NOV DEC

Flora & Fauna JULY

WEEK 1

BIRDS: Goldfinches may be gathering thistledown for nesting material as Canada thistles begin to go to seed. **WILDFLOWERS:** Canada lily and other lilies begin to bloom along Cleveland Metroparks roadsides this week. Buckwheat begins to bloom. Later in the fall, this wildflower's seeds become an important part of the diet of migrating waterfowl. It is planted in many wet places by Cleveland Metroparks wildlife management staff

WEEK 2

BIRDS: Mallards and wood ducks begin to change color as they go into their summer "eclipse" plumage. This is an especially wary time for them, as they are unable to fly for several weeks. **WILDFLOWERS:** Queen Anne's lace, yarrow, milkweed, ox-eye daisy, butter-and-eggs, evening primrose, and enchanter's nightshade should all be in full bloom by now. Teasel heads, looking like tall purple burrs, are beginning to bloom along roadsides and in open meadows.

WEEK 3

WILDFLOWERS: Early goldenrod, first of many goldenrods to bloom, becomes a harbinger of autumn as it adds bright yellow to shady open places along parkways. The tall lavender blossoms of joe-pye weed may stand six feet tall in low wet places like Lake Isaac, in Big Creek Reservation, in Mill Stream Run Reservation, and along Brecksville's Riverview Road. **SHRUBS:** Crab apples become ripe this week, much to the delight of Cleveland Metroparks deer!

WEEK 4

BIRDS: As the days grow shorter, blackbirds begin to flock together to prepare for the long journey south. Surprisingly, the young of some species, who have never migrated before, often leave before the adults. Young house wrens should have fledged by this week. **WILDFLOWERS:** The brilliant reds of cardinal flowers contrast with the golds and greens of cattails and sedges in wet meadows and woods this week. White boneset flowers and the rich purple of ironweed brighten marsh edges. **INSECTS:** Katydids and cicadas should be in full chorus by the end of the week. **TREES:** Tulip trees are turning orange, black tupelo is turning crimson, and sassafras is turning orange. Can autumn be far away?

Adapted from the Nature Almanac by Robert Hinkle, with permission from Cleveland Metroparks.

HOW A CAR CAN TURN QUICKLY INTO AN OVEN

Temperatures rise in a closed car in varying weather conditions. Researchers placed sensors in a dark blue 2000 Honda Accord and recorded these results:

Outside Temp.	Temperature inside closed automobile after ...				
	10 min.	20 min.	30 min.	40 min.	50 min.
72	94	99	104	108	111
75	97	104	111	115	118
79	100	106	110	114	116
84	109	119	125	128	130
88	105	117	125	130	133

Reprinted from the Plain Dealer.
Source: San Francisco State University

{ DICK'S **BIRD** OF THE YEAR }

OF CARDINAL IMPORTANCE

· DICK GODDARD ·

Why anything with wings would spend the usually frigid and punishing winter in Northeast Ohio has always been a mystery to me.

Ohio's state bird, the northern cardinal, is one of those who resist the temptation to fly to a warmer southern clime. (Contrary to popular wisdom, many robins also spend the winter with us. Every winter I get dozens of calls from surprised viewers who report robins in their backyards. They appreciate any raisins or fruit you can toss out for them.)

Our year-round red-feathered companion the cardinal gets its name from the Latin

JAN FEB MAR APR MAY JUN JUL AUG SEP OCT NOV DEC

word *cardinalis*, which means "important." The adult male cardinal sports flashy red plumage, while the female wears a more conservative buff-brown outfit with flashes of red on her head, crest, and wings. The handsome male also shows off a dramatic black face mask that extends from the face down to the chin and throat. Add a large red bill, and you've got one handsome bird dude. The lady cardinal makes do with a black mask and large red bill. Both have long tails, and both sexes serenade us with songs all year long.

In winter, flocks of 50 or more cardinals will congregate. Against the brilliant white snow of the northern Ohio winter, the flaming red of the cardinal in combination with the color of another nonmigrating bird, the blue jay, makes a beautiful red-white-and-blue All-American combination. In spring—when they are dating—the male brings food for his lady love (look for small candelabras). The courtship continues with soft singing, outstretched necks, erect crests, and bodies swaying from side to side. Cardinals are monogamous in spring, and they sing "whata-cheer-cheer-cheer" as they stake out their territory.

In the nest, three to four eggs may range in color, but most are bluish-white with brown markings. There can be two to four broods per season, with the male cardinal caring for the first clutch while the female incubates the next. Eggs hatch in about two weeks, and the young leave the nest at around ten days old.

If you should find a fledgling of any species out of its nursery, do not hesitate to pick up the baby bird and return it to its nest. Don't believe the old wives' tale about mother birds rejecting their young if the babies have been touched by human hands. If any baby bird is prematurely out of its nest, you can bet that mama is watching its every movement.

Cardinals enjoy a wide-ranging diet that includes insects, fruits, and seeds. Black sunflower seeds are a favorite.

So let's hear it for the tough and faithful cardinal. Hang on, Sloopy!

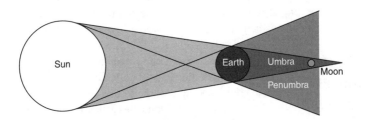

2003 Eclipses:
By the (Rosy) Light of the Silvery Moon

Clyde Simpson

Astronomical highlights this year include two total eclipses of the moon and an exceptionally close passage between the planet Mars and the earth. These visually striking events have a couple of things in common—they're very easy to see, and they're both a vivid red.

The moon blushes over the skies of Ohio in the mid- and early evening hours of May 15 and November 8, and Mars will dominate the night sky from August through the fall season. Information on the appearance of Mars can be found on page 117.

A total lunar eclipse occurs when the moon passes through the earth's dark shadow in space, which extends away from the sun like a long narrowing tail into the midnight sky. The darkest inner portion of the earth's shadow, the "umbra," stretches nearly a million miles into space before tapering to a point.

You can actually see a part of this shadow on any clear evening by looking to the east about a half hour after sunset. Note a deep blue band rising higher and higher in the east as the sun sets to the west— you are looking at the earth's shadow projected through the atmosphere. The effect is heightened [ahem] when there is a lot of dust in the atmosphere. Countless dust particles form a pinkish band that can be seen above the dark blue band, faintly illuminated by the reddened light of the setting sun.

The moon moves about one lunar diameter per hour in its stately orbit across the sky.

The moon orbits the earth about a quarter of a million miles away, and at that distance, the earth's umbral shadow is over 5,000 miles wide. This looming dark hole in space spans more than $2\frac{1}{2}$ times the diameter of the moon.

Although we generally don't notice it, the moon moves about one lunar diameter per hour in its stately orbit across the sky. The great size of the earth's umbral shadow and the moon's slow transit through it mean that viewing a lunar eclipse is a delightful, leisurely event that can last over three hours. Get out the lawn chairs and throw a party!

The maximum amount of time that the moon can be entirely within the umbra (called "totality") is about an hour and a half. Totality for the May 15 lunar eclipse lasts from 11:14 p.m. to 12:06 a.m., and the moon will be fully eclipsed from 8:06 p.m. to 8:30 p.m. the evening of November 8.

Partial phases of the eclipses, when the moon first enters and then progresses through the earth's dark umbral shadow, are the most dramatic part of the lunar eclipse experience. It's at this time that you can directly witness the moon's orbital motion, as our celestial companion appears to be gradually swallowed by the earth's giant shadow.

On May 15, the moon first enters the earth's umbra at 10:03 p.m. (keep the kids up for this one). Within a minute or two of "first contact" you will easily see the earth's dark shadow creep upwards from the lower left lunar limb. Keep in mind it's really the moon that is moving into the earth's shadow. Partial eclipse for the November 8 event starts at 6:33 p.m. The earth's umbral shadow on the moon's surface will show an obvious broad curvature—this feature convinced many observers even in ancient times that the planet we live on is round.

The umbral shadow will be quite fuzzy, due to the fact that the source of light casting the shadow (the sun) is an extended object rather than a point source. The outer and lighter shadow of the earth, the penumbra, grades rather gently into the umbra, yielding the blurred appearance. You're already familiar with a penumbral shadow if you've ever noticed how the shadow of a distant building on a brightly lit sidewalk appears fuzzy. Objects closer to the sidewalk cast sharper shadows, although even these have tiny penumbrae.

"Second contact" of the umbra marks the beginning of totality, when the moon is completely immersed in the earth's shadow. It occurs at 11:14 p.m. for the May eclipse, and at a slightly more reasonable time, 8:06 p.m., for the November event. Even at totality, the moon never completely vanishes, but rather takes on a darkish appearance that can range from dusky brown-gray to a deep coppery-red to a light orange color.

During a lunar eclipse the earth's atmosphere works like a prism to bend, or refract, sunlight toward the moon, giving it a reddish cast. The daytime sky is blue because blue light waves, which are short, are easily scattered all around us by molecules and dust in the earth's atmosphere. Longer red waves can penetrate farther and are responsible for colorful red sunrises and sunsets.

Imagine standing on the moon during a total lunar eclipse. Looking earthward, you would witness a total eclipse of the sun! The earth's atmosphere would glow as a brilliant orange-red ring surrounding the darkened hemisphere of nighttime earth. The brightness and color of that gleaming ring during totality (and hence the brightness and hue of the moon) are variable, due to a combination of atmospheric conditions here on earth. Extreme cloud cover and the presence of volcanic dust and aerosols in the atmosphere tend to deepen and redden the appearance of the moon's disk.

Indonesia has the inauspicious reputation of gumming up lunar eclipses. The August 1883 eruption of Krakatoa was followed by a lunar eclipse in 1884 in which the blackened moon all but disappeared. An eruption of Agung in Bali in 1963 resulted in extraordinarily dark lunar eclipses during that year and the following one. A 1982 lunar eclipse was significantly darkened by the eruption of El Chichon in Mexico. Most recently, the remarkable June 1991 eruption of the volcano Pinatubo in the Philippines tossed enough high-altitude volcanic dust in the atmosphere to noticeably dim a lunar eclipse a full year and a half later, in December 1992!

The third contact of the moon with the earth's umbra marks the end of totality, and the moon slowly parades out of the earth's shadow. Understandably, far fewer people view this phase of the eclipse than the preceding ones, their minds turning to late-night TV or sleep. Let's face it, it's less interesting to see the tape rewind than to watch it roll in the first place. The moon will begin to leave the earth's umbra six minutes after midnight on May 16, and at 8:30 p.m on November 8. Partial eclipse ends when the moon bids a final farewell to the dark umbra—1:17 a.m. for the May eclipse, 10:05 p.m. in November (just in time to catch Dick's forecast).

The show isn't really over, however, until the moon finally leaves the earth's faint outer penumbral shadow, which will occur at 2:15 a.m. on May 16 and 11:22 p.m. on November 8. The penumbral phases of a lunar eclipse are subtle, and really noticeable only within about 20 minutes before and after the partial phases of the eclipse. Beginning and ending times of the penumbral phases of an eclipse are not generally given in newspaper accounts, since they are virtually imperceptible. Penumbral eclipse begins at 9:05 p.m. for the May 15 event (the sky won't even be completely dark by that time of the evening) and 5:15 p.m. on November 8 (almost right at sunset).

Something that might not be immediately obvious is that lunar eclipses always occur at full moon.

Something that might not be immediately obvious is that lunar eclipses always occur at full moon. At that time the sun, earth, and moon lie in a straight line, with the moon opposite the sun in the sky. We would see a lunar eclipse once a month—at each full moon—if the moon revolved around the earth in the exact same plane as that in which the earth orbits the sun. It turns out, however, that the moon's orbit around the earth is slightly tilted in relation to the earth's orbit around the sun, so that the full moon usually passes well above or below the earth's shadow. Hold two hula hoops together and then pivot them apart a couple of inches and you get an idea of how the earth's and moon's orbits are slightly misaligned.

Lunar eclipses occur about as often as solar eclipses, but more people have witnessed an eclipse of the moon simply because the event is observable from the entire nighttime side of the earth. And unlike a solar eclipse, everybody on the dark hemisphere gets the same view at exactly the same time. Make sure you're one of those observers on the evenings of May 15 and November 8. Dick has personally guaranteed that there is a 100% probability it might be clear those nights!

Clyde Simpson is the Observatory Coordinator at the Cleveland Museum of Natural History, and has been with the museum for 18 years. He is a native Clevelander who grew up watching Dick Goddard (and paying particular attention to the astronomical details always included in his broadcasts). Proceeds from his contribution benefit the Cleveland Museum of Natural History.

PLANET VISIBILITY

Planet	Morning Visibility	Evening Visibility
Mercury	January 1–January 6 January 18–March 12 May 16–June 28 September 18–October 13	March 31–April 28 July 13–September 4 November 10–December 21
Venus	January 1–July 31	September 25–December 31
Mars	January 1–August 28	August 28–December 31
Jupiter	January 1–February 2 September 5–December 31	February 2–August 9
Saturn	July 13–December 31	January 1–June 6

Source: Nautical Almanac Office, United States Naval Observatory

JAN FEB MAR APR MAY JUN JUL AUG SEP OCT NOV DEC

OHIO'S RECORD FISH

Fish	Size	Where caught	by Whom	Date caught
Bass, Hybrid Striped	17.68 lb., 31"	Deer Creek Lake	Rosemary Shaver, Logan	May 4, 2001
Bass, Largemouth	13.13 lb., 25 1/16"	Farm pond	Roy Landsberger, Kensington	May 26, 1976
Bass, Rock	1.97 lb., 14 3/4"	Deer Creek	George A. Keller, Dayton	Sept 3, 1932
Bass, Smallmouth	9.5 lb., 23 1/2"	Lake Erie	Randy Van Dam, Kalamazoo, Mich.	June 16, 1993
Bass, Spotted	5.25 lb., 21"	Lake White	Roger Trainer, Waverly	May 2, 1976
Bass, Striped	37.10 lb., 41 1/4"	West Branch Reservoir	Mark Chuifo, Ravenna	July 2, 1993
Bass, White	4 lb., 21"	Gravel pit	Ira Sizemore, Cincinnati	July 1, 1983
Bluegill	3.28 lb., 12 3/4"	Salt Fork Reservoir	Willis D. Nicholes, Quaker City	April 28, 1990
Bowfin	11.69 lb., 33 1/4"	Nettle Lake	Christopher A. Boling, Montpelier	May 9, 1987
Bullhead	4.25 lb., 18 1/2"	Farm pond	Hugh Lawrence Jr., Keene	May 20, 1986
Burbot	17.33 lb., 36"	Lake Erie	Bud Clute, Chardon	Dec 20, 1999
Carp	50 lb., 40"	Paint Creek	Judson Holton, Chillicothe	May 24, 1967
Catfish, Channel	37.65 lb., 41 1/2"	LaDue Reservoir	Gus J. Gronowski, Parma	Aug 15, 1992
Catfish, Shovel/Flathead	76.5 lb., 58 5/8"	Clendening Lake	Richard Affolter, New Philadelphia	July 28, 1979
Crappie, Black	4.5 lb., 18 1/8"	Private lake	Ronald Stone, Wooster	May 24, 1981
Crappie, White	3.90 lb., 18 1/2"	Private pond	Kyle Rock, Zanesville	April 25, 1995
Drum, Freshwater (Sheepshead)	23.5 lb., 37 1/8"	Sandusky River	James S. Williams, Fremont	July 21, 2001
Gar, Longnose	25 lb., 49"	Ohio River	Flora Irvin, Cincinnati	Aug 31, 1966
Muskellunge	55.13 lb., 50 1/4"	Piedmont Lake	Joe D. Lykins, Piedmont	April 12, 1972
Muskellunge, Tiger	31.5 lb., 47"	Turkeyfoot Lake	Ronald P. Kotch, Canal Fulton	April 22, 1999
Perch, White	1.42 lb., 14 1/16"	Green Creek	John Nause, Fremont	May 3, 1988
Perch, Yellow	2.75 lb., 14 1/2"	Lake Erie	Charles Thomas, Lorain	April 17, 1984
Pickerel, Chain	6.25 lb., 26 1/4"	Long Lake	Ronald P. Kotch, Akron	March 25, 1961
Pike, Northern	22.38 lb., 43"	Lyre Lake	Chris Campbell, Dayton	Oct 3, 1988
Salmon, Chinook	29.5 lb., 42 7/8"	Lake Erie	Walter Shumaker, Ashtabula	Aug 4, 1989
Salmon, Coho	13.63 lb., 34 3/4"	Huron River	Barney Freeman, Kansas	Dec 1, 1982

Fish	Size	Where caught	by Whom	Date caught
Salmon, Pink	OPEN			
Sauger	7.31 lb., 24 ½"	Maumee River	Bryan Wicks, Maumee	March 10, 1981
Saugeye	12.42 lb., 29"	Lake Logan	Daniel D'Amore, Swanton	March 29, 1993
Sucker, Buffalo	46.01 lb., 42"	Hover Reservoir	Tim Veit, Galena	July 2, 1999
Sucker (other than buffalo)	9.25 lb., 27 ½"	Leesville Lake	Wayne Gleason, Wellsville	April 3, 1977
Sunfish, Green	.75 lb., 10 ½"	Private pond	Edward J. Alltop, Utica	May 28, 1994
Sunfish, Hybrid	1.67 lb., 12"	Jackson County farm pond	Peggy Johnson, Oak Hill	July 30, 2000
Sunfish, Longear	OPEN			
Sunfish, Pumpkinseed	.75 lb., 9 ½"	Farm pond	Terry Rush, Edison	Jan 6, 2001
Sunfish, Redear	3.58 lb., 15"	Licking County farm pond	Bert Redman, Newark	Oct 2, 1998
Sunfish, Warmouth	1 lb., 9 ⅞"	Private Pond	Rich Campitalli, Athens	Sept 6, 1994
Trout, Brown	14.65 lb., 29 ¼"	Lake Erie	Timothy L. Byrne, Brooklyn, Mich.	July 15, 1995
Trout, Lake	20.49 lb., 34"	Lake Erie	Tom Harbison, Natrona, PA	April 20, 2000
Trout, Rainbow (Steelhead)	20.97 lb., 36 ½"	Lake Erie	Mike Shane, New Middletown	Oct 2, 1996
Walleye	16.19 lb., 33"	Lake Erie	Tom Haberman, Brunswick	Nov 23, 1999

BOWFISHING

Fish	Size	Where caught	by Whom	Date caught
Bowfin	8.79 lb., 31"	East Harbor	John Ehrman, Brook Park	April 30, 1989
Carp	39 lb., 40"	Farm pond	Dennis Derheimer, Canton	May 3, 1981
Gar, Longnose	14.57 lb., 48"	Ohio Brush Creek	Ronald L. Cross, Russellville	April 14, 2001
Sucker, Buffalo	37 lb., 40 ¼"	Hoover Reservoir	Don Paisley, Columbus	May 14, 1983
Sucker (other than buffalo)	7.36 lb., 26 ¾"	Big Walnut Creek	Michael Stumph, Columbus	May 18, 1997

For further information about the state record fish program, contact Outdoors Writers of Ohio State Record Fish Committee Chairman, Tom Cross, 1497 Cross Rd., Winchester, OH, 45697, ph/fax (937) 386-2752.

JAN
FEB
MAR
APR
MAY
JUN
JUL
AUG
SEP
OCT
NOV
DEC

JAN FEB MAR APR MAY JUN JUL AUG SEP OCT NOV DEC

THE HEAT INDEX

The Heat Index serves as a diagnostic measure of the combination of temperature and relative humidity. The resulting "apparent" temperature (when the meteorologist says "it feels like …") gives an estimation of what the hot, humid air feels like to the average person.

Exceptional heat indices (which can endanger your life) occur mostly during the muggy summer months. The abundance of moisture and increased heat keeps you perspiring, which is your body's involuntary attempt to cool itself. Those with health concerns should keep a close eye on the heat index during prolonged spells of hot weather, as dehydration and heat exhaustion are very serious matters.

APPARENT TEMPERATURE READINGS

Caution: 85° to 94° F
Physical activity can cause fatigue.

Extreme Caution: 95° to 105° F
Possible heat cramps and/or heat exhaustion with lengthy exposure to the heat.

Danger: Above 105° F
Conditions for heat stroke if exposure to heat is prolonged; heat exhaustion and heat cramps likely.

DATES WHEN CLEVELAND'S TEMPERATURE REACHED 100°

June 25, 1988 (104°)
July 27, 1941 (103°)
August 27, 1948 (102°)
September 1–3, 1953 (101°)
June 28, 1944 (101°)
July 16, 1988 (100°)
August 19, 1955 (100°)
June 28, 1934 (100°)
August 6, 1918 (100°)

HEAT INDEX CHART

Temp (F)	Relative Humidity (%)								
	90.0	80.0	70.0	60.0	50.0	40.0	30.0	20.0	10.0
65	65.6	64.7	63.8	62.8	61.9	60.9	60.0	59.1	58.1
70	71.6	70.7	69.8	68.8	67.9	66.9	66.0	65.1	64.1
75	79.7	76.7	75.8	74.8	73.9	72.9	72.0	71.1	70.1
80	88.2	85.9	84.2	82.8	81.6	80.4	79.0	77.4	76.1
85	101.4	97.0	93.3	90.3	87.7	85.5	83.5	81.6	79.6
90	119.3	112.0	105.8	100.5	96.1	92.3	89.2	86.5	84.2
95	141.8	131.1	121.7	113.6	106.7	100.9	96.1	92.2	89.2
100	168.7	154.0	140.9	129.5	119.6	111.2	104.2	98.7	94.4
105	200.0	180.7	163.4	148.1	134.7	123.2	113.6	105.8	100.0

Source: National Oceanic and Atmosphere Agency

AUGUST STATISTICS

SUNSHINE %	63
DRIEST MONTH	0.17"/1881
WARMEST MONTH	77.8°/1995
COLDEST MONTH	65.4°/1927
LIQUID PCPN AVG.	3.40"
RAINIEST DAY	3.65"/1994
RAINIEST MONTH	8.96"/1975
THUNDERY DAYS	5
SNOWIEST DAY	None
DAYS ONE INCH SNOW	0

The Perseids are coming! One of the most reliable of the meteor showers, the Perseids are most frequent around the 11th night. These night lights of August may be no larger than a bean, or grain of sand, as they become super-heated after entering our atmosphere at about 65 miles up, traveling at 150,000 mph. Shooting stars that make it through the atmosphere and strike earth are called meteorites. An especially bright meteor, called a bolide, was seen blazing across the Northeast Ohio sky in October of 1992; the bolide eventually struck the trunk of a car in New York State.

While May is the month of woodland flowers, August is the month of field flowers. New England asters, with bright yellow centers and purple petals, adorn the untended countryside.

Creating a summertime symphony will be the stridulation of crickets and red-legged grasshoppers. Personally, I'll take the noise of summer over the silence of winter.

On extremely hot August afternoons the refraction of light over Lake Erie has created a mirage, allowing the Canadian shoreline to appear—upside down.

JAN FEB MAR APR MAY JUN JUL AUG SEP OCT NOV DEC

DAILY DATA FOR AUGUST

Date	Moon Phase	Day	Day of Year	Days Left in Year	Sunrise	Sunset	Length of Day	Avg. Hi	Avg. Lo
1		Fri	213	152	6:21	8:44	14:23	82	62
2		Sat	214	151	6:22	8:43	14:21	82	62
3		Sun	215	150	6:23	8:42	14:19	82	62
4		Mon	216	149	6:24	8:41	14:17	82	62
5	◑	Tue	217	148	6:25	8:40	14:15	82	61
6		Wed	218	147	6:26	8:38	14:12	82	61
7		Thu	219	146	6:27	8:37	14:10	82	61
8		Fri	220	145	6:28	8:36	14:08	82	61
9		Sat	221	144	6:29	8:34	14:05	82	61
10		Sun	222	143	6:30	8:33	14:03	82	61
11		Mon	223	142	6:31	8:32	14:01	81	61
12	○	Tue	224	141	6:32	8:30	13:58	81	61
13		Wed	225	140	6:33	8:29	13:56	81	61
14		Thu	226	139	6:34	8:28	13:54	81	61
15		Fri	227	138	6:35	8:26	13:51	81	61
16		Sat	228	137	6:36	8:25	13:49	81	60
17		Sun	229	136	6:37	8:24	13:47	81	60
18		Mon	230	135	6:38	8:22	13:44	81	60
19	◐	Tue	231	134	6:39	8:21	13:42	80	60
20		Wed	232	133	6:40	8:19	13:39	80	60
21		Thu	233	132	6:41	8:18	13:37	79	60
22		Fri	234	131	6:42	8:16	13:34	79	60
23		Sat	235	130	6:43	8:15	13:32	79	60
24		Sun	236	129	6:44	8:13	13:29	79	59
25		Mon	237	128	6:45	8:11	13:26	79	59
26		Tue	238	127	6:46	8:10	13:24	79	59
27	●	Wed	239	126	6:47	8:08	13:21	79	59
28		Thu	240	125	6:48	8:07	13:19	79	59
29		Fri	241	124	6:49	8:05	13:16	79	59
30		Sat	242	123	6:50	8:03	13:13	76	58
31		Sun	243	122	6:51	8:02	13:11	78	58

JAN FEB MAR APR MAY JUN JUL AUG SEP OCT NOV DEC

Rec. Hi°	Rec. Lo°	Avg. Lake°	On This Date ...
95/1917	47/1960	73	1st U.S. census (population 3,939,214) (1790)
97/1988	50/1962	73	Horror movie director Wes Craven born in Cleveland (1939)
97/1944	58/1976	73	1st aerial cropdusting (Troy, Ohio) to kill caterpillars (1921)
97/1930	46/1966	74	Circus fire at E. 9th & Lakeside kills dozens of animals (1942)
94/1947	46/1972	74	Browns coach Paul Brown dies at 82 (1991)
100/1918	45/1997	74	Actor Dorian Harewood born in Dayton (1950)
95/1918	48/1997	74	Shotzie, Cincinnati Reds dog mascot, dies at age 9 (1991)
96/1941	47/1975	74	Actress Suzee Pai born in Toledo (1962)
96/1949	50/1972	74	Richard Nixon resigns presidency (1974)
97/1944	47/1972	74	Race riots in Cincinnati (1827)
96/1944	48/1965	74	Singer Eric Carmen born in Cleveland (1949)
99/1881	44/1967	74	Space shuttle Enterprise makes 1st atmospheric flight (1977)
95/1995	47/1982	74	Annie Oakley born in Drake Ohio (1860)
97/1944	46/1964	74	Actress Halle Berry born (1968)
96/1944	44/1962	74	Wayne County incorporated (1796)
96/1944	45/1979	74	Indians' Ray Chapman dies after being hit by pitch (1920)
99/1988	48/1971	74	World's 1st Moon probe explodes (1958)
96/1947	46/1981	74	Actor Trey Ames born in Canton (1971)
100/1955	47/1964	74	Hurricane Diane kills 200 & 1st billion $ damage storm (N.E. US) (1955)
95/1947	46/1998	74	Benjamin Harrison born in North Bend, OH (1833)
96/1947	45/1950	74	Next total solar eclipse visible from North America (2017)
94/1936	45/1982	74	Hurricane Camille strikes U.S. Gulf Coast kills 255 (1969)
93/1914	48/1969	74	Mars's closest approach to Earth since the 10th century (1924)
94/1947	44/1952	74	-127 F (-88 C), Vostok, Antarctica (world record) (1960)
97/1948	45/1951	73	Voyager 2's closest approach to Saturn (1981)
97/1948	47/1958	73	19th Amendment adopted (1920)
102/1948	49/1963	73	Earliest recorded hurricane in US (Jamestown, Virginia) (1667)
98/1953	42/1968	73	1st known photograph of a tornado made near Howard, SD (1884)
98/1953	38/1982	73	Inventor Charles F. Kettering born in Ohio (1876)
96/1953	45/1976	73	William H. Taft dies (1930)
99/1953	46/1890	73	Comet Howard-Koomur-Michels collides with the Sun (1979)

JAMES A. GARFIELD
20TH PRESIDENT (1881)

Dick Goddard

On November 19, 1831, in Orange Township in eastern Cuyahoga County, James Abraham Garfield became the last American president to be born in a log cabin. He was born into poverty and raised by his widowed mother. His father died when James was less than two years of age while helping neighbors fight a wildfire. His mother was forced to take up sewing and farmwork in order to survive.

Muscular and handsome, he grew to be six feet tall and weigh 185 pounds. Garfield had light brown hair, blue eyes, and an aquiline (eagle beak-like) nose. He was the youngest of four children who lived to maturity. Growing up as an underprivileged child, Garfield was precocious, quick tempered, and more than willing to duke it out with any of his peers. He walked at nine months, and by the age of three he had learned to read. In adulthood, Garfield's personality changed. He became amicable and good-natured, often putting his arm around those to whom he was speaking.

At 17 he went to work on a Great Lakes freighter, then worked as a mule skinner (driving mules that pulled the boats) on the Ohio & Erie Canal. By his own count he fell into the canal six times. Garfield figured this rough and rowdy life made him "ripe for ruin," and he decided to purge his soul by entering Ohio's Geauga Seminary for two years. He completed his formal education at Williams College in Massachusetts, where he became class president. He studied law and became a professor of classics before becoming president at what was to become Hiram College in Ohio. Garfield was an exceptional speaker and, inspired by a traveling preacher, became a lay minister in the Disciples of Christ. He was the only preacher to become president.

At the age of 26 Garfield married 26-year-old Lucretia (Crete) Rudolph of Hiram. He admitted to one indiscretion during his marriage, and Lucretia forgave him, blaming the episode on lawless passion. Joining the Union Army as a lieutenant colonel in the Civil War, he became the youngest major general and was cited for heroism and bravery at the battle of Chickamauga. He also fought at Shiloh. After his military discharge he returned to his Mentor home, which was called Lawnfield. He left Lawnfield in 1863 for the United States Congress and served with distinction for 18 years.

Although Garfield generally favored his left hand, he was ambidextrous and would amaze friends by writing simultaneously with both hands in both Latin and Greek. An ardent abolitionist, he became a compromise choice for president in 1880. His vice president was Chester A. Arthur, who would succeed Garfield following his assassination less than eight months after his inauguration in March of 1881. Although he was in office for too brief a time for a critical assessment, Garfield showed all the prerequisites for becoming an outstanding president. Tragically, on July 2, 1881, at 9:30 a.m., a religious zealot, Charles J. Guiteau, carried out a cowardly attack on the president, shooting him twice in the back as he was walking through the Baltimore & Potomac railroad station in Washington.

Although in agony, Garfield lived for 80 days, sustained by his excellent general health, before he died at 10:35 p.m. on September 18, 1881, at Elberon, New Jersey, with his loving wife, Crete, at his bedside. Garfield had been president for less than eight months.

Guiteau, the assassin, was a rejected office seeker. The deranged man chose an expensive .44 British Bulldog pistol for the deed, later saying that he wanted a pricey weapon so that "it would look good in a museum."

On the day of his hanging, Guiteau mounted the gallows reading aloud from the Bible and singing a "hymn" he had written for the occasion. It began, "I am going to the Lordy, I'm so glad." He was quickly accommodated. In honor of the internationally admired Garfield, the royal courts of Europe broke precedent by observing a day of mourning for the president. Garfield's body was brought back to Ohio on a special train, and he was buried in Cleveland's Lake View Cemetery. His wife died in 1918 and rests next to her husband at Lake View.

JAN
FEB
MAR
APR
MAY
JUN
JUL
AUG
SEP
OCT
NOV
DEC

NORTHEAST OHIO
COUNTY FAIRS

Ashland County
Dates for 2003: September 14-20
Location: Ashland County Fairgrounds
Contact: 419-281-6831
Year Founded: 1859
Average Annual Attendance: 120,000
Attendance for 2001: 118,000

Ashtabula County
Dates for 2003: August 5-10
Location: Ashtabula County Fairgrounds
Contact: 440-576-7626
Year Founded: 1846
Average Annual Attendance: 43,000
Attendance for 2001: 38,000

Carroll County
Dates for 2003: July 15-20
Location: Carroll County Fairgrounds
Contact: 330-627-2300
Year Founded: 1850
Average Annual Attendance: 30,000
Attendance for 2001: 30,318

Columbiana County
Dates for 2003: July 28 - August 3
Location: Columbiana County Fairgrounds
Contact: 330-424-5531
Year Founded: 1845
Average Annual Attendance: 45,000
Attendance for 2001: 45,000

Coshocton County
Dates for 2003: September 26 - October 2
Location: Coshocton County Fairgrounds
Contact: 740-622-2385
Year Founded: 1851
Average Annual Attendance: 80,000
Attendance for 2001: 80,000

Cuyahoga County
Dates for 2003: August 4-10
Location: Cuyahoga County Fairgrounds
Contact: 440-243-0090
Year Founded: 1895
Average Annual Attendance: 150,000
Attendance for 2001: 131,000

Erie County
Dates for 2003: August 5-10
Location: Erie County Fairgrounds
Contact: 419-625-1000
Year Founded: 1848 (joint fair with Huron County)/1856 (separate)
Average Annual Attendance: 48,000
Attendance for 2001: 48,000

Geauga County
Dates for 2003: August 28 - September 1
Location: Geauga County Fairgrounds
Contact: 440-834-1846
Year Founded: 1823
Average Annual Attendance: 200,000
Attendance for 2001: 212,000

Harrison County
Dates for 2003: July 8-13
Location: Harrison County Fairgrounds
Contact: 740-942-8332
Year Founded: 1846
Average Annual Attendance: 12,000
Attendance for 2001: 11,500

Holmes County
Dates for 2003: August 11-16
Location: Holmes County Fairgrounds
Contact: 330-674-0869
Year Founded: 1923
Average Annual Attendance: 25,000
Attendance for 2001: 19,041

Huron County
Dates for 2003: August 11-16
Location: Huron County Fairgrounds
Contact: 419-744-2116
Year Founded: 1921
Average Annual Attendance: 50,000
Attendance for 2001: 48,000

Jefferson County
Dates for 2003: August 12-17
Location: Jefferson County Fairgrounds
Contact: 740-765-5156
Year Founded: 1871
Average Annual Attendance: 75,000
Attendance for 2001: 75,500

JAN FEB MAR APR MAY JUN JUL AUG SEP OCT NOV DEC

Lake County
Dates for 2003: August 12-17
Location: Lake County Fairgrounds
Contact: 440-354-3339
Year Founded: 1911
Average Annual Attendance: 100,000
Attendance for 2001: 105,000

Lorain County
Dates for 2003: August 18-24
Location: Lorain County Fairgrounds
Contact: 440-647-2781
Year Founded: 1845
Average Annual Attendance: 145,000
Attendance for 2001: 143,495

Mahoning County
Dates for 2003: August 27 - September 1
Location: Canfield Fairgrounds
Contact: 330-533-4107
Year Founded: 1846
Average Annual Attendance: 325,000
Attendance for 2001: 475,000

Medina County
Dates for 2003: July 27 - August 3
Location: Medina County Fairgrounds
Contact: 330-723-9633
Year Founded: 1845
Average Annual Attendance: 130,000
Attendance for 2001: 126,000

Portage County
Dates for 2003: August 19-24
Location: Portage County Fairgrounds
Contact: 330-325-7476
Year Founded: 1858
Average Annual Attendance: 130,000
Attendance for 2001: 130,000

Richland County
Dates for 2003: August 3-9
Location: Richland County Fairgrounds
Contact: 419-747-3717
Year Founded: 1850
Average Annual Attendance: 70,000
Attendance for 2001: 65,000

Stark County
Dates for 2003: August 26 - September 1
Location: Stark County Fairgrounds
Contact: 330-452-0621
Year Founded: 1849
Average Annual Attendance: 100,000
Attendance for 2001: 92,000

Summit County
Dates for 2003: July 22-27
Location: Summit County Fairgrounds
Contact: 330-633-6200
Year Founded: 1852
Average Annual Attendance: 60,000
Attendance for 2001: 70,000

Trumbull County
Dates for 2003: July 7-13
Location: Trumbull County Fairgrounds
Contact: 330-637-6010
Year Founded: 1846
Average Annual Attendance: 54,000
Attendance for 2001: 61,000

Tuscarawas County
Dates for 2003: September 15-21
Location: Tuscarawas County Fairgrounds
Contact: 330-343-0524
Year Founded: 1850
Average Annual Attendance: 60,000
Attendance for 2001: 43,998

Wayne County
Dates for 2003: September 6-11
Location: Wayne County Fairgrounds
Contact: 330-262-8001
Year Founded: 1849
Average Annual Attendance: 110,000
Attendance for 2001: 107,000

Information compiled from county offices. Unofficial dates, subject to approval by the State.

JAN FEB MAR APR MAY JUN JUL AUG SEP OCT NOV DEC

IT HAPPENED 1ST IN OHIO:
Ohio was the 1st state created from the Northwest Territory.
Ohio's James A. Garfield was the 1st left-handed president.
The world's 1st commercial chick hatchery was founded in Ohio in 1897.

JAN FEB MAR APR MAY JUN JUL AUG SEP OCT NOV DEC

⚡ STORM SAFETY *Lightning*

Lightning kills more people in the U.S. each year than hurricanes and tornadoes combined. Eighty percent of those struck by lightning are male. Two of every three live to tell their story. Victims often recall these sensations just prior to the strike: a tingling sensation in the hands and feet, hair standing on end, and a pungent smell of sulfur. If you realize that you have suddenly become a human lightning rod, immediately drop to your knees, cover your head with your hands, and curl up into a tight ball.

Many victims who have been struck and appear to be dead can be revived with artificial respiration (CPR). The body does not carry an electric charge after being struck. If the victim is not breathing and has no pulse, CPR must be given within four to six minutes in order to prevent irreversible brain damage.

LIGHTNING SAFETY RULES:

1. A home or large building offers good protection. Avoid using the telephone and stay away from open doors, windows, and all plugged-in electrical appliances.

2. Automobiles (but not convertibles) with windows rolled up offer good protection. Stay off of and away from lawn mowers, tractors, motorcycles, scooters, bicycles, and golf carts.

3. Avoid wide open areas such as beaches, football and baseball fields, and golf courses. Avoid hilltops and high ground; seek out a ravine or low ground. Avoid isolated tall objects such as trees and poles. In a heavily wooded area, seek shelter on low ground under a thick growth of small trees. Stay away from wire fences, railroad tracks, and all metal objects.

4. Swimmers should immediately leave the water. Boats should be taken ashore. If you are caught far from shore in an electrical storm, curl into a ball and stay low in the boat.

fun facts NORTHEAST OHIO

A quarry hole in Amherst known as Buckeye Number One is believed to be the largest sandstone quarry in the world. It can easily be seen from Quarry Road, which runs from South Amherst to Amherst. Sandstone from here was used to build the John Hancock Building in Boston, the Hockey Hall of Fame in Toronto, and Buffalo's City Hall.

{ DICK'S **ANIMAL** OF THE YEAR }

OH, THOSE WHITE TAILS

· DICK GODDARD ·

Ohio's state animal is the white-tailed deer, one of the most numerous large animals in North America. As opposed to the buffalo and other game animals that have been hunted relentlessly to near extinction, there are more white-tailed deer now than when settlers first arrived in the New World.

The deer population in Ohio, which stood at less than 20,000 in 1965, exploded to more than 400,000 by 1995. This massive increase has taken place to the detriment of the deer and the vegetation they need to survive. Many deer starve in a hard winter when food becomes increasingly scarce.

Deer primarily browse on trees and shrubs, eating up to seven pounds of food each day. They do not graze on grass but will eat corn and alfalfa. And your spring flowers. One lady reported that all 600 of her tulips were pulled up and the tops eaten. Due to the overpopulation of deer, countless thousands of the beautiful white spring wildflowers known as trillium have disappeared.

Deer management is critical. In 2001 the Cleveland Metroparks initiated a nonlethal deer fertility project. Female deer (does) are captured using either a drop-net or tranquilizing darts. A fertility control agent is then injected into the animal, which prevents fawn delivery in the spring. The does are then fitted with radio transmitter collars, ear-tagged, and released.

Deer proliferation has also increased the incidence of deer–car accidents by 30 percent over the last 10 years. Deer are nocturnal, and are most active in the early morning and at dusk. If you see a deer cross the road in front of you, there's a good chance that another deer—or several—will follow. Fifty percent of deer–car collisions occur during the amorous rutting months of October, November, and December.

Male deer (bucks) grow a new set of antlers every year. Contrary to popular wisdom, the number of points and the size of a buck's antlers (rack) are a better indication of nutrition than of age.

Does give birth to one to four spotted fawns in late spring. The mother deer places the fawns in woods or fields, and she only returns to nurse them. The ability to lie still usually offers good protection for the fawns. At about three weeks of age, the fawns will begin to follow their mother. By autumn the fawns' spots will disappear, and their reddish coats will be replaced by (surprisingly) thinner gray coats. The new gray hairs are hollow, trapping air inside to protect and insulate the deer from the cold.

Speed is the best recourse the deer has to avoid predators. The gracefully bounding animals can reach speeds of 40 miles per hour, and they can easily jump eight feet as they head for protective cover. The tail of the deer (the flag) will flash upright, revealing a white underside, to signal other deer of danger.

While starvation and attacks by predators such as the coyote pose continual dangers for the beautiful and gentle deer, the unethical hunter will forever be the animals' greatest enemy. As Bambi's mother warned, man is the most dangerous animal in the forest.

TALES FROM THE NEWS DESK

TIM TAYLOR

There are many ways we mark the passage of time. I seem to measure the past 25 years by the arrivals and departures of many talented and dramatically unique news co-anchors.

My personal Independence Day was July 4, 1977, following a five-year stint at Channel 5, where I was getting a surprising amount of recognition as the city's first consumer ombudsman, known as the Eyewitness News action reporter. No one was more surprised than I was to learn my "Q rating," which measures how many people know and like you, was, inexplicably, nearly on a par with those of the news anchors in town. And happily that bought me a one-way ticket to an anchor chair at TV8, sitting next to Judd Hambrick, brother of TV5 star anchor, John.

JAN
FEB
MAR
APR
MAY
JUN
JUL
AUG
SEP
OCT
NOV
DEC

The Hambricks shared brains and good looks, but Judd was the business-man. He had a Hollywood smile, but was not the kind of guy with whom you could share a belly laugh—except on Friday nights. After we'd put the 11 o'-clock news to bed, Judd would plop himself down in front of the tube to just howl at how J. R. Ewing would royally screw his business competitors. It's the first time I thought of *Dallas* as a comedy—if only to Judd. In fact, Judd pulled one out of J. R.'s playbook when he "retired" from TV8 to pursue out-side business interests and then showed up at TV3 a year later.

Enter the first female co-anchor in the history of Cleveland television! Tana Carli was a Miss Ohio who came within an eyelash of the Miss America crown. The most gorgeous girl-next-door you'd ever seen would show up at work every day with her hair in rollers, hauling bags of clothes and shoes from her favorite discount stores. It was a daily ritual!

When we won the highest 11 o'clock news ratings despite TV5's huge lead-in from the *Winds of War* blockbuster, we knew Miss Ohio had become Miss Cleveland. The new general manager, Joe Dimino, was also smitten by "Mama Tana," as we called her, because of all the food she'd lug in with her daily clothes booty. In fact, the GM liked her so much, he married her!

The story of the wedding ceremony is known in the annals of TV8 as "The Great Camera Caper." It was a high mass during which we knew picture snap-ping was simply not appropriate. The seriousness of the occasion apparently escaped our esteemed weather legend, Dick Goddard. Even a direct glare from the priest couldn't stop his pictorial frenzy. In fact, when he finally ran out of film, Dick was eager to reload as quickly as possible. Whether it was carelessness or just plain bad luck is inconsequential. The end result was the celluloid springing loudly from the back of the camera and wrapping, like a coiled snake, around Dick's fingers, which worked feverishly to stuff the spaghetti-like mess back into the camera. Dick finally managed to slam the camera shut, film oozing from the edges. Adding to the comedy of this aus-tere event was Dick's checkered sport coat amid a sea of somber black, gray, and navy. When asked about his choice, Goddard said he didn't realize it was such a serious occasion.

Enter Denise D'Ascenzo, another beautiful and intelligent young woman, but much more serious than we were used to. In fact, during the relatively short time she spent with Goddard and me, Denise became known as the nothing-to-live-for queen. We eventually learned that much of her reserve stemmed from a long-distance relationship—her fiancé ran a family busi-ness in New England.

What was perhaps the defining moment of her Cleveland career came at

Goddard's annual Woollybear Festival parade. Denise, late as usual, ran toward an already-moving open convertible along the Vermilion parade route. She jogged toward the convertible we were to share just as the driver reached the reviewing stand. Just as she raised one of her extraordinarily long legs to jump over the closed door, the driver's wife tried to help her by suddenly flinging the door open, with disastrous results. As the door sent Denise flying, the cheering and clapping instantly turned to a subdued Ohhhh, followed by a deadly silence as my embarrassed co-anchor sprawled on her back, attempting to maintain what was left of her dignity in the middle of Vermilion's main drag. Seeing that only her ego was injured, Dick tried to save the day by asking the crowd to clap long and hard if they wanted Denise to remain in Cleveland. This would be Denise's last Woollybear Festival. She's now happily married in New England.

It's the quirky, unplanned things that break me up on the air.

Enter the irrepressible Robin Swoboda, about whom I could write a novel. What's Robin really like? What you see is no less than what you get. She's the same bright, clever, wacky person off the air as on the air. I don't know why, but my normally staid self-control on the air went right out the window when sitting next to Robin. First, you need to know that it's the quirky, unplanned things that break me up on the air, not someone setting out to make me laugh. And because we often saw irreverent humor in the same things, our breaking up became part of what people tuned in to see. Take, for example, one election night, when serious journalists studiously read the reams of often boring returns. On just this night, our entire computer system went south. Lacking update returns on an election night is like a play-by-play announcer looking at a baseball field with no players—no place to run, no place to hide. So Robin just started laughing. Not giggling a little, but that hearty Swoboda laugh that quickly infected my psyche in the same way as laughing in church. Needless to say, our election coverage that night wasn't very precise, but it was highly entertaining. At Robin's wedding to then Browns punter Bryan Wagner in San Diego, Robin again showed her sense of humor—and her good sense—by insuring there would be no repeat of the Tana Carli wedding debacle. After we were all seated and the minister was about to begin, the ushers suddenly did a quick search and seizure, confiscating all cameras. The lightning raid happened so quickly the usually nimble-witted Goddard was for the first time at a loss for words.

Enter Denise Dufala, truly the girl next door, raised in North Olmsted and often claimed by our Italian viewers. But I'm afraid the vowels are misleading—Denise proudly claims to be of Slovak and Irish descent. On one memorable night, an on-air situation went south so quickly that we could do nothing but break into an instant sweat that left us glistening, very much the way Albert Brooks looked during his anchoring debut in *Broadcast News*. Kelly O'Donnell, now of NBC, was the on-set reporter describing a bullet fired through a local couple's bedroom wall, nearly hitting them as they slept in their bed. During the on-camera tag, Kelly's last line of this very serious story was supposed to express concern that the "Clymos" sleep well tonight. Instead, the spoonerism trap opened wide, as it has with all of us, and instead of calling them the Clymo family, Kelly uttered, with all the sincerity she could muster, "We can only hope the Slymos sleep well tonight." The serious nature of the story, along with the stunned look on Kelly's face, only made the torture of restrained laughter more difficult to endure. But besides the beet-red faces and exploding sweat glands, we dutifully restrained ourselves. And, of course, in the very next story, Denise found herself reading another deadly serious account of the human condition, during which she claims to have lost five pounds.

Enter Wilma Smith, elegant, extremely bright, and already a star in Cleveland for many years.

Enter Wilma Smith, elegant, extremely bright, and already a star in Cleveland for many years. What you may not know from her always ladylike demeanor is that Wilma has a terrific sense of humor. When one of Wilma's dogs, Clarence, was attacked by a wolf, we did a series of stories on this growing problem, including an on-set look at the little guy's injuries. Not wanting Clarence's brother Clifford to feel left out, Wilma had her husband, Tom, sit with him off-camera, and at the end of the segment he introduced Clifford. Well, no one could have possibly anticipated how much Clifford would savor the moment. As the camera moved in for a tight shot, it quickly became obvious he was thoroughly in love with the experience. Wilma quickly and accurately pointed out that Clarence was obviously "very excited" to be here. Yes, little Clifford had a "cliffy."

With the inevitable changing of the guard in this crazy business, it's my hope that someone else will chronicle the passage of the next quarter-century with gentle humor that nurtures, empowers, and renews all those good people who take broadcast journalism—but never themselves—seriously.

Tim Taylor serves as the Chief Anchor of FOX 8 NEWS at 6 and 10 p.m., Monday through Friday on WJW. He is a member of the prestigious "Silver Circle," honored for his more than a quarter of a century of contributions to Cleveland television by the National Academy of Television Arts and Sciences. He is also a longtime member of the Ohio Broadcasters Hall of Fame and is a charter member of the Bedford High School Hall of Fame. Tim was also voted "Favorite Male News Anchor" in polls conducted by both *Cleveland Magazine* and the *Akron Beacon Journal.*

Flora & Fauna ❦ AUGUST

WEEK 1

BIRDS: Immature hummingbirds begin to appear at Cleveland Metroparks feeders as the young finally leave their thimble-sized nests. **WILDFLOWERS:** Evening primrose unfolds its pale yellow petals at sunset to be pollinated by night-flying insects. Giant dandelions? A closer look reveals that this flower is actually a sow thistle, a similar yellow flower, whose stems and blossoms may reach two feet in height

WEEK 2

BIRDS: Blue and green-winged teal ducks reappear at Baldwin Lake and Lake Isaac as their fall migration southward continues. **WILDFLOWERS:** Mountain mint, a species of wildflower with a green flowerhead and "dusted white" leaves, blooms in many places in Mill Stream Run, Rocky River, and Hinckley reservations. This mint is considered rare throughout most of Ohio, yet blooms commonly in certain locations here.

WEEK 3

BIRDS: The first black ducks reappear at Lake Isaac and Sunset Pond. Some may stay for the winter, but most pause for a few days and then move on southward. **WILDFLOWERS:** Wingstem, a seven-foot-tall yellow flower, begins to bloom in low wet places throughout Cleveland Metroparks. When it has "set seed," the seeds contain a two-pronged spear. The seeds latch onto an animal host and travel far away from the parent plant. New England aster, perhaps the most attractive of the fall asters, begins to bloom this week and continues through September; its purple flowers with bright yellow centers set it apart from all others.

WEEK 4

BIRDS: Nighthawks form flocks to prepare for their autumn migration. By Labor Day, most will be gone from the skies of Cleveland. Migrating warblers this week include Cape May, Tennessee, magnolia, and blackburnian. Migrating shorebirds at Baldwin Lake's mud flats may include Caspian terns, dowitchers, semipalmated and pectoral sandpipers, and lesser yellowlegs. **WILDFLOWERS:** Bottle gentian, an extremely rare and protected plant, begins to bloom at secret places near Lake Isaac. Poison ivy and deadly nightshade set fruit this week. Chickadees, not affected by the irritating oils, eagerly search for the white poison ivy berries as they ripen.

Adapted from the Nature Almanac by Robert Hinkle, with permission from Cleveland Metroparks.

More Tang Toungelers

Dick Goddard

Coming off the popularity of my last essay on the speaking affliction known as metathesis, I'm sure we could all use another round of verbal malapropria.

The common word for the dysphasia caused by unconscious consonant transposition is spoonerism. The word was created to acknowledge the person who made a cottage industry out of butchering the King's English, Reverend William Archibald Spooner, a beloved academician from Oxford University in England.

After more than four decades of trying to talk on television, I've accumulated a wonderful assortment of verbal gaffes. My favorite came during the FOX 8 Jerry Lewis Telethon in 1989, when it was my turn to announce our new venue, Stouffer's Tower City Plaza. With the ever faithful and always smiling Sister Angela at my side, I graciously invited viewers to come to Cleveland and join us at "Stouffer's Sour Titty Plaza."

It wasn't that long ago that I told weather viewers that we had to be concerned about an on-rushing and bitterly cold Canadian air mass. To the delight of viewers, and to my dismay, it came out "a cold mare's ass."

I put Robin Swoboda on the ropes one evening when I told her and our viewers to stay tuned because I would be showing a photograph of the tiny cricket frog known as a spring peeper. I unfortunately left out a key word. What I said was, "coming back I'm going to show you my peeper!" Robin's laser eyes grew to Orphan Annie dimensions as our director mercifully faded to blue.

A news anchor who prides himself on his composure is my colleague, Tim Taylor. He recalls his early days in local radio and how eager he was to impress management when he began his big upgrade to Cleveland's WHK. He mellifluously concluded his first newscast with the obligatory area temperature update: "And now, scanning the Cleveland climatological area for Parma, Parma Heights, and Pecker Pipe ..."

But, back to the legendary father of verbal somersaults, the Reverend Spooner: Spooner augmented his speech problems with the absent-minded-professor syndrome. After a lengthy treatise to an auditorium filled with students, he suddenly realized that his train of thought had wandered off track. As he concluded his lecture he told the bemused audience that "during the presentation I have just given, whenever I said Aristotle, I meant St. Paul."

Spooner once invited a man he had just met to attend a tea for a newly appointed archeology professor. "I *am* the new archeology professor," explained the man. "Never mind," said Spooner, "come just the same."

Spooner had reprimanded a student who had wasted two academic terms and continually missed his history lectures. Chastising the student, Spooner accused him of "not only hissing my mystery lectures, but tasting two worms."

To a miscreant who had set a fire on the Oxford campus, Spooner charged him with "fighting a liar in the Quadrangle."

We'll let up on Reverend Spooner and turn to another form of speech dysphasia, the mixed metaphor.

In his career as manager of the Cleveland Indians, Charlie Manuel showed promise of becoming the poor man's Yogi Berra. Charlie had a lot of trouble crossing bridges. After one of those uncomfortable postgame interviews, Charlie explained to reporters, "We'll tackle that bridge when we come to it." After another quizzing, Charlie announced, "We'll jump off that bridge when we come to it."

Charlie summed up the Indians' scoring problems with this explanation: "If we don't score more runs than they do, we're gonna lose."

The Cleveland radio team did a great job of broadcasting first-place games for an also-ran this past season. I knew that it was going to be a long year when early on I heard Mike Hegan put his meteorological seal of approval in jeopardy by announcing that "it's raining harder now than it was before it started."

I'll conclude this essay with a few of those hilarious linguistic distortions that are known as mondegreens. The word mondegreen was coined in 1914 by Sylvia Wright. In a mondegreen, the listener misinterprets words to mean something entirely different from what was intended. A classic example would be hearing "Jose, can you see?" instead of "Oh, say can you see?"

Children, naturally, are most subject to this confusion, and here are some of their precious mondegreens:

God bless America, land that I love,
Stand aside, sir, and guide her,
With delight through the night from a bulb.

Our Father, Art, in heaven,
Harold be Thy name.
Thy King done come, Thy will be done,
On Earth as it is in heaven.
Give us this day our jelly bread,
And forgive us our press passes,
As we forgive those who press past against us.
And lead us not into Penn Station,
But deliver us some e-mail.
A-men.

My favorite is a child's interpretation of the events that gave us our Declaration of Independence:

"America was founded by four fathers. Delegates from the original thirteen states formed the Contented Congress. Benjamin Franklin and Thomas Jefferson, a Virgin, were two singers of the Decoration of Independence, which says that all men are cremated equal and are well endowed by their creator."

Autumn

Many Ohioans call early autumn their favorite time of the year. September is usually a pleasantly warm month with mild days followed by refreshingly cool nights. This early fall period, with its light winds, brings a series of sunny, often hazy days.

NORTHEAST OHIO'S WARMEST AND COLDEST AUTUMNS
(by Median Temp)

....

WARMEST
Cleveland: 59.8° / 1931
Akron-Canton: 58.9° / 1931

....

COLDEST
Cleveland: 47.6° / 1976
Akron-Canton: 46.5° / 1976

The first snow of the season, most often in the form of hard snow grains, or soft snow pellets, falls over the northeastern counties about the third week in October. Sharp cold fronts are often followed by several days of moderating temperatures and calm weather.

November begins a new chapter in the Ohio weather story: the cold fronts are increasingly colder and more vigorous. November also brings the "cloud season" to the northeastern quarter of Ohio. Cold Canadian air crossing the still-warm waters of Lake Erie picks up water vapor that quickly condenses into a thick stratocumulus cloud layer upon reaching land.

The first heavy snows of the season can be expected over the extreme northeastern counties of Ohio by mid to late November. Snow bursts of one foot or more are not uncommon under sustained and gusty west-to-northwest winds across Lake Erie. This lake-effect snow causes heavy accumulations over the high-ground snowbelt regions east and southeast of Cleveland. The primary snowbelt is in Lake, Geauga, and Ashtabula counties, and the eastern portion of Cuyahoga County.

IN THE
✴ Northeast Ohio Sky ✴
THIS SEASON

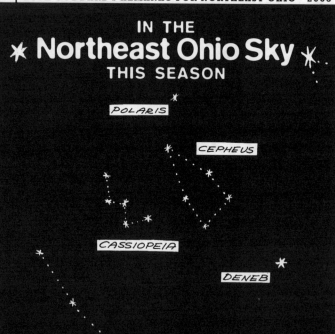

POLARIS

CEPHEUS

CASSIOPEIA

DENEB

PEGASUS

fall

Autumn

While mid-August is great for watching shooting stars (which, of course, are not really stars, but meteors), it is the poorest season for real star watching. You'll need your Clark Kent eyes; stars in the autumn sky are faint and subtle.

Mythology tells us that Queen Cassiopeia (KASS-ee-oh-PEE-ah) was punished for her vain boasting by being placed forever in the heavens. Cassiopeia makes her regal appearance (as a lazy "W") with her much fainter consort, King Cepheus (SEE-fee-us). (She wants it that way.)

If you use your imagination, the legendary winged horse of mythology, Pegasus (PEG-uh-suss), can be seen galloping across the firmament.

SEPTEMBER STATISTICS

SUNSHINE %	60
DRIEST MONTH	0.48"/1908
WARMEST MONTH	72.4°/1881
COLDEST MONTH	58.2°/1918
LIQUID PCPN AVG.	3.44"
RAINIEST DAY	5.24"/1996
RAINIEST MONTH	11.05"/1996
THUNDERY DAYS	3
SNOWIEST DAY	Trace/1993
DAYS ONE INCH SNOW	0

A magnificent, yet melancholy, sight as this month goes by is the southward migration of those big and beautiful orange, black, and white monarch butterflies. One of the few insects to migrate (Ohio's green darner dragonfly is another), the fragile monarchs are known to fly 50 miles every day, sometimes up to 200 miles if a blustery cold front cooperates. This incredible odyssey will take the butterflies some 3,000 miles from Ohio, to such exotic places as Mexico's Quintana Roo (on the Yucatan Peninsula), a place they have never been. The departure of the monarch and the green darner, as much as the migration of birds, foretells the early-morning frosts that are just ahead.

The autumnal equinox (from Latin meaning "equal night") occurs around the 22nd. At the equinox each place on earth shares in 12 hours of darkness and 12 hours of light, and with the diminishing duration of sunlight, temperatures of 85° are seldom experienced after the 15th of the month. September did establish a Cleveland benchmark for extreme heat in 1953, when the high temperature on each of the first three days of the month hit a sizzling 101°F.

September 24, 1950, will forever be remembered as Dark Sunday throughout Ohio. The cause was ash and smoke from a major forest fire in Canada's Alberta province. September 29th is St. Michael's Day; folklore says that if there has been a heavy fall of acorns (mast), a very hard, cold winter is ahead.

JAN FEB MAR APR MAY JUN JUL AUG SEP OCT NOV DEC

DAILY DATA FOR SEPTEMBER

Date	Moon Phase	Day	Day of Year	Days Left in Year	Sunrise	Sunset	Length of Day	Avg. Hi	Avg. Lo
1		Mon	244	121	6:52	8:00	13:08	78	58
2		Tue	245	120	6:53	7:59	13:06	78	58
3	◑	Wed	246	119	6:54	7:57	13:03	77	58
4		Thu	247	118	6:56	7:55	12:59	77	57
5		Fri	248	117	6:57	7:54	12:57	77	57
6		Sat	249	116	6:58	7:52	12:54	77	57
7		Sun	250	115	6:59	7:50	12:51	76	57
8		Mon	251	114	7:00	7:48	12:48	76	57
9		Tue	252	113	7:01	7:47	12:46	76	56
10	○	Wed	253	112	7:02	7:45	12:43	75	56
11		Thu	254	111	7:03	7:43	12:40	75	56
12		Fri	255	110	7:04	7:41	12:37	75	56
13		Sat	256	109	7:05	7:40	12:35	75	55
14		Sun	257	108	7:06	7:38	12:32	74	55
15		Mon	258	107	7:07	7:37	12:30	74	55
16		Tue	259	106	7:08	7:35	12:27	74	54
17		Wed	260	105	7:09	7:33	12:24	73	54
18	◐	Thu	261	104	7:10	7:31	12:21	73	54
19		Fri	262	103	7:11	7:30	12:19	73	53
20		Sat	263	102	7:12	7:28	12:16	72	53
21		Sun	264	101	7:13	7:26	12:13	72	53
22		Mon	265	100	7:14	7:24	12:10	72	52
23		Tue	266	99	7:15	7:23	12:08	71	52
24		Wed	267	98	7:16	7:21	12:05	71	52
25	●	Thu	268	97	7:17	7:19	12:02	70	51
26		Fri	269	96	7:18	7:18	12:00	70	51
27		Sat	270	95	7:19	7:16	11:57	70	51
28		Sun	271	94	7:20	7:14	11:54	69	50
29		Mon	272	93	7:21	7:12	11:51	69	50
30		Tue	273	92	7:22	7:11	11:49	69	49

JAN FEB MAR APR MAY JUN JUL AUG SEP OCT NOV DEC

Rec. Hi°	Rec. Lo°	Avg. Lake°	On This Date ...
101/1953	42/1970	73	Baseball season ends due to WW I (1918)
101/1953	45/1970	73	Rock and Roll Hall of Fame opens (1995)
101/1953	44/1976	73	Dirigible Shenandoah crashed near Caldwell Ohio, 13 die (1925)
95/1953	41/1946	72	U.S. authorizes Agency for International Development (1961)
99/1954	44/1974	72	Indians stage 1st "I hate the Yankee Hanky Night" (1977)
98/1954	40/1976	72	Actor Otto Kruger born in Toledo (1885)
94/1939	43/1962	72	Severance Hall dedicated (1931)
95/1978	41/1951	72	Ohio Senator Robert A. Taft born (1889)
94/1959	44/1986	72	Musician Macy Gray born in Canton (1970)
93/1964	39/1883	72	W. 117th St. sewer explosion (1953)
92/1952	42/1995	72	World Trade Center disaster (2001)
98/1952	40/1943	72	Indians sweep Yanks at Muni. Stad; largest AL crowd: 86,563 (1954)
96/1952	38/1964	72	Author Sherwood Anderson born in Camden, Ohio (1876)
94/1939	37/1975	71	President William McKinley dies in Buffalo (1901)
93/1991	37/1871	71	Mayflower departs from Plymouth, England (1620)
96/1944	45/1979	71	Cleveland Rams play 1st NFL game, beat Phila. 35-10 (1650)
95/1955	37/1984	70	19 students attend opening class at OSU (1873)
94/1955	39/1959	70	Indians clinch AL pennant, beat Tigers (3-2) (1954)
93/1955	40/1973	70	James A. Garfield dies (1881)
92/1978	40/1956	70	Washington D.C. abolishes slave trade (1850)
90/1931	35/1956	69	Sandra Day O'Connor 1st female Supreme Court Justice (1981)
92/1895	36/1904	69	Indians pitcher Bob Lemon born (1920)
88/1936	36/1995	69	1st female pres. candiate Victoria Chaflin Woodhull born in Ohio (1838)
87/1941	36/1995	69	1st Supreme Court of the U.S. established (1789)
88/1900	35/1976	68	Columbus sails on 2nd voyage to America (1493)
89/1908	37/1947	68	FCC formed (1914)
88/1946	33/1947	68	Actor Greg Morris born in Cleveland (1934)
89/1949	34/1984	68	Euclid Beach Park closes forever (1969)
95/1953	32/1942	67	1st congress adjourns (1789)
86/1881	35/1963	67	Ohio Turnpike opens (1955)

Left margin: JAN FEB MAR APR MAY JUN JUL AUG SEP OCT NOV DEC

Flora & Fauna SEPTEMBER

WEEK 1

BIRDS: Labor Day marks the traditional migration of the nighthawks, a common bird throughout our suburban area. This whippoorwill-like bird zooms through the summer night skies hunting for insects and creating a loud "b-u-z-z-t" sound as it power-dives in flight. Look for their long narrow wings with white wing bars in flight. Shortly behind the nighthawk migration the chimney swifts also leave. These small swallow-like birds gather in wheeling flocks of a hundred or more around inactive chimneys in the summer. A spectacular migration at Baldwin Lake in Rocky River Reservation presents rare and unusual shorebirds using the exposed mud flats as a feeding area. Among September stopovers, look for semipalmated plovers, greater and lesser yellowlegs, great egrets, and hundreds of killdeers. Small sandpipers, called "peeps," are difficult to identify, but fun to watch as they probe the soft mud in search of small invertebrates. **MAMMALS:** Fawns (without their spots) appear more frequently in Cleveland Metroparks meadows and open areas at dusk. Their watchful mothers are never far behind.

WEEK 2

WEEK 3

BIRDS: Although most warblers are in their confusing fall colors, watch for blackburnian, hooded, Tennessee, Cape May, and magnolia warblers in and around Cleveland Metroparks forests. Black ducks and blue-winged teal return from northern haunts this week. Watch Cleveland Metroparks rivers and ponds for them. **WILDFLOWERS:** The cardinal flower reaches its peak of blooming this week. The vibrant red flowers dot many Cleveland Metroparks marshes and river edges. A stroll through Cleveland Metroparks meadows reveals the beauties of gray goldenrod, bottle gentian, great lobelia, and turtlehead. **TREES:** Ohio buckeye nuts are ripe! Can you find them before the squirrels do? Look for the polished-looking "buck's eye" beneath the tough green husk. A good crop of hickory nuts and other "mast" may take the squirrels away from your bird feeders starting this week. To your delight (or dismay) they will soon return!

WEEK 4

BIRDS: Hummingbirds may still be flitting around your flower garden if the days have not grown too cold, but most will be gone by the end of the month. Their migration may include a non-stop trip of over 500 miles across the Gulf of Mexico! Dark-eyed juncos—sometimes called "snow-birds"—may appear at feeders beginning this week. Legend says that they appear just before the first snow of winter and leave after the last snow of spring. Previous years' observations show that their timing is considerably off, fortunately. Flocks of robins increase their numbers daily as they prepare for migration. Fall-ripened crab apples are a favorite high-energy food. **WILDFLOWERS:** New England aster, perhaps the most beautiful of all fall asters, begins to bloom this week. The bright yellow center is surrounded by deep purple petals, making a lovely contrast of colors on the fall landscape. Ironweed's bright burgundy flowers top its stems at heights of five feet or more in Cleveland Metroparks meadows. Look for it among the bright yellows of goldenrods blooming nearby. **TREES AND SHRUBS:** The first blush of autumn colors is now found on red and sugar maples, tulip trees, ashes, and dogwoods.

BIRDS: Grackles accumulate in flocks numbering in the thousands as they prepare for migration. They may be joined by a few cowbirds and red-winged blackbirds as well. The woods grow silent as most non-resident songbirds leave for warmer climates. Cardinals and robins still serenade the dawn. White-throated sparrows begin to appear this week on their annual migration from Canada through Cleveland to warmer climates. Listen to their half-hearted "old Sam Peabody-Peabody-Peabody" calls.

Adapted from the Nature Almanac by Robert Hinkle, with permission from Cleveland Metroparks.

RUTHERFORD B. HAYES
19TH PRESIDENT 1877–1881

Dick Goddard

Rutherford Birchard Hayes was born in his family's home in Delaware, Ohio, on October 4, 1822.

He was delivered for a doctor's fee of $3.50. His father died 11 weeks before his birth.

Broad-shouldered and handsome with a large head and high forehead, Hayes stood 5 feet, 8 1/2 inches tall and weighed about 175 pounds. Nicknamed "Rud," he had deep-set blue eyes and a straight nose. He also had straight teeth, not a common feature in the 19th century. His hair was auburn in his youth, then dark brown and eventually snow white. Hayes wore a full beard beginning with his service in the Civil War.

In robust good health, Hayes neither drank nor smoked, and his only exercise was fast-paced walks. He spoke in a clear and pleasing voice, but was not considered a great orator. Hayes dressed simply, and often sloppily, in ill-fitting clothes.

The modest Hayes had a vanilla personality and a steady-as-rent temperament. Although not given to mood swings, he was a bit fear-

OHIO'S MAGNIFICENT SEVEN

JAN FEB MAR APR MAY JUN JUL AUG SEP OCT NOV DEC

ful of the family legacy of insanity. He surmounted this fear and got along very well in society, becoming a relaxed and easygoing conversationalist who treasured his friendships and possessed a keen memory for names and faces. Descended from Vermont Puritans with scrupulous ethics, Hayes was considered an honorable man of unbending propriety. He also welcomed constructive criticism.

A hunter and fisherman, Hayes was an avid outdoorsman. Hayes had only one sibling, his sister Fanny, who lived to maturity. He had an unusually close bond with his sister and was devastated when she died in 1856 after delivering stillborn twins.

Hayes's First Lady was Lucy Ware Webb of Chillicothe, the first of the presidential mates to graduate from college (Wesleyan). Lucy was a doozy. Hayes's detractors said that Lucy was the real chief executive. A strict Methodist, Lucy ruled the roost and would not allow dancing, card-playing, or low-necked dresses in the White House. A staunch advocate of temperance, she also prohibited booze, becoming known as "Lemonade Lucy."

Remarkably, Hayes did not support his wife's Methodist beliefs, and he was not a member of any church. In his diaries Hayes said he believed in the "good parts" of the Bible—kindness and humanity—but he did not believe in any orthodox creed (as was the case with so many of our presidents). He was generous with his money and time, and if any belief system could claim him it would be Unitarianism.

In the Civil War Hayes served with the 23rd Ohio Volunteer Infantry Regiment from June 1861 to June 1865, rising from major to major general. He took part in 50 engagements, was seriously wounded in the left arm, and had four horses shot out from under him. He participated in the savage battle at Antietam.

Hayes grew up as an overprotected, fatherless child. His mother, Sophie, supported her family by renting a farm in exchange for one-third of the crops and one-half of the fruit. The youthful Hayes won many spelling contests and was tutored by a harsh schoolmaster, Daniel Granger. At 16 he enrolled in Kenyon College at Gambier, Ohio. He loathed science, and loved philosophy. Graduating as valedictorian in 1845, he went on to graduate from Harvard with a law degree.

Hayes said that he always felt ambitious, but the more he learned the more he felt his "littleness."

In politics, Hayes had been a Whig, but he later became instrumental in founding the Republican Party. In 1864 he was elected to Congress, and between 1868 and 1876 he served as governor of Ohio. With his gallantry and heroism in war and his established reputation for integrity and honesty, he was encouraged to run for the presidency in 1876. His opponent was reform candidate Samuel Tilden, who achieved fame by helping to throw out the infamous Tammany Hall–Boss Tweed Ring in New York City. A lot of mud was slung in the campaign. While Tilden won the popular vote by about a 250,000 plurality, he was one vote shy of winning the necessary electoral college majority. With national violence threatening to erupt, the Republicans and Democrats agreed to what became known as the Great Swap: Hayes would become president in exchange for concessions to the white southern Democrats, who were trying to recover from the ravages of the recent Civil War. Hayes thus came to power through what many critics labeled as fraud. In his four-year term Hayes labored mightily to restore dignity and respect to the office that was so tainted by the Grant administration. Hayes had to make so many promises and compromise on so many issues that he lost much of his power before taking office.

True to his word, Hayes served only one term as president. In 1881 he and Lucy retired to Spiegel Grove in Fremont. Lucy died of a stroke in 1889; Hayes died on January 17, 1893, after suffering a heart attack. His last words as he lay dying in the arms of his son Webb were "I know that I am going where Lucy is."

In 1915 the bodies of Mr. and Mrs. Hayes were reinterred at the Spiegel Grove estate, which had been deeded over to the state of Ohio.

Of the 41 United States presidents rated in the recent C-SPAN survey, Hayes was ranked 26th.

CAPTION CONTEST

Thanks for entering this year's caption contest on the FOX 8 web site. The winning caption was submitted by **Bonnie Hershey** of Garrettsville.

"Look, Dick, this woollybear is as big as me!"

Distance Learning

DAN COUGHLIN

When I was young and foolish (now I am old and foolish) I bought a brand-new 1967 Jaguar XKE two-passenger roadster, a car so beautiful that I should have worn a tuxedo whenever I drove it.

It is good that I did not buy a tuxedo because the Jaguar spent more time in the shop than on the road. The speedometer went up to 160 miles per hour, but this was an unrealistic expectation, as the needle was usually stuck on zero. If the weather was too cold, too hot, or too humid, it wouldn't run.

On one of the days when it actually started, I drove it down to the Indianapolis Motor Speedway when Firestone was testing its racecar tires. I was friendly with the Firestone people, and they said, "Let's see how fast it will go." Mario Andretti, one of the drivers testing the racing tires, jumped in for the ride. Andretti is not a big man—he is almost elfin—and he fit easily into the passenger seat. The Speedway technical staff turned on the automatic timing devices, and I pulled out of the pits, shifting quickly through the four gears.

Earlier that summer I had asked Andretti about his strategy for the Indianapolis 500. "I'm gonna stand on it," he said.

So I stood on it.

Andretti must have been crazy to ride around the Speedway with an amateur who had never driven on a race course. The centrifugal force of the banked turns pushed us outward, within inches of the wall, and I backed off the gas. If I had hit the wall, Andretti would have been the first to get it.

After three or four trips around the concrete oval, I pulled into the pits to see how we were doing. The electronic timers clocked me at 117 miles an hour. That wasn't my average speed, it was my top speed on the straightaways. So much for the manufacturer's claims. It was embarrassing. Andretti usually went down those straightaways at 240 miles an hour.

The Jaguar was nothing more than an overpriced driveway decoration. I should have gotten a silver ball or a pink flamingo. If I had used that money for the down payment on two duplexes in Lakewood, I would be a wealthy man today.

My thumb was a far more reliable mode of transportation in the old days.

I notice that no one hitchhikes anymore. Maybe it's a fear of perverts. When I was young, we never thought of perverts. Random murders, serial killers, and perverts were never in the news. We trusted people.

I frequently hitchhiked back and forth to college, even in bitter winter weather. I would hang a sign around my neck that said "Notre Dame" on one side and "Cleveland" on the other. Because my father worked on the railroad, I could ride the New York Central for half price, only $10 between the Linndale Station and South Bend, Indiana, but that was still a lot of money for a college kid. I could subsist for a week on $10 in those days.

I once persuaded my old friend Jim Flannery to ride my thumb home during our semester break in January. In the winter, when the trees are barren, the Golden Dome is clearly seen from the Indiana Toll Road. It looks like an easy hike. But on foot, in the snow and carrying a suitcase, it was more like a forced march. At the end we still had to climb a six-foot wire fence and scale a 10-foot embankment to reach the berm of the highway. That's not the ideal location. Cars whizzing by at 70 miles an hour are not likely to stop, and they didn't.

Finally, I said to Flannery, "Lie down." "What?" Flannery said. "Lie down, right here in the snow," I said. "Somebody will think you're hurt and they'll stop."

Naturally, a good Samaritan stopped. Flannery hopped to his feet, and we jumped in before the driver knew he had been flimflammed.

I was not proud about resorting to trickery, but we were desperate. Our relationship with the driver was chilly, needless to say. He resented the deceit, and I don't blame him. It was the only time I did that. Trust is important when you're hitching a ride. He dropped us off at the next service plaza.

I always preferred to work service plazas. In bad weather you could stay warm and dry. Nobody bothered you (at toll gates the state police might hassle you). Most importantly, at service plazas drivers could get a good look at you. I always wore a sports coat and tie. A friendly, nonthreatening appearance was important. People were comfortable with cleancut college boys and soldiers in uniform.

Some of my adventures were exhilarating. For example, in October of 1957 I hitchhiked from New York City to South Bend, a trip that took 20 hours.

It began when an upperclassman with a car stashed off campus sought riders to share the cost of a trip to the Notre Dame–Army football game in Philadelphia. Army was a national power, led by Pete Dawkins, who won the Heisman Trophy that year. I signed up.

The game was a classic. Notre Dame won, 23–21, on Monty Stickles's last-minute field goal, and we were feeling pretty chipper. Off we went to New York to celebrate.

But our group became separated in McSorley's Saloon in Lower Manhattan, and I found myself alone and virtually broke in New York City at 3 a.m. Live, from New York, it's Sunday morning, but it wasn't funny.

The streets of New York actually grow quiet at that hour. I walked them until I came upon a church. Churches were like convenience stores in those days. They were open 24 hours.

The tiny flicker of votive candles in a far corner was the only light. I stretched out in the last pew and went to sleep. The footsteps and muted voices of those arriving for the six o'clock Mass woke me up in time to fulfill my Sunday obligation.

After Mass I stepped into the sunlight and asked someone how to get to the Pennsylvania Turnpike.

"I don't know. I guess I'd start in Philadelphia," the man said.

"Which way is that?" I asked. He pointed south.

I stepped off the curb and stuck out my thumb. I was more than 700 miles from school, and I had 24 hours to get there.

It was early afternoon when I was rescued from a service plaza in eastern Pennsylvania by a family that was crowded into an old two-door Chevrolet. Mom and Dad were in the front seat with one of the kids. They rearranged some boxes and suitcases and said I could get in back with Grandma and another youngster if I held one of their suitcases on my lap. As for me, I was traveling light. I didn't even have a toothbrush.

They seemed like devout Protestants, or maybe Quakers, and they actually lived their faith. I was broke, and they didn't have much more. The man counted out exact change when he paid for his gas.

They weren't much for small talk, and they never turned on the radio. I didn't expect them to spin the dial and find a pro football game, but some music would have helped. I never mentioned it. After a while Grandma found her Bible in her bundles and began reading aloud. I had already been to church so—what the hell—I went to sleep.

It was dark when they dropped me off at a service plaza in the middle of Pennsylvania. The pace quickened when a trucker picked me up. He didn't say anything worth remembering, but he was gabby. At least he kept me awake—as if that were necessary after he started ramming the slower truck in front of him.

He seemed to know the driver of the slower rig, because he kept ramming him from behind, laughing like a fiend. This ramming game continued up and down the mountains and through the tunnels. I actually wished I had Grandma and her Bible next to me.

The trucker got me to the other side of Pittsburgh and then two more rides got me into Indiana, but I was horrified when one of the drivers suddenly pulled off at an exit in Indiana, not a service plaza, at about two in the morning. It was dark and cold, and there wasn't a car in sight. Two hours passed before I got my last ride. I got to bed at seven Monday morning, two hours before my first class. I had been up for 48 hours.

I actually wished I had Grandma and her Bible next to me.

My thumb was exhausted.

When I was in the army in the early sixties I hitchhiked around the country in military planes by hanging around Air Force bases until a flyboy going my way had room for an extra body. One time, though, the best I could do was the cargo hold of a fat old helicopter.

The last time I put miles on my thumb was in January 1963, when I was returning to my army base from Christmas furlough. My mother drove me to a service plaza on the Ohio Turnpike near Elyria and kissed me good-bye. This time I was not wearing a spiffy tweed sports coat and tie. I was wearing army dress grays, and the sign around my neck said, "Fort Hood, Texas." It was snowing, and I was lugging my big army duffle bag. In my day, when you went on leave, you had to take all your equipment with you except your rifle. I even had my mess kit and my tent in there. If we had broken down in Missouri, I would have been ready. Welcome to 1,400 miles of rough road in the cabs of a dozen Mack trucks.

Most of the truckers of that era had been in the service during World War II or Korea, so when they saw a dogface, they'd say, "Get in." They didn't share many stories, however. I might have been riding with heroes, but heroes never brag. The trip took almost 30 hours. That's a lot of country songs on small-town radio stations.

That was my last adventure. A few years later I bought the Jaguar, proving that I traveled a great distance and learned nothing.

Emmy-award winning sports journalist **Dan Coughlin** delivers sports reporting and commentary as a member of the FOX 8 news team. He is a Cleveland native currently residing in Rocky River. Coughlin is a trustee of St. Edward High School, serves on the board of directors of the Cleveland National Air Show, and is a past president of the Press Club of Cleveland.

City-by-City Weather Statistics

Temperature and Precipitation Averages

AKRON/CANTON (Elev. 1,209 ft.)

Month	Max	Min	Pcpn	Snow
Jan	33	17	2.16	12
Feb	36	19	2.23	10
Mar	47	29	3.33	9
Apr	59	38	3.16	3
May	70	48	3.73	T
Jun	79	57	3.18	0
Jul	82	62	4.08	0
Aug	80	60	3.32	0
Sep	74	54	3.32	0
Oct	62	43	2.35	1
Nov	50	34	3.01	5
Dec	38	24	2.95	10

ASHLAND (Elev. 1,050 ft.)

Month	Max	Min	Pcpn	Snow
Jan	30	14	2.12	10
Feb	33	15	1.88	8
Mar	44	25	2.95	7
Apr	55	36	3.23	1
May	69	46	3.86	0
Jun	78	55	3.40	0
Jul	83	59	3.56	0
Aug	80	57	3.63	0
Sep	73	51	2.96	0
Oct	61	39	2.06	T
Nov	48	31	3.10	3
Dec	34	20	2.70	8

ASHTABULA (Elev. 690 ft.)

Month	Max	Min	Pcpn	Snow
Jan	31	17	2.35	20
Feb	53	19	1.78	15
Mar	43	27	2.40	11
Apr	55	36	2.98	3
May	68	48	3.41	0
Jun	78	57	3.52	0
Jul	81	61	4.07	0
Aug	80	60	3.81	0
Sep	74	54	3.63	0
Oct	63	44	3.29	T
Nov	50	25	3.48	7
Dec	38	25	2.85	17

CHARDON (Elev. 1,210 ft.)

Month	Max	Min	Pcpn	Snow
Jan	30	13	2.64	29
Feb	33	14	2.51	21
Mar	43	24	3.33	17
Apr	56	34	3.55	5
May	68	44	3.57	T
Jun	77	53	4.18	0
July	81	58	3.53	0
Aug	79	57	3.61	0
Sep	72	50	3.75	0
Oct	60	40	3.75	2
Nov	48	32	4.05	12
Dec	35	21	3.79	27

CINCINNATI (Elev. 869 ft.)

Month	Max	Min	Pcpn	Snow
Jan	37	20	2.59	7
Feb	41	23	2.69	5
Mar	53	33	4.24	4
Apr	64	42	3.75	1
May	74	52	4.28	T
Jun	82	60	3.84	0
Jul	86	65	4.24	0
Aug	84	63	3.35	0
Sep	78	57	2.88	0
Oct	66	44	2.86	T
Nov	53	35	3.46	2
Dec	42	25	3.15	4

COLUMBUS (Elev. 813 ft.)

Month	Max	Min	Pcpn	Snow
Jan	34	19	2.18	8
Feb	38	21	2.24	6
Mar	51	31	3.27	5
Apr	62	40	3.21	1
May	72	50	3.93	T
Jun	80	58	4.04	0
Jul	84	63	4.31	0
Aug	82	61	3.72	0
Sep	76	55	2.96	0
Oct	65	43	2.15	T
Nov	51	34	3.22	2
Dec	39	25	2.86	5

DAYTON (Elev. 995 ft.)

Month	Max	Min	Pcpn	Snow
Jan	34	18	2.13	8
Feb	33	21	2.17	6
Mar	50	31	3.42	5
Apr	62	41	3.46	1
May	73	51	3.88	T
Jun	82	59	3.82	0
Jul	85	63	3.54	0
Aug	83	61	3.20	0
Sep	77	55	2.54	0
Oct	65	44	2.48	T
Nov	51	34	3.07	2
Dec	39	24	2.93	6

ELYRIA (Elev. 730 ft.)

Month	Max	Min	Pcpn	Snow
Jan	36	20	1.83	11
Feb	39	21	1.85	10
Mar	50	31	2.80	8
Apr	62	41	2.82	1
May	73	50	3.51	T
Jun	82	59	3.76	0
Jul	86	63	3.39	0
Aug	84	62	3.00	0
Sep	78	56	3.03	0
Oct	67	45	2.30	0
Nov	53	37	3.14	4
Dec	40	26	3.05	10

ERIE, PA (Elev. 731 ft.)

Month	Max	Min	Pcpn	Snow
Jan	33	18	2.22	23
Feb	34	18	2.28	16
Mar	44	28	3.00	11
Apr	55	38	3.24	3
May	66	48	3.44	T
Jun	75	58	4.09	0
Jul	80	63	3.43	0
Aug	79	62	4.06	0
Sep	72	56	4.39	T
Oct	61	46	3.77	1
Nov	49	37	4.02	10
Dec	38	25	3.59	22

JAN FEB MAR APR MAY JUN JUL AUG SEP OCT NOV DEC

IRONTON (Elev. 555 ft.)

Month	Max	Min	Pcpn	Snow
Jan	41	21	2.55	7
Feb	46	24	2.78	5
Mar	58	33	3.06	3
Apr	67	42	3.50	0
May	78	51	3.98	0
Jun	85	60	3.57	0
Jul	88	64	4.58	0
Aug	87	63	3.77	0
Sep	81	56	2.59	0
Oct	70	44	2.80	0
Nov	58	35	2.93	1
Dec	46	27	3.13	3

MANSFIELD (Elev. 1,295 ft.)

Month	Max	Min	Pcpn	Snow
Jan	32	17	1.65	10
Feb	35	19	1.66	9
Mar	47	29	2.88	7
Apr	59	38	3.43	2
May	69	48	4.15	0
Jun	78	57	3.68	0
Jul	82	62	3.67	0
Aug	80	60	4.00	0
Sep	74	54	3.25	0
Oct	62	43	2.08	T
Nov	49	34	3.12	2
Dec	37	23	2.82	9

NEW PHILA/DOVER (Elev. 890 ft.)

Month	Max	Min	Pcpn	Snow
Jan	34	16	2.37	9
Feb	38	17	2.46	7
Mar	49	27	3.49	5
Apr	61	36	3.52	1
May	72	46	3.93	T
Jun	81	55	4.06	0
Jul	85	59	4.28	0
Aug	83	58	3.35	0
Sep	76	51	3.06	0
Oct	64	39	2.48	T
Nov	51	32	2.55	2
Dec	39	23	2.94	6

KENT/RAVENNA (Elev. 1,150 ft.)

Month	Max	Min	Pcpn	Snow
Jan	34	17	2.30	12
Feb	38	18	2.15	11
Mar	48	28	3.21	9
Apr	59	38	3.20	2
May	71	48	3.42	T
Jun	80	57	3.33	0
Jul	82	62	3.88	0
Aug	81	60	3.38	0
Sep	75	54	3.14	0
Oct	63	43	2.39	1
Nov	49	33	2.92	5
Dec	39	24	2.59	10

MARIETTA (Elev. 580 ft.)

Month	Max	Min	Pcpn	Snow
Jan	39	21	2.36	8
Feb	43	22	2.49	5
Mar	54	32	3.11	4
Apr	65	40	2.84	T
May	75	50	3.62	0
Jun	83	59	3.64	0
Jul	86	63	3.90	0
Aug	84	62	3.33	0
Sep	78	55	3.01	0
Oct	67	43	2.69	0
Nov	55	35	2.77	2
Dec	44	26	2.91	4

NORWALK (Elev. 670 ft.)

Month	Max	Min	Pcpn	Snow
Jan	31	15	1.46	9
Feb	34	17	1.83	7
Mar	44	27	2.69	6
Apr	58	36	3.28	1
May	70	47	3.76	0
Jun	79	56	3.84	0
Jul	83	61	3.37	0
Aug	81	59	3.25	0
Sep	75	52	2.90	0
Oct	62	41	1.83	0
Nov	50	33	2.56	2
Dec	36	22	2.77	7

LIMA (Elev. 860 ft.)

Month	Max	Min	Pcpn	Snow
Jan	31	15	1.75	7
Feb	34	17	1.59	6
Mar	45	27	2.65	5
Apr	58	37	3.03	T
May	72	49	3.79	0
Jun	81	58	3.09	0
Jul	85	63	3.44	0
Aug	82	60	2.67	0
Sep	76	54	2.95	0
Oct	63	42	1.95	0
Nov	49	33	2.51	2
Dec	37	22	2.50	4

MEDINA (Elev. 1,192 ft.)

Month	Max	Min	Pcpn	Snow
Jan	31	14	2.01	12
Feb	35	15	2.13	10
Mar	46	25	3.12	7
Apr	58	35	3.25	3
May	69	46	3.86	0
Jun	78	55	3.61	0
Jul	82	59	3.86	0
Aug	80	57	3.24	0
Sep	74	51	3.39	0
Oct	62	39	2.29	1
Nov	49	31	3.33	4
Dec	36	21	3.00	10

PAINESVILLE (Elev. 600 ft.)

Month	Max	Min	Pcpn	Snow
Jan	34	20	2.33	15
Feb	36	21	1.82	13
Mar	46	29	2.62	9
Apr	57	38	3.20	1
May	68	48	3.06	0
Jun	77	58	3.37	0
Jul	81	62	3.31	0
Aug	80	61	3.44	0
Sep	75	53	3.30	0
Oct	64	46	3.04	T
Nov	51	36	3.44	5
Dec	40	26	2.77	15

fun facts OHIO

ASTRONAUTS

James Arthur Lovell, Jr. was born in Cleveland (Spacecraft Commander of the Apollo 13 mission in 1970.)

G. David Low was born in Cleveland.

Robert F. Overmyer was born in Lorain. Sadly, In 1996, he was killed when a small plane he was test piloting crashed near Duluth, Minnesota.

SANDUSKY (Elev. 606 ft.)

Month	Max	Min	Pcpn	Snow
Jan	31	17	1.29	9
Feb	33	19	1.71	7
Mar	43	29	2.18	S
Apr	55	39	2.80	T
May	68	50	3.68	0
Jun	78	60	3.26	0
Jul	83	65	3.27	0
Aug	80	63	3.17	0
Sep	74	56	2.53	0
Oct	61	45	2.01	0
Nov	49	35	2.50	2
Dec	37	24	2.82	7

TIFFIN (Elev. 760 ft.)

Month	Max	Min	Pcpn	Snow
Jan	33	18	2.44	8
Feb	36	20	1.98	6
Mar	47	29	3.12	5
Apr	61	39	3.54	1
May	72	49	3.55	0
Jun	81	59	3.46	0
Jul	84	62	3.88	0
Aug	82	61	3.22	0
Sep	76	54	2.74	0
Oct	65	44	2.05	0
Nov	50	34	2.65	2
Dec	38	29	2.62	7

WOOSTER (Elev. 1,020 ft.)

Month	Max	Min	Pcpn	Snow
Jan	32	17	1.60	9
Feb	35	19	2.01	8
Mar	47	28	2.60	6
Apr	59	37	3.00	1
May	69	47	3.73	0
Jun	78	56	3.37	0
Jul	82	60	3.97	0
Aug	80	58	3.58	0
Sep	73	52	2.78	0
Oct	62	41	1.78	T
Nov	49	33	2.72	3
Dec	37	23	2.50	7

STEUBENVILLE (Elev. 992 ft.)

Month	Max	Min	Pcpn	Snow
Jan	37	19	2.97	12
Feb	40	21	2.47	10
Mar	50	29	3.87	7
Apr	63	39	3.58	2
May	73	49	3.88	0
Jun	81	58	4.16	0
Jul	84	62	3.97	0
Aug	83	61	3.43	0
Sep	77	55	2.84	0
Oct	65	43	2.65	T
Nov	52	34	2.64	3
Dec	41	25	2.87	8

TOLEDO (Elev. 669 ft.)

Month	Max	Min	Pcpn	Snow
Jan	30	15	1.75	10
Feb	33	17	1.73	8
Mar	46	27	2.66	6
Apr	59	36	2.96	2
May	71	47	2.91	T
Jun	80	56	3.75	0
Jul	83	61	3.27	0
Aug	81	58	3.25	0
Sep	74	52	2.85	0
Oct	62	40	2.10	T
Nov	49	32	2.81	3
Dec	35	21	2.93	8

YOUNGSTOWN (Elev. 1,178 ft.)

Month	Max	Min	Pcpn	Snow
Jan	31	16	2.13	13
Feb	34	18	2.03	11
Mar	45	27	3.11	11
Apr	58	37	3.06	3
May	69	46	3.52	T
Jun	77	55	3.94	0
Jul	81	59	4.07	0
Aug	80	58	3.32	0
Sep	73	52	3.48	0
Oct	61	42	2.62	1
Nov	48	34	3.11	6
Dec	36	23	2.93	12

AREA 2001-2002 STATE CHAMPIONS
OHIO HIGH SCHOOL ATHLETIC ASSOCIATION

Boys Golf, Division I: **St. Ignatius High School**, *Cleveland*

Boys Golf, Division II: **John F. Kennedy**, *Warren*

Girls Golf, Division I: **Walsh Jesuit**, *Cuyahoga Falls*

Boys Cross Country, Division I: **Hudson High School**, *Hudson*

Girls Cross Country, Division II: **Beaumont Girls School**, *Cleveland Heights*

Girls Soccer, Division II: **Walsh Jesuit High School**, *Cuyahoga Falls*

Volleyball, Division III: **Villa Angela-St. Joseph Academy**, *Cleveland*

Football, Division I: **St. Ignatius High School**, *Cleveland*

Football, Division III: **Lake Catholic Academy**, *Mentor*

Football, Division V: **St. Peter Chanel High School**, *Bedford*

Gymnastics, Division I: **Magnificat Girls School**, *Rocky River*

Ice Hockey, Division I: **St. Edward High School**, *Lakewood*

Wrestling, Division I: **St. Edward High School**, *Lakewood*

Girls Basketball, Division I: **Hoover High School**, *North Canton*

Girls Basketball, Division II: **East Tech High School**, *Cleveland*

Girls Basketball, Division III: **Regina High School**, *South Euclid*

Boys Tennis, Division I, Singles: **Stephen Rozek**, *Chardon High School*

Girls Tennis, Division II, Singles: **Lara Mauer**, *Bay Village High School*

Boys Track & Field, Division II: **Edison High School**, *Milan*

Girls Track & Field, Division I: **Beaumont Girls School**, *South Euclid*

Baseball, Division I: **St. Ignatius High School**, *Cleveland*

Baseball, Division II: **Tallmadge High School**, *Tallmadge*

Softball, Division I: **Elyria High School**, *Elyria*

Softball, Division II: **Walsh Jesuit High School**, *Cuyahoga Falls*

Softball, Division III: **Loudonville High School**, *Loudonville*

(left margin: JAN FEB MAR APR MAY JUN JUL AUG SEP OCT NOV DEC)

⚡ STORM SAFETY: *Flash Flood*

The flash flood has become this nation's deadliest weather event. The average annual death toll is 160, with yearly property losses of more than $1 billion. The reasons: denuding of the landscape by developers and the general public; more people setting up homesites in flood plains; more vacationers camping in flood-prone areas; more mobile home parks locating near rivers and streams.

The National Weather Service is responsible for issuing flash flood watches and warnings, based on current and past rainfall amounts, land configuration, and drainage potential. It is vital that communities set up local "river watches." The NWS, aided by ham radio and CB operators, will help establish that network.

FLOOD SAFETY RULES:

1. Never attempt to drive across a flooded area, since just two feet of water can float an automobile.

2. Never try to walk across a rapidly moving stream if the water is above your knees.

3. Never allow children to play near drainage ditches during or after heavy rains.

fun facts OHIO

ODDS AND ENDS:

The National Football League (NFL) was organized in Canton, Ohio in 1920.

Dr. B. F. Goodrich introduced the rubber industry to Akron, "the Rubber Capital of the World," in 1870.

The American Federation of Labor (AFL) was founded in Columbus in 1886.

Jesse Owens, (1913–1980), won four gold medals during the 1936 Olympics in Berlin, grew up in Cleveland and graduated from The Ohio State University.

The first successful blood transfusion was performed in Cleveland in 1905 by Dr. George Crile.

W.F. Semple of Mount Vernon patented chewing gum in 1869.

Sources:http://www.ohiotourism.com/industry/grouptour/overview/ ohio_facts.html; http://my.ohio.voyager.net/~ohivesta/tidbits.htm

OCTOBER STATISTICS

SUNSHINE %	62
DRIEST MONTH	0.47"/1886
WARMEST MONTH	61.4°/1947
COLDEST MONTH	45.2°/1925
LIQUID PCPN AVG.	2.54"
RAINIEST DAY	3.44"/1954
RAINIEST MONTH	9.50"/1954
THUNDERY DAYS	2
SNOWIEST DAY	6.7"/1962
LEAST SNOWFALL	Trace
	(most recently in 1997)
DAYS ONE INCH SNOW	0

October's arrival means that the season of the sun is gone in Northeast Ohio. The first three weeks of the month are usually very pleasant with comfortably mild days and cool nights. It'll turn frosty by mid-month in many nooks and crannies, and the arrival of steadily colder air over the still-warm waters of Lake Erie will often cause waterspouts and cold-air funnels to develop over the lake.

Leaf color often peaks in Northeast Ohio during the third week, but it can vary if the growing season has been very wet or very dry. Most Ohioans are not aware of how lucky we are to be treated to the flaming foliage. More than 90 percent of earth's inhabitants, and three-quarters of the United States, never see the dazzling colors of autumn.

October is the Woollybear Festival and the Pumpkin Festival and apple cider. Ohio groundhogs are growing fat on clover and alfalfa as they prepare to enter their winter hibernation chambers. Turtles and frogs are likewise burying themselves in muddy pond and river bottoms. Hornets will be killed by the frosts of late October, but the queens are checking out attics for the long winter to come.

The return to Standard Time the last Sunday in October means we'll regain the hour of sleep we lost in early April.

JAN FEB MAR APR MAY JUN JUL AUG SEP OCT NOV DEC

DAILY DATA FOR OCTOBER

JAN
FEB
MAR
APR
MAY
JUN
JUL
AUG
SEP
OCT
NOV
DEC

Date	Moon Phase	Day	Day of Year	Days Left in Year	Sunrise	Sunset	Length of Day	Avg. Hi	Avg. Lo
1		Wed	274	91	7:23	7:09	11:46	68	49
2	◑	Thu	275	90	7:24	7:07	11:43	68	48
3		Fri	276	89	7:25	7:06	11:41	67	48
4		Sat	277	88	7:26	7:04	11:38	67	48
5		Sun	278	87	7:27	7:02	11:35	66	47
6		Mon	279	86	7:28	7:00	11:32	66	47
7		Tue	280	85	7:29	6:59	11:30	66	46
8		Wed	281	84	7:31	6:57	11:26	65	46
9		Thu	282	83	7:32	6:56	11:24	65	46
10	○	Fri	283	82	7:33	6:54	11:21	65	45
11		Sat	284	81	7:34	6:52	11:18	64	45
12		Sun	285	80	7:35	6:51	11:16	64	45
13		Mon	286	79	7:36	6:49	11:13	63	44
14		Tue	287	78	7:37	6:48	11:11	63	44
15		Wed	288	77	7:38	6:46	11:08	62	43
16		Thu	289	76	7:39	6:45	11:06	62	43
17		Fri	290	75	7:40	6:43	11:03	62	43
18	◑	Sat	291	74	7:42	6:41	10:59	61	43
19		Sun	292	73	7:43	6:40	10:57	61	42
20		Mon	293	72	7:44	6:38	10:54	61	42
21		Tue	294	71	7:45	6:37	10:52	60	42
22		Wed	295	70	7:46	6:36	10:50	60	41
23		Thu	296	69	7:47	6:34	10:47	59	41
24		Fri	297	68	7:49	6:33	10:44	59	41
25	●	Sat	298	67	7:50	6:31	10:41	59	41
26		Sun	299	66	7:51	6:30	10:39	58	40
27		Mon	300	65	7:52	6:29	10:37	58	40
28		Tue	301	64	7:53	6:27	10:34	57	40
29		Wed	302	63	7:54	6:26	10:32	57	40
30		Thu	303	62	6:56	5:25	10:29	57	39
31	◑	Fri	304	61	6:57	5:23	10:26	56	39

Rec. Hi °	Rec. Lo °	Avg. Lake °	On This Date ...
87/1952	34/1947	66	Bob Feller 348th strikeout of the season (1946)
86/1919	32/1975	66	Bob Feller strikes out 18 Detroit Tigers (1938)
89/1953	29/1975	66	Indians' Frank Robinson becomes baseball's 1st black mgr (1974)
88/1952	33/1981	66	1st AL playoff game, Indians beat Red Sox, 8-0 (1948)
88/1951	32/1980	65	Browns' guard Bill Willis born (1921)
90/1946	34/1964	65	1st train robbery in US (1866)
88/1946	30/1964	65	Far side of Moon seen for 1st time (1959)
88/1939	31/1952	64	U.S. Rep. Dennis Kucinich born in Cleveland (1946)
86/1947	30/1876	64	American Humane Association organized in Cleveland (1877)
86/1949	30/1895	63	Great Hurricane of 1780 kills 20,000–30,000 in Caribbean (1780)
86/1928	25/1964	63	Actor Luke Perry born in Mansfield (1966)
85/1893	26/1876	63	City Club of Cleveland incorporated (1912)
82/1969	29/1875	63	White House cornerstone laid (1792)
84/1989	30/1988	62	Cavs lose to Buffalo Braves in their 1st game 107-92 (1970)
86/1947	29/1876	62	Clarence Thomas confirmed as Supreme Court Justice (1991)
83/1962	29/1944	61	Disney Company founded (1923)
82/1953	32/1981	61	Actor Tom Poston born in Columbus (1921)
84/1950	28/1876	61	Hurricane Hazel (3rd of 1954) becomes most severe to hit US (1954)
84/1953	29/1986	60	Actress LaWanda Page born in Cleveland (1920)
83/1953	27/1992	60	East Ohio Gas Co. explosion and fire (1944)
83/1953	26/1952	60	1st recorded total eclipse of the sun (2137 b.c.)
81/1947	27/1976	59	NFL Hall of Famer Joe Carr born in Ohio (1880)
80/1963	25/1976	59	Football legend John William Heisman born in Cleveland (1869)
80/1920	22/1969	59	1st telegram sent; Pony Express ends (1861)
80/1963	28/1982	59	Postcards 1st used in U.S. (1870)
81/1963	24/1976	58	Cleveland Coliseum opens (1974)
78/1927	23/1962	58	Actress Ruby Dee born in Cleveland (1924)
81/1927	24/1976	58	Coach Lenny Wilkens born (1937)
78/1946	24/1980	57	William Walker, publisher of the Cleveland Call & Post, dies at 85 (1981)
79/1950	23/1980	57	"War of the Worlds" broadcast (1938)
82/1950	19/1988	56	Conjuror/magician Harry Houdini dies (1926)

JAN FEB MAR APR MAY JUN JUL AUG SEP OCT NOV DEC

JAN FEB MAR APR MAY JUN JUL AUG SEP OCT NOV DEC

Go Bucks!

Dick Goddard

Ohio is known as the Buckeye State, and the nickname was likely born on September 2, 1788. It was on that date that Colonel Ebenezer Sproat, representing the United States government, met with American Indians in the part of Ohio that was then known as the Northwest Territory.

The Indians greeted Colonel Sproat with cries of "Hetuck, hetuck, hetuck." The word hetuck was Indian for "eye of the buck," and it was taken as a compliment since deer were a very important food source for the nature-dependent tribes.

An ashy-gray tree with scaly bark was found throughout the Northwest Territory, and since the fruit (seeds) that appeared on the tree in autumn resembled the eye of a male deer, it was logical to name the tree "buckeye."

It wasn't until 1840, however, that Ohio became recognized nationally as the Buckeye State. The notoriety came when presidential candidate William Henry Harrison used a log cabin made from buckeye wood as part of his campaign tactics. The image of a rough-and-ready president who lived in a log cabin (he hadn't) and drank hard cider (he did) proved so appealing to the common folk that Harrison won election in a landslide over Martin Van Buren.

Ohio's state flag, which was created in 1902, features a red orb inside a white circle, which represents a buck's eye and the letter O. It was not until 1953, however, that Buckeye became Ohio's official nickname.

The buckeye tree displays flowers at the ends of branches in spring. During summer, five elliptical leaflets are attached to each stalk at a single point. In autumn the leaves take on a showy orange to yellow-brown color. My aunt's buckeye tree, next to Buchtel High School in Akron, has grown to an impressive and symmetrical 35 feet. Some buckeye trees can tower to 70 feet.

In summer the tree seeds are enclosed in a brownish-green pod that will split open in autumn to reveal the one to three seeds (nuts) that, like a male deer's eye, are shiny and dark brown with one large tan spot. Unfortunately, the buckeye nuts—along with the tree's early leaves—are poisonous (crush a seed or twig, and you'll experience a foul odor).

American Indians would mash the seeds and twigs and spread the material on lakes and ponds in order to stun fish and make them easy pickings (literally). Don't think about trying this today, since it is illegal in Ohio.

Buckeye wood has been used for log cabins, furniture, flooring, and musical instruments. Pioneers believed that carrying a buckeye nut in your pocket would ward off the pain of rheumatism.

Brutus Buckeye is the mascot of the Ohio State University sports teams. Brutus is very familiar to fans of the University of Michigan, but the only pain that the Maize and Blue occasionally feel is centralized in a lower part of the anatomy.

WOOLLYBEAR RACE WINNERS

YEAR, NAME, HIGHLIGHTS

1998, Skeeter Thousands cheered as this fellow (who trained on dandelion juice exclusively) beat out Lightning II and Woobie.

1999, Hayden II On a wet track with wind chills in the 30s Hayden the deuce out-slogged Cater P and Roadrunner.

2000, Gump On the coldest day since 1977 Gump took 26 seconds to dump Maisy and Rolly Polly.

2001, Comet was more like an asteroid as he blazed to the finish line in 16 seconds. Accompanied, trained, and coached by Alydia Lemon of Medina.

2002, Fast 'n Furious was just that.

JAN FEB MAR APR MAY JUN JUL AUG SEP OCT NOV DEC

NATIONAL OR INTERNATIONAL
AWARD WINNERS
~ FROM ~
NORTHEAST OHIO

Major League Baseball All-Stars Team:
Omar Vizquel, *Shortstop, Cleveland Indians*

National Football League All-Pro Team:
Jamir Miller, *Linebacker, Cleveland Browns*

Academy Award for Best Actress in a Leading Role for her performance in *Monster's Ball*: **Halle Berry**, *Native of Bedford*

Inducted into Television Hall of Fame:
Tim Conway, *Native of Chagrin Falls*

Presidential Medal of Freedom for Serving as Head of World Health Organization's Smallpox Eradication Campaign in the '60s and '70s: **Donald A. Henderson**, *Native of Lakewood*

2002 Institute of Electrical and Electronics Engineers, Edison Gold Medal: **Edward Hammer**, *Retired Global Fluorescent Technical Advisor, General Electric Lighting at Nela Park, East Cleveland*

Accountant Advocate of the Year in Ohio and the Cleveland District, U.S. Small Business Administration: **Rita Singh**, *S&A Consulting Group, Beachwood*

2002 National Jewelers Retailer Hall of Fame Award, Jewelry Chains/Supersellers Category: **Terry Burman**, *Chairman and CEO*, and **Harriet Schreiner**, *Executive Vice President and General Merchandising Manager, Sterling Jewelers, Inc., Akron*

American ORT Jurisprudence Award:
U.S. District Judge Donald Nugent and attorney **Robert Duvin**, *Duvin, Cahn & Hutton, Cleveland*

American Heart Association, Merit Award:
Meredith Bond, *Molecular Cardiologist, Cleveland Clinic Foundation and Professor of Physiology and Biophysics at Case Western Reserve University*

American Heart Association, Award of Excellence: **John Warfel**, *President of Westfield Financial Corp., Westlake*

American Heart Association, Distinguished Service Award: **Lois Carnes**, *Elementary School Physical Education Teacher, Solon Schools*

American Nationalities Movement Award for Exceptional Services to Immigrants: **Richard Herman**, *Founder, Richard T. Herman & Associates, Cleveland*

2002 RadioShack National Teacher Award:
Robert Seitz, *Chairman of the Mathematics Department at Collinwood High School, Cleveland*

Communicator Awards' 2002 Print Media Competition, Award of Distinction, and Awards for Publication Excellence of Communications Concepts Inc., Award of Excellence: **Nina Messina**, *President, The Graphic Edge Professional Design Inc., North Royalton*

American Medical Technologists, Silver Service Award: **Daniel Liska**, *Retired Certified Medical Technologist, Parma*

American Society for Gastrointestinal Endoscopy, Rudolf Schindler Award: **Jeffrey Ponsky, M.D.**, *Director of Endoscopic Surgery, The Cleveland Clinic Foundation*

Southern Christian Leadership Conference, Outstanding Humanitarian Award: **The Rev. Richard E. Sering**, *Executive Director, Lutheran Metropolitan Ministry, Cleveland*

The American Red Cross, The Chapter and Blood Region Community Award: **Summit County Chapter of the American Red Cross and the Northern Ohio Blood Region**, *Akron*

Honorary Doctorates from State University of St. Petersburg, Russia; and Certificates of Appreciation and Medal, Novgorod State University, Russia: **Sidney Picker, Jr.**, *Retired Professor of the Case Western Reserve University School of Law*, and **Jane Picker**, *Retired Professor of the Cleveland-Marshall College of Law at Cleveland State University*

Council of Independent Colleges, The Heuer Award for Outstanding Achievement in

Undergraduate Science Education: **Chemistry Department**, *John Carroll University, University Heights*

Cross of the Knight of the Order of the Lithuanian Grand Duke Gediminas (for medical humanitarian efforts in Lithuania): **Dr. Jerold Goldberg, D.D.S.**, *Dean of the Dental School at Case Western Reserve University*

Council on Social Work Education, 2002 Significant Lifetime Achievement in Social Work Education Award: **M.C. "Terry" Hokenstad, Ralph S. and Dorothy P. Schmitt**, *Professor, Mandel School of Applied Social Sciences, Case Western Reserve University*

National Black Caucus of State Legislators, National State Legislator of the Year: **State Sen. C.J. Prentiss** *(D), Cleveland; President, Ohio Legislative Black Caucus, Columbus*

Presidential Award for Excellence in Mathematics and Science Teaching: **Stephanie Eagleton**, *Second-Grade Teacher at Boulevard Elementary School in Shaker Heights* and **Amy Harker**, *Sixth-Grade Teacher at Dale R. Rice Elementary School in Mentor*

Presidential Award for Excellence in Mathematics and Science Teaching in Ohio: **Christine Milcetich**, *Science Teacher at Firestone High School, Akron*

U.S. Junior Figure Skating Championship, Silver Medal: **Victor Travis**, *Cleveland Heights*

National Recreation and Park Association, 2001 Gold Medal Award: **The Cleveland Metroparks**

National Multiple Sclerosis Society, Norman Cohn Hope Award (for Outstanding Community and Civic Leadership): **David A. Daberko**, *Chairman and CEO, National City Corp., Cleveland*

International Black Women's Congress, Oni Award: **Mary Saunders**, *Faculty, Breen School of Nursing, Ursuline College, Pepper Pike*

Environmental Technology Council, Washington, D.C., Industry Award (First-Ever): **Maureen Cromling**, *President and CEO, Ross Environmental Services, Inc., Grafton*

Fulbright Memorial Fund Master Teacher Program Award: **Jane Maczuzak**, *Dean of Students and Upper School, Lake Ridge Academy, North Ridgeville*

National Alliance for the Mentally Ill, Top Crisis Intervention Team Member: **Sgt. Michael R. Yohe**, *Akron Police Department*

National Alliance for the Mentally Ill, Sam Cochran Compassion in Law Enforcement Award: **Lt. Michael S. Woody**, *Akron Police Department*

World's Best Jump Ropers, World Jump Rope Title, Ghent, Belgium: **Mike Fry**, *Richfield*; **Lindsey Gronauer and Elizabeth Michalos**, *Akron*; **Emily Moore**, *Akron*; and **Rachel Smik**, *Richfield*

American Bar Association, 2001-2002 Outstanding Young Military Lawyer: **Lt. Cmdr. Clay Diamond**, *Principal Assistant Legal Officer, U.S. Coast Guard, Ninth District, Cleveland*

National Cartoonists Society, 2002 Magazine Gag Cartoons Award: **Jerry King**, *North Canton*

National Association of Police Organizations, 2002 Top Cop, Honorable Mention (for his heroic actions taken on April 4, 2001): **Patrol Officer Michael Fox**, *Cleveland Police Department*

JAN FEB MAR APR MAY JUN JUL AUG SEP OCT NOV DEC

Zoos in the **Future**

Steve Taylor

Zoos have many stakeholders: wildlife under their care, guests, members, board members and commissioners, donors, staff, volunteers. The best zoos in the 21st century will meet (or exceed) the expectations of all these.

What will it take to be the best of the best in the 21st century? Future efforts can be divided into three categories. First, the zoo needs a clear and concise vision and mission. Second, it must show leadership in living that vision and achieving that mission. Third, it must thrive through the use of good business practices.

The great zoo will have a clear, concise, and exciting vision, mission, set of values, and both long- and short-term goals.

These must be clearly understood, even embraced, up and down the organization and by all stakeholders. The cornerstone of these guiding principles must continue to be the conservation of the world's declining wildlife.

Great zoos must be leaders.

They have a moral obligation to "step up to the plate" and positively affect environmental change. Here are just a few facts regarding our ever-changing world and the challenges we face:

In the last 50 years, the world's population has grown from 2.5 billion people to 6 billion people, putting a tremendous strain on the earth's resources.

Global warming could easily result in climate change by the end of the century by 2 to 6 degrees centigrade—a little less than the change during the recession of the last ice age.

If we conclude that we have about 10 million species, then we are losing about 1,000 species a year.

If we continue to lose rain forests at the present rate, the last tree will fall in 2050.

I believe E.O. Wilson put the environmental challenge in perspective best when he stated, "It would take two more earths to give everyone on this planet a standard of living equal to what we have in North America." Zoos now clearly see their mission as conservation of wildlife, but making a change from community zoological parks to conservation agencies is not simple. Here is what I believe we need to do to accomplish this conservation-driven mission:

Great zoos will move their education programs from enlightenment and awareness to influence. These zoos will help create a world that understands that nonsustainable use of resources cannot continue (it's like winning a million dollars in the lottery and spending $250,000 a year—how long would that last!). They will advocate for wildlife.

The zoo's exhibits and programs will tell a conservation story and inform and inspire guests to take personal action for the good of wildlife. At Cleveland Metroparks Zoo, The RainForest encourages guests to donate to a rain forest conservation project before leaving the building.

Zoos will build networks. Even the greatest zoos cannot save wildlife alone. Since successful zoos are very popular, others will want to join them in their efforts to save wildlife. For instance, Cleveland Metroparks has a long-standing partnership with the local Earth Day Coalition.

Great zoos will "walk the talk." They will be heavily engaged in resource management, recycling, water conservation, constructing "green buildings," and composting, etc. How can we be taken seriously if we are not leaders in resource management?

Zoos will continue to coordinate their captive breeding programs and collectively manage some of the most endangered species on earth. They will continually learn from the animals they maintain. Most of what we know about the biology of the cheetah, for example, is a result of excellent work in zoos. Understanding the complicated biology and unique genetic makeup of the cheetah (they are basically all related) has helped save this beautiful cat, not only in zoos, but also in the wild.

Learning more about the management of small populations of animals will help us manage animals in the future. Even in the most optimistic view of the future, we know that many isolated populations of species will need intensive scientific management. At Cleveland Metroparks Zoo, we house over 50 species that are part of the American Zoo and Aquarium Association's Species Survival Plan (SSP). Great zoos no longer compete to have animals that no one else has in their zoo, but work to be part of cooperative programs that manage endangered species collectively.

Zoos in the U.S. and other developed countries will continue expansion of zoo-sponsored conservation programs in underdeveloped countries. As Dr. William Conway, former director of the Bronx Zoo, stated, if that trend continues "We will easily become the most significant non-government field conservation organization in the world." Cleveland Metroparks Zoo has been very active in the last five years working with BioAndina, a Venezuelan non-government conservation organization, helping to release zoo-born Andean condors in the mountains of Venezuela. Until this release program began, condors had not been seen in Venezuela for 50 years.

The best zoos in the 21st century will be beautiful, dynamic, and exciting places to visit. They will be the pride of their community. They will be the most heavily attended institutions in their communities. They will have huge memberships and donor bases. And they will need to consider the following:

The best exhibits tell an exciting story and immerse guests in a wonderful natural setting that will temporarily transport them to another place or another habitat. Cleveland Metroparks Zoo's RainForest, Wolf Wilderness, African Savanna, and Australian Adventure were designed with this principle in mind.

Zoos will be "Disney-like" in their upkeep, maintenance, and attention to detail. This is a challenge for all great zoos because it is continual and not very exciting.

Guests visiting a great zoo will feel welcome. They will be both invigorated and relaxed. They will learn and have fun. Guest services, such as restrooms, gift shops, food facilities, directional signs and gate handouts, ticketing, and rides will be first rate. Staff on all levels will need to continually evaluate guest reactions and take appropriate action to improve the experience.

Great zoos will be the most diverse institutions, not only in work force, but also in visitation, membership, and support. At Cleveland Metroparks, we are committed to diversity and have created several very successful diversity initiatives. Our Park Pathway Intern Partnership (PPIP) is a partnership with the Cleveland Municipal School District and the Urban League of Cleveland. We take 12 local high school students and work with them during the summer to expose them to interesting careers in Cleveland Metroparks.

Great zoos will have staffs and volunteers who are committed to the zoo's mission and who will constantly seek improvement—both personally and professionally. They will work in teams. They will embrace change. They will be empowered and will feel ownership. They will be proud.

Great zoos will have an absolute commitment to the health and well-being of the animals. In 2004, Cleveland Metroparks Zoo will open its new state-of-the-art 23,000-square-foot Center for Zoological Medicine. This will be quite an improvement over our current 6,000-square-foot facility.

While no zoo will ever be absolutely financially secure, great zoos will be entrepreneurial. Most will put new emphasis on endowment. While zoos will be less dependent on government, the government (local, state, and federal) will still be very important.

> *Great zoos will have an absolute commitment to the health and well being of the animals.*

Historically, zoos did not start out as conservation institutions, but as menageries with diverse collections of animals kept in sturdy but unaesthetic cages. Over the last few decades, zoos evolved into zoological parks with an emphasis on education and new, modern exhibits. For the last decade, zoos have been challenged to evolve into significant conservation centers. The opportunity for zoos to play an important role in the conservation of the world's disappearing wildlife is a most worthy goal. While the transition is certainly accepted by the zoo community, the full transition is still to occur. The question remains: If we do not change fast enough, will there be any wildlife left to save?

Steve Taylor is director of the Cleveland Metroparks Zoo, the ninth oldest zoo in the United States. He is a member of the Board of Directors of the Cleveland Convention and Visitors Bureau, a member of the Greater Cleveland Growth Association, an alumnus of Leadership Cleveland, and serves on the Admissions Committee of United Way. Taylor's wife, Sarah, is controller for the Cleveland Indians. Proceeds from his contribution benefit the Cleveland Metroparks Zoo.

JAN FEB MAR APR MAY JUN JUL AUG SEP **OCT** NOV DEC

Flora & Fauna OCTOBER

WEEK 1

BIRDS: Chickadees at feeders now wear sharp new winter feather coats. The fall migration continues with yellow-rumped warblers becoming common in the Rocky River Valley. The first of the golden-crowned kinglets, residents of Canada's boreal forests, also begin to appear. **MAMMALS:** Ever wary of winter, portly skunks intently prowl open grassy fields in search of their fall diet of insect larvae. They grow rounder as the month passes and will be in winter sleep by late November. **WILDFLOWERS:** Most asters are at their peak of blooming this week and will quickly decline

WEEK 2

after mid-month. Jewelweed is in seed. Touch the cigar-shaped green seed pods and find out why they're called "touch-me-nots"!

WEEK 3

BIRDS: Wood ducks begin their migration southward in earnest. Many begin to appear this week at Lake Isaac and Sunset Pond. A few will stay the winter but most migrate farther south. Ruby-crowned kinglets follow in their golden-crowned relatives' migration paths this week. The peak of the invasion of the white-throated sparrows should occur this week. They scamper through the underbrush in small flocks looking for insects and seeds, making a great deal of noise for such small birds. **TREES:** The peak of fall color arrives this week, generally between the 10th and 20th of the month. Due to local variations in climate and moisture, different parts of Cleveland Metroparks may offer views of peak color at different times.

WEEK 4

BIRDS: The first of the wintering black ducks are now at Lake Isaac in Big Creek Reservation. Other earlier arrivals have passed on to the south, but these birds will stay for most of the winter in small, reclusive flocks. Ducks appearing on Cleveland Metroparks ponds with long, pointed bills are mergansers, sometimes called "fish ducks." They may gather off the Lake Erie shoreline in rafts numbering in the thousands. **MAMMALS:** Woodchucks wax fat on the last of the green grasses. Some are seen feeding far into the night, preparing for their long hibernation to come. They will disappear into their wintering forest burrows by late November. **INSECTS:** Crickets may still call on warm autumn nights before the first hard frost. **WILDFLOWERS:** New England aster and small white aster, the last of the autumn wildflowers, should be at their peak of bloom by now. They will quickly decline and leave the meadows a gentle brown haze of stems and seeds. *Reptiles*— Small and gentle DeKays snakes can often be found sunning themselves along Cleveland Metroparks trails this week as they prepare for a long winter hibernation.

BIRDS: Whistling (now called tundra) swans begin to appear throughout Cleveland Metroparks as winter begins in the far north. Red-bellied and downy woodpeckers return to feeders as cooler weather approaches. **MAMMALS:** Deer begin their fall breeding season in the meadows of the Cleveland Metroparks, which will last until January. If you see a female deer, stand quietly and watch for a buck to follow in her tracks. **WILDFLOWERS:** Milkweed pods open and fill the air with their fluffy parachute seeds this week. **TREES:** By month's end, the appearance of flowers on witch-hazel announces the final act of the plant world's play for the year

Adapted from the Nature Almanac by Robert Hinkle, with permission from Cleveland Metroparks.

2003 HURRICANE NAMES

Ana, Bill, Claudette, Danny, Erika, Fabian, Grace, Henri, Isabel, Juan, Kate, Larry, Mindy, Nicholas, Odetta, Peter, Rose, Sam, Theresa, Victor, Wanda

JAN FEB MAR APR MAY JUN JUL AUG SEP OCT NOV DEC

NOVEMBER STATISTICS

SUNSHINE %	31
DRIEST MONTH	0.41"/1904
WARMEST MONTH	51.2°/1931
COLDEST MONTH	31.3°/1880
LIQUID PCPN AVG.	3.17"
RAINIEST DAY	2.73"/1985
RAINIEST MONTH	8.80"/1985
THUNDERY DAYS	1
SNOWIEST DAY	15.0"/1950
SNOWIEST MONTH	23.4"/1996
LEAST SNOWFALL	Trace
	(most recently in 1994)
DAYS ONE INCH SNOW	2

One of the electrifying sounds of November is the gabbling of Canada geese as they wing their way southward. The geese fly in their classic V formation for a reason. As each bird flaps its wings, it creates uplift for the bird immediately behind, thus allowing the flock to expand its flying range by about 70 percent. As the bird at the point of the V tires, it will drop back into the flock and another bird will become the leader. If the point bird is so worn out that it falls to the ground to rest, other birds will join their leader until he is able to return to the flock.

Ohio's state animal, the white-tailed deer, is now rutting and can be very dangerous to unwary woodsmen and hunters. Motorists need to be especially alert for the next three months since deer will be constantly crossing the highways. If one deer crosses in front of you, you can expect another close behind. Lake-effect snows can be expected before the month is over. The Thanksgiving week snowstorm of 1950 dumped record amounts of snowfall around the state of Ohio, with upwards of 20 to 40 inches around Greater Cleveland and Northeast Ohio. In November of 1996, 69 inches of snow fell on Chardon in the heart of the Northeast Ohio snowbelt in Geauga County—in only five days. It was Ohio's greatest single storm snowfall. Great Lakes seamen fear the west-to-northwest gale wind of November, the "Witch."

JAN FEB MAR APR MAY JUN JUL AUG SEP OCT NOV DEC

DAILY DATA FOR NOVEMBER

Date	Moon Phase	Day	Day of Year	Days Left in Year	Sunrise	Sunset	Length of Day	Avg. Hi	Avg. Lo
1		Sat	305	60	6:58	5:22	10:24	56	39
2		Sun	306	59	6:59	5:21	10:22	55	38
3		Mon	307	58	7:00	5:20	10:20	55	38
4		Tue	308	57	7:02	5:18	10:16	54	38
5		Wed	309	56	7:03	5:17	10:14	54	37
6		Thu	310	55	7:04	5:16	10:12	53	37
7		Fri	311	54	7:05	5:15	10:10	53	37
8	○	Sat	312	53	7:06	5:14	10:08	53	37
9		Sun	313	52	7:08	5:13	10:05	52	36
10		Mon	314	51	7:09	5:12	10:03	52	36
11		Tue	315	50	7:10	5:11	10:01	51	36
12		Wed	316	49	7:11	5:10	9:59	51	35
13		Thu	317	48	7:12	5:09	9:57	50	35
14		Fri	318	47	7:14	5:08	9:54	50	35
15		Sat	319	46	7:15	5:07	9:52	50	35
16	◑	Sun	320	45	7:16	5:06	9:50	49	34
17		Mon	321	44	7:17	5:05	9:48	49	34
18		Tue	322	43	7:19	5:05	9:46	48	34
19		Wed	323	42	7:20	5:04	9:44	48	33
20		Thu	324	41	7:21	5:03	9:42	47	33
21		Fri	325	40	7:22	5:03	9:41	47	32
22		Sat	326	39	7:23	5:02	9:39	46	32
23	●	Sun	327	38	7:24	5:01	9:37	46	32
24		Mon	328	37	7:26	5:01	9:35	46	32
25		Tue	329	36	7:27	5:00	9:33	45	31
26		Wed	330	35	7:28	5:00	9:32	45	31
27		Thu	331	34	7:29	4:59	9:30	44	31
28		Fri	332	33	7:30	4:59	9:29	44	30
29		Sat	333	32	7:31	4:58	9:27	43	30
30	◐	Sun	334	31	7:32	4:58	9:26	43	30

JAN FEB MAR APR MAY JUN JUL AUG SEP OCT NOV DEC

Rec. Hi°	Rec. Lo°	Avg. Lake°	On This Date ...
82/1950	25/1988	56	1st President to live in white house (John Adams) (1800)
77/1938	25/1895	56	James A Garfield elected president (1880)
79/1961	19/1951	55	Bob Feller born (1918)
77/1935	16/1991	55	First uniform election day (1845)
75/1948	16/1991	55	Roy Rogers born in Cincinnati (1911)
76/1977	17/1951	55	President William McKinley re-elected (1900)
79/1938	23/1971	54	Carl Stokes elected first black mayor of Cleveland (1967)
72/1945	19/1976	54	Actor Joe Flynn born in Youngstown (1924)
74/1975	22/1976	54	Actress Dorothy Dandridge born in Cleveland (1922)
70/1991	19/1991	53	TV host Jack McCoy born in Akron (1918)
73/1915	21/1957	53	Comedian Jonathan Winters born in Dayton (1925)
74/1949	18/1911	53	Criminal Charles Manson born in Cincinnati (1934)
72/1989	15/1911	52	Mariner 9, 1st to orbit another planet (Mars) (1971)
72/1994	13/1986	52	Herman Melville's *Moby Dick* published (1851)
72/1931	14/1996	51	Detroit-Superior Bridge opens to traffic (1917)
72/1931	12/1933	51	Actor Burgess Meredith born in Cleveland (1907)
72/1954	14/1959	51	Congress held 1st session in DC (1800)
71/1954	10/1959	50	Time zones established by railroads in US & Canada (1883)
72/1908	4/1880	50	James A. Garfield born in log cabin in Orange Twp. (1803)
73/1931	15/1951	50	Actress/comedienne Kaye Ballard born in Cleveland (1926)
70/1930	3/1880	49	1st US postage stamp in 2 colors (1952)
73/1934	0/1880	49	Ernie "Ghoulardi" Anderson born (in Massachusetts) (1923)
75/1931	7/1880	49	1st issue of Life magazine
70/1931	7/1950	48	Dante Lavelli born (1930)
67/1906	15/1950	48	Former Browns quarterback Berni Kosar born in Youngstown (1963)
70/1896	9/1880	47	1st national Thanksgiving (1789)
71/1990	7/1880	47	Earliest photo of a meteor shower made (1885)
68/1990	8/1955	47	Paul Warfield born (1942)
67/1933	6/1976	47	Mercury-Atlas 5 carries chimp (Enos) to orbit (1961)
71/1934	3/1976	46	Baseball's Negro National League disbands (1948)

ULYSSES S. GRANT
18TH PRESIDENT 1869–1877

Dick Goddard

Hiram Ulysses Grant, who became the commanding general of the Union forces in the Civil War, was named after the tragic hero of Greek mythology. Grant's life was, in its own way, tragic as well.

Born April 27, 1822, at Point Pleasant, Ohio, a village on the Ohio River upstream from Cincinnati, Grant was the oldest of six children. He remained nameless for an entire month after his birth. The burden of anyone named Ulysses is that in childhood his schoolmates dubbed him "Useless."

It was through a mix-up at West Point that his name became Ulysses Simpson Grant.

Of English and Scottish heritage, Grant was only five feet, one inch tall when he entered West Point at the age of 17. He grew another seven inches by the time he graduated, placing 23rd among the 39 cadets in his class.

With wavy brown hair and soft blue eyes, Grant had the long, slim fingers of a concert pianist. He had a full beard and moustache, wore false teeth, and was a victim of migraine headaches all his life. He survived a family history of tuberculosis.

It is assumed that the nearly 20 cigars he smoked every day of his adult life were the cause of his painful death from throat cancer at the age of 63 in 1885. After his penchant for stogies was revealed while he was president, some 10,000 cigars arrived at the White House.

Modest, humble, and self-deprecating, Grant was squeamish for a military man who attained everlasting fame on the battlefield. He could not stand the sight of blood and even rare steak would make him nauseous. He never ate fowl, saying, "I can't eat anything that went around on two legs." Even as a farm boy growing up in southern Ohio he did not like to hunt.

Never punished as a child, Grant was very close to his mother. He disdained off-color jokes, and when in the field he always bathed alone in a closed tent. A disciplined soldier, Grant did not care for military pomp and ceremony. Being superstitious, he would never retrace his steps.

Grant loved to draw and paint as a child and was fascinated with horses. At the age of five he was a remarkable horseman, even riding while standing up. His only early goals in life were to be a farmer or a down-the-Ohio-River trader. A peace-loving man, Grant accepted an appointment to West Point to better his status. The plainspoken Grant hated war, the military life, and—ironically—politics. Nonreligious, he did not believe in organized religion and was not baptized. While at West Point he received eight demerits for missing church services and was briefly placed under house arrest. He was also reprimanded for sloppy dressing (this trait continued through his presidency).

After satisfying his military commitment (he actually was forced to resign because of heavy drinking), Grant returned to civilian life and failed both in farming and business.

When the Civil War began, he quit his job as a clerk at his brother's store in Galena, Illinois, and applied for a commission as a colonel in an Illinois regiment. He never received a reply. Grant then mobilized a group of volunteers from Galena and was appointed mustering officer under the Illinois adjutant general. That launched a new career with the Twenty-first Illinois Infantry, and his capture of Fort Donelson, Tennessee, in 1862 was the first major Union victory of the war. Grant's ultimatum to the beleaguered Confederate troops was so stern that he was christened "Unconditional Surrender" Grant. He immediately became President Lincoln's favorite general and in 1864 was given the command of all Union forces. Victory followed upon victory, and Grant's reputation rose to heroic proportions.

When a field officer complained to Lincoln about General Grant's drinking, Abe replied, "Find out what Grant is drinking and send a barrel to all the other generals!" Gracious in the ultimate Union victory, Grant would not accept the sword of Confederate General Robert E. Lee, and he allowed all the

Confederate soldiers to keep their horses for the upcoming spring planting.

Never wanting to be president ("Just the mayor of Galena"), Grant was propelled to the White House by his Civil War fame in 1869, for the first of two terms. Grant freely admitted that he came to the presidency totally unqualified and with no political credentials.

An honest and trusting person, Grant always tried to do right. Unfortunately he appointed an unending parade of scoundrels, liars, and cheats to high positions in his administration. Grant refused to believe the treachery of his friends. He governed at an impossible time—during Reconstruction— and critics said he ruled mainly by neglect.

Grant's love of horses continued in the White House, and he was once arrested for speeding as he was piloting a horse and buggy on the streets of Washington. He praised the black officer for doing his duty, and Grant walked back to the White House. He paid a 20-dollar fine and apologized for his recklessness. Grant's favorite horses were named Cincinnati, Egypt, and Jeff Davis. Davis, named after the president of the Confederacy, bit everyone but Grant.

At the age of 26 Grant had married 23-year-old Julia Dent Boggs, "a plain lady who squinted through crossed eyes." Julia delighted in lavish White House parties. Tough times followed the Grants after the presidency. Penniless only eight years before becoming president, Grant was once again near rock bottom financially several years after he left Washington. A stock scandal involving his (innocent) son wiped out the Grants' bank account, and he was forced to sell most of his mementos. When the general and Julia emptied their pockets they had a net worth of $180.

Having become terminally ill with throat cancer, Grant embarked, with the help of his friend and publisher Mark Twain, on the venture of writing and publishing his personal memoirs. He died a few days after finishing the book, and it became a huge bestseller, providing Julia with half a million dollars and comfortable circumstances for the remainder of her life. Grant died at about 8 a.m. on July 23, 1885, at Mount McGregor, New York. Julia died in December of 1902, and she lies with her husband at Grant's Tomb in New York City.

Of the 41 United States presidents rated in the recent C-SPAN survey, Grant is ranked 33rd.

WHY I LIVE IN CLEVELAND

ROBIN BENZLE

**If anybody asks you why on earth you
live in Cleveland, do what I do.
Tell them it's because of the weather.**

Then watch as their eyebrows rise to the top of their forehead and their mouth curls into one of those sour milk smiles. They may think you're kidding. But you're not, if you appreciate living on the North Coast like I do.

Long the target of jokes, my city has taken many a beating from visitors who happen to visit on one of those Cleveland days that is so gray and cold and rainy, life appears to be happening in black and white. Little do they know that you must experience days like this to know the exhilaration of one of our blindingly brilliant, sunny days, when the fall foliage appears to be painted in Day-Glo colors. Or those winter evenings when the moon lights up the sky and huge, lacy snowflakes float down and frost the trees like marshmallow fluff.

JAN FEB MAR APR MAY JUN JUL AUG SEP OCT NOV DEC

It seems to me the times I hear most about how horrible the weather is in Cleveland is when it comes from my friend who lives in Southern California, Mecca of Eternal Sunshine. Well, my friend, I've got news for you. If I lived in a climate where every day was 80 degrees and sunny, it would be like my husband telling me he loved me three times a day. I would become immune to it. Totally numb. Alas, I need the excitement of Cleveland weather, where one day can be 70 and sunny and 24 hours later there are light snow flurries.

Let's compare:

Spring in Southern California: Warm, sunny, flowers blooming.

Summer in Southern California: Warm, sunny, flowers blooming.

Fall in Southern California: Warm, sunny, flowers blooming.

Winter in Southern California: Sort of warm, sunny, flowers blooming.

Spring in Cleveland: The dormant brown earth begins coming to life before your eyes, giving birth to gardens of grape-purple and blue-white crocuses, fields of creamy jonquils and smile-face yellow daffodils, and more colors of tulips than the paint-chip display at the hardware store. Some days are gray with gentle rains—perfect for cleaning out closets and packing away the winter wardrobe. Some days the sky is so blue you find yourself going outside and just standing there, looking up for a while and thinking it looks fake, like the backdrop on a movie set. Spring fever in Cleveland can make you naturally higher than a kite on the moon.

Summer in Cleveland: The season is short, prompting people to celebrate for three months straight. Hot, sunny days spent on the shore of (sharkless) Lake Erie; barbecues and picnics and impromptu gin-and-tonics even on a Tuesday. And everyone racing to fill their gardens with impatiens, snapdragons, zinnias, petunias, and geraniums the color of cheap pink lipstick. Then, there are those summer days where it becomes pitch black at two in the afternoon – and a huge thunderstorm rolls in, bringing with it deafening rains and bolts of thunder cracking giant Z's in the sky, making you want to run for cover and curl up with a good book.

Fall in Cleveland: Mixed in with the chilly, damp days that cause you to suddenly think about getting together with friends for a cup of Irish coffee, are those days that Clevelanders know as Indian Summer, where you're blessed with just a few more hot days. Just enough to have one last barbecue, one last porch party, and one more chance to pack up the lawn furniture and unpack the bird feeder. It's a time to take long drives in the countryside to buy a bushel of apples right from the orchard, being careful not to run off the road as you soak in the fall colors.

Winter in Cleveland: At first, it's wonderful. You place your bets on when the first snow will fall (it only counts when it "sticks"), and when it finally happens, the earth becomes covered in a big, white blanket as if to keep it warm until spring. The days are short and busy, and at night you can drive down the street and see people inside their homes, parked in front of the fireplace or stirring a pot of soup. The holidays are coming, company's coming, and you're praying for postcard-perfect snowfalls.

Toward the end of winter, the weather grows tiresome, like a never-ending lecture from your ninth-grade algebra teacher. The snow isn't quite as white as before, and you're sick of cold tile on your feet and runny noses and pale skin. You may even briefly think to yourself, "Why do I live in Cleveland?"

And then one of those completely exhilarating, indescribably gorgeous spring days appears out of nowhere like a gift from the heavens.

Robin Benzle is co-host of The Morning Show with Trapper Jack on WDOK 102.1 FM. She is also the author of two cookbooks and an award-winning writer of food, travel, and everyday life.

Flora & Fauna NOVEMBER

WEEK 1 — **BIRDS:** Birds of all kinds from the Canadian northland pour into the area. Canada geese by the hundreds stop by to rest and refuel on their way south. Among the smaller birds, the most common might be tree sparrows (light breast with a single spot), fox sparrows (larger than most sparrows and showing a rusty-red color), and juncos, sometimes called snowbirds. **MAMMALS:** November is the peak of the white-tailed deer's breeding season. Adult bucks polish their antlers on small trees and shrubs to mark territory.

WEEK 2 — **BIRDS:** Tundra swans appear in the Rocky and Chagrin river valleys. Some stop by Lake Isaac in Big Creek Reservation or Baldwin Lake in Mill Stream Run Reservation to rest and feed. Others feed in cornfields along River Road between North and South Chagrin reservations. Flocks of over 300 have been counted as they head south. Purple finches reappear throughout the area. Look closely at the reddish-colored house finches you have seen all summer and watch for a slightly larger bird, more purple than red, without stripes on its breast. **MAMMALS:** New beaver cuttings mark the last month of frenzied activity by these industrious creatures. They must set aside enough tender branches beneath the water's surface to provide winter food for a family of six or more.

WEEK 3 — **BIRDS:** Rufous-sided towhees, singing "drink-your-tea," can still be found where crab apple trees bear fruit in meadows. Dark-eyed juncos, apparently sensing the same day length as spring, begin spring songs each morning. As days shorten, songs will cease. **MAMMALS:** Fox, gray, and black squirrels are busy adding insulation to winter tree dens. Squirrels of all kinds return to bird feeders as the autumn crop of nuts has been eaten or stored for winter

WEEK 4 — **BIRDS:** The last autumn waterfowl appear at Cleveland Metroparks refuges. Look for hooded mergansers, buffleheads, and goldeneye ducks. Shoveler ducks with attractive bright green heads and large, scoop-shaped bills graze among shallow water plants. **MAMMALS:** Hardy woodchucks still browse among frost-laden grasses, storing up a few more days of food for the long winter.

Adapted from the Nature Almanac by Robert Hinkle, with permission from Cleveland Metroparks.

WINNERS
~ OF ~
ANNUAL NORTHEAST OHIO AWARDS

2002 Governor's Awards for the Arts in Ohio, Irma Lazarus Award (for generating public support for the arts): **Christoph von Dohnanyi**, *Music Director, Cleveland Orchestra*

Cleveland Fire Department, Firefighter of the Year: **David Meade**, *Cleveland*

2001 Weatherhead 100, #1 Winner: **Wolcott Systems Group**, *Fairlawn*

Cleveland Technical Council, Technical Achievement Award: **David Ball**, *Professor of Chemistry at Cleveland State University*

Cleveland Technical Council, Technical Educator Award: **Paul Mathews**, *Self-Employed Consultant, Cleveland*

Cleveland Technical Council, Distinguished Leadership Award: **Michael Salkind**, *President of the Ohio Aerospace Institute, Cleveland*

Ohio Society of Certified Public Accountants' 2002 Gold Medal for Meritorious Service to the Accounting Profession: **Gary Previts**, *Professor of Accountancy, Case Western Reserve University*

American Business Women's Association, Western Reserve Chapter, "Woman of the Year": **Patricia Bruckner**, *Accounting Manager, Innovative Data Solutions, Bedford Heights*

The Allan Severson, AB8P, Memorial Award (bestowed on an amateur radio operator in the Ohio Section who has demonstrated a continuing dedication to the advancement of amateur radio): **David Kersten**, *Medina*

Ohio eCorridor (Ohio Department of Development), 2001 Edison Award: **NASA Glenn Research Center**, *Cleveland*

Ohio eCorridor (Ohio Department of Development), 2001 Emerging Technology Award Winners: **ACCELENT SYSTEMS, Inc.** *(Akron)*, **AlphaMicron, Inc.** *(Kent)*, **Cleveland Medical Devices, Inc.** *(Cleveland)*, **Fiberland, Inc.** *(Cleveland)*, **Secant Technologies** *(Cleveland)*

2001 Governor's Awards for Excellence in Energy Efficiency: **Ashland University** in Partnership with **Johnston Controls, Inc.** for the Energy Management/Deferred Maintenance Project

2001 Governor's Awards for Excellence in Energy Efficiency: **Cuyahoga County** in Partnership with **The Brewer Garrett Company** for the Energy Efficiency and Renewable Energy Awareness Education Project

Mt. Sinai Health Care Foundation, Maurice Saltzman Award: **Joyce Lee, RN**, *President of the Greater Cleveland Health Education and Service Council*

Cleveland Association of School Psychologists, 2002 School Psychologist of the Year: **Ralph S. Pajka**, *Psychologist in the Lakewood School System*

West Side Ecumenical Ministry, 9th Annual Lamplighter Humanitarian Award: **Jack Kahl**, *Retired Founder and CEO of Manco Inc., Avon Lake*

Ohio Senior Citizens Hall of Fame: **Everett Hosack**, *Chagrin Falls*, who also set three world records and one U.S. record at the 2002 National Indoor Championships for the 100-104 age category

League of Women Voters, 2002 Belle Sherwin Democracy in Action Award: **Jane Campbell**, Mayor of Cleveland

Soap Box Derby, 2nd Place, World Rally Masters Champion Title: **Katie Levy**, *Cleveland*

Ohio Chapter of the National Association of Social Workers, Akron Region, 2002 Public Official of the Year Award: **Sylvester Small**, *Akron Schools Superintendent*

Ceska sin Karlin (a Czech Fraternal Organization), 2002 Good Joe of the Year: **Edward Motyka**, *Northfield*

United Irish Societies of Greater Cleveland, 2002 Irish Mother of the Year: **Mary McCluskey**, *Euclid*

(Continued on page 192)

DECEMBER STATISTICS

SUNSHINE %	26
DRIEST MONTH	0.71"/1958
WARMEST MONTH	42.0°/1889
COLDEST MONTH	19.2°/1989
LIQUID PCPN AVG.	3.09"
RAINIEST DAY	2.81"/1992
RAINIEST MONTH	8.59"/1990
THUNDERY DAYS	0
SNOWIEST DAY	12.2"/1974
SNOWIEST MONTH	30.3"/1962
LEAST SNOWFALL	Trace
(most recently in 1931)	
DAYS ONE INCH SNOW	4

Northeast Ohioans have now entered the dark weather tunnel from which we will not emerge for many months. In dark December Greater Clevelanders will experience only 26 percent of possible sunshine. From now through January, Cleveland will rank with such places as Seattle, Washington, Portland, Oregon, and Syracuse, New York, as the nation's cloudiest cities.

The sun (if seen) will reach its lowest point in the sky around December 21, the time of the winter solstice. It has taken 365 days for our small planet to complete its elliptical (not circular) orbit around the sun. Four hundred million years ago there were 400 days in a year, because our favorite planet was spinning much faster and days were shorter. It's been discovered that earth has nine separate movements as it wobbles, whirls, and nods while traveling at 1,100 miles per minute.

While many Ohio animals are in their deep winter snooze, raccoons, opossums, and skunks may awaken to forage for food. If you started to feed the birds in autumn you must keep it up, since they now depend on you for a handout.

Ohio's coldest Christmas was in 1983, with area high temperatures only around zero and a -50° wind chill; Ashtabula and Conneaut were snowbound.

DAILY DATA FOR DECEMBER

Date	Moon Phase	Day	Day of Year	Days Left in Year	Sunrise	Sunset	Length of Day	Avg. Hi	Avg. Lo
1		Mon	335	30	7:33	4:58	9:25	43	29
2		Tue	336	29	7:34	4:58	9:24	42	29
3		Wed	337	28	7:35	4:57	9:22	42	28
4		Thu	338	27	7:36	4:57	9:21	41	28
5		Fri	339	26	7:37	4:57	9:20	41	28
6		Sat	340	25	7:38	4:57	9:19	40	27
7		Sun	341	24	7:39	4:57	9:18	40	27
8	○	Mon	342	23	7:40	4:57	9:17	40	27
9		Tue	343	22	7:41	4:57	9:16	39	27
10		Wed	344	21	7:42	4:57	9:15	39	26
11		Thu	345	20	7:43	4:57	9:14	39	26
12		Fri	346	19	7:43	4:57	9:14	38	26
13		Sat	347	18	7:44	4:57	9:13	38	25
14		Sun	348	17	7:45	4:57	9:12	38	25
15		Mon	349	16	7:46	4:58	9:12	37	25
16	◑	Tue	350	15	7:46	4:58	9:12	37	24
17		Wed	351	14	7:47	4:58	9:11	37	24
18		Thu	352	13	7:48	4:59	9:11	37	24
19		Fri	353	12	7:49	4:59	9:10	36	24
20		Sat	354	11	7:49	4:59	9:10	36	23
21		Sun	355	10	7:50	5:00	9:10	36	23
22		Mon	356	9	7:50	5:00	9:10	36	23
23	●	Tue	357	8	7:51	5:01	9:10	35	23
24		Wed	358	7	7:51	5:01	9:10	35	22
25		Thu	359	6	7:51	5:02	9:11	35	22
26		Fri	360	5	7:52	5:03	9:11	35	22
27		Sat	361	4	7:52	5:03	9:11	34	22
28		Sun	362	3	7:52	5:04	9:12	34	21
29		Mon	363	2	7:53	5:05	9:12	34	21
30	◐	Tue	364	1	7:53	5:06	9:13	34	21
31		Wed	365	0	7:53	5:06	9:13	34	21

Rec. Hi°	Rec. Lo°	Avg. Lake°	On This Date ...
65/1970	7/1929	45	LPGA golfer Barb Mucha born in Parma (1961)
70/1982	-5/1976	45	Actor Robert F Simon born in Mansfield (1908)
77/1982	-7/1976	45	77°F highest temp ever recorded in Cleve in Dec (1982)
70/1982	8/1871	44	Cleveland Cavaliers retire jersey #7, Bingo Smith (1979)
71/2001	2/1871	44	George Armstrong Custer born in New Rumley (1839)
68/1956	7/1977	44	Otto Graham born (1921)
66/1892	-5/1882	43	Pearl Harbor bombed (1941)
67/1966	-9/1882	43	John Lennon shot (1980)
62/1952	-5/1917	43	Cavs guard World B Free born (1953)
69/1971	-5/1958	42	WSTV (now WTOV) channel 9 in Steubenville begins (1953)
64/1931	-2/1977	42	"Mike Douglas Show" first airs in Cleveland (1961)
63/1949	-1/1962	41	Bank of the US opens (1791)
65/1901	-3/1962	41	Indians' Larry Doby born (1st black in baseball's AL) (1924)
64/1901	0/1914	41	1st state road authorized, Frankfort KY to Cincinnati (1793)
67/1971	-1/1958	40	Actor Tim Conway born in Willoughby (1933)
64/1984	-9/1951	40	Cleveland Rams win NFL championship (1945)
61/1984	-7/1989	40	WEWS TV channel 5 in Cleve begins broadcasting (1947)
62/1939	-5/1989	39	Director Steven Spielberg born in Cinci (1947)
61/1939	-5/1884	39	WJW TV channel 8 in Cleveland begins broadcasting (1949)
62/1895	-4/1963	38	Rockers' guard Jenny Boucek born (1973)
65/1967	-7/1972	38	TV host Phil Donahue born in Cleveland (1935)
64/1949	-15/1989	37	1st string of Christmas tree lights created by Edison (1882)
61/1933	-7/1960	37	Voyager completes global flight (1986)
65/1964	-10/1983	37	Luna 13 lands on Moon (1966)
66/1982	-10/1983	37	Centigrade temperature scale introduced (1741)
64/1875	-8/1983	36	Lorain County incorporated (1822)
64/1936	-5/1944	36	Writer Louis Bromfield born in Mansfield (1896)
68/1982	-3/1880	36	Newscaster Jack Perkins born in Cleveland (1933)
66/1889	-12/1880	36	U.S. patent for chewing gum granted to W. F. Semple of Mt. Vernon (1869)
63/1971	-12/1880	36	Actor Jack Riley born in Cleveland (1935)
68/1875	-11/1880	36	Toboggan Chutes begin operation in Cleveland Metroparks (1966)

JAN FEB MAR APR MAY JUN JUL AUG SEP OCT NOV **DEC**

In the Name of Religion

Dick Goddard

You've got to be taught to hate and fear,
You've got to be taught from year to year,
It's got to be drummed in your dear little ear,
You've got to be carefully taught.

—Sung by Lieutenant Joe Cable in "South Pacific"

There's an old song that says, "Love Makes the World Go 'Round." It's hate that could stop it. It is ironic to realize, with deep regret, that the main reason for the horrible hatred and terrorism on this small planet comes from the thing that gives comfort, hope, and solace to so many: religion.

I must confess that I am an infidel. Don't cluck your tongue.

You are also an infidel, since whatever creed you profess makes you an infidel to the "other guy's" religion. Because you are an "unbeliever" you are destined to spend eternity wearing asbestos underwear (I subscribe to the idea that our worst enemies cannot create the hell that we make for ourselves on earth). While most religions begin with a philosophy of love and compassion, somewhere along the line the zealots and militants try to take control. Of the 30 wars in progress in October of 2001, 28 were based on religious intolerance (incredibly, some within the same religion!). Including the 2,823 who died in the United States on September 11, 2001, at the hands of religious terrorists, at least 300,000 have been killed for the same reason over the last six years.

The type of perverted behavior by a minority of religious teachers that is making headline news today has unquestionably been going on ever since men of faith have been "guiding" their innocent prey. These clerics should be given a few years of expenses-paid vacation at Club Fed.

A television colleague of mine recalls how he and his childhood friends were terrified by other children who said that they would be going to hell because they didn't belong to the right church. You can imagine who inculcated the children with such hatred. It is also apparent that most adults never examine or question the beliefs of their childhood. (At the other extreme are the atheists and agnostics who believe that all religions are simply guilt trips with different holidays.)

You've got to be taught to be afraid,
Of people whose eyes are oddly made,
Of people whose skin is a different shade,
You've got to be carefully taught.

History has revealed countless cruel horrors based on religious intolerance. As the 17th-century French scientist and philosopher Blaise Pascal lamented, "Men never do evil so completely and cheerfully as when they do it from religious conviction." Whatever your religion or philosophy of life, we need to realize, as the great pacifist Mohandas K. Gandhi said, "All men are brothers." (Gandhi was assassinated by a religious fanatic.) He had proclaimed that he was a Hindu, a Shinto, a Christian, a Jew, a Muslim, a

JAN FEB MAR APR MAY JUN JUL AUG SEP OCT NOV **DEC**

Confucian, a Buddhist, and a Taoist.

For so many on earth, simply being alive is a treadmill to oblivion. Some 800 million live in poverty and are on the verge of starvation (every 3.6 seconds someone dies of hunger). At least 15 million children die of starvation each year. Our goal in this brief life should be to relieve as much pain and suffering as possible. To quote English author George Eliot (actually Mary Ann Evans), "What do we live for, if it is not to make life less difficult for others?"

When asked about my beliefs—after more than seven decades of observations—I confess to being a skeptic (I believe not only that Humpty Dumpty was pushed, but that a bird in the hand is a dead bird). I feel like a rabbi watching a Notre Dame–Southern Methodist football game. I'm pulling for everybody, but I have no favorites. We need to spend more time easing the suffering of both humans and animals. Too many of us are so worried about making it to that Theme Park in the Sky that we neglect the only reason we have for living.

You've got to be taught before it's too late,

Before you are six, or seven, or eight,

To hate all the people your relatives hate,

You've got to be carefully taught.

NORTHEAST OHIO'S WETTEST AND DRIEST AUTUMNS
(Liquid)

. . . .

WETTEST

Cleveland: 20.73" / 1996

Akron/Canton: 19.59" / 1926

. . . .

DRIEST

Cleveland: 2.37" / 1908

Akron/Canton: 2.52" / 1953

Northeast Ohio
COUNTY STATISTICS

ASHLAND

Name: Named for Henry
  Clay's
  Kentucky estate
  (a Whig presidential
  candidate)

Established:
  Feb 24, 1846

Size: 424.4
  square miles

Population: 52,523

Projected population
  for 2015: 56,950

Persons under
  5 years old: 6.6%

Persons 65 years
  old and over: 13.9%

Persons per
  square mile: 123.9

Average personal
  per capita income:
  $20,739

County Seat:
  Ashland City

House Districts: 90, 97

Senate Districts:
  19, 22

ASHTABULA

Name: Named for
  the Ashtabula River,
  a Native American
  word meaning "River
  of Many Fish"

Established:
  June 7, 1807

Size: 702.7
  square miles

Population: 102,728

Projected population
  for 2015: 113,500

Persons under
  5 years old: 6.5%

Persons 65 years old
  and over: 14.7%

Persons per
  square mile: 146.3

Average personal
  per capita income:
  $21,685

County Seat:
  Jefferson Village

House District: 99

Senate District: 32

CARROLL

Name: Named for
  Charles Carroll, last
  surviving signer
  of the Declaration
  of Independence

Established:
  Jan 1, 1833

Size: 394.7
  square miles

Population: 28,836

Projected population
  for 2015: 29,400

Persons under
  5 years old: 6.0%

Persons 65 years old
  and over: 14.2%

Persons per
  square mile: 73.0

Average personal
  per capita income:
  $21,652

County Seat:
  Carrollton Village

House District: 61

Senate District: 33

COLUMBIANA

Name: Named for
  Christopher Columbus
  and "Anna"

Established:
  May 1, 1803

Size: 532.5
  square miles

Population: 112,075

Projected population
  for 2015: 116,700

Persons under
  5 years old: 5.9%

Persons 65 years old
  and over: 15.0%

Persons per
  square mile: 210.7

Average personal
  per capita
  income:: $21,159

County Seat:
  Lisbon Village

House District: 1

Senate District: 30

COSHOCTON

Name: Named for
  a Delaware Native
  American word
  meaning "Black Bear
  Town"

Established:
  Jan 31, 1810

Size: 567.6
  square miles

Population: 36,655

Projected population
  for 2015: 35,400

Persons under
  5 years old: 6.4%

Persons 65 years old
  and over: 14.7%

Persons per
  square mile: 65.0

Average personal
  per capita income:
  $21,130

County Seat:
  Coshocton City

House District: 94

Senate District: 20

CUYAHOGA

Name: Named for
  the Cuyahoga River,
  a Native American
  word meaning
  "Crooked River"

Established:
  June 7, 1807

Size: 458.3
  square miles

Population: 1,393,845

Projected population
  for 2015: 1,392,900

Persons under
  5 years old: 6.5%

Persons 65 years old
  and over: 15.6%

Persons per square mile:
  3,043.6

Average personal
  per capita income:
  $32,241

County Seat:
  Cleveland City

House Districts:
  7, 8, 9, 10, 11, 12, 13,
  14, 15, 16, 17, 18, 98

Senate Districts:
  18, 21, 23, 24, 25

ERIE

Name: Named for Lake
  Erie and Erie
  Indians, a Native
  American word
  meaning "cat"

Established:
  March 16, 1838

Size: 245.5
  square miles

Population: 79,551

Projected population
  for 2015: 80,700

Persons under 5 years
  old: 6.0%

Persons 65 years old
  and over: 15.6%

Persons per
  square mile: 312.0

Average personal
  per capita income:
  $28,210

County Seat:
  Sandusky City

House District: 80

Senate District: 2

GEAUGA

Name: Named for a
Native American word
meaning "raccoon"
Established:
March 1, 1806
Size: 404.1
square miles
Population: 90,895
Projected population
for 2015: 100,000
Persons under
5 years old: 6.8%
Persons 65 years old
and over: 12.0%
Persons per
square mile: 225.0
Average personal
per capita income:
$34,027
County Seat:
Chardon
House District: 98
Senate District: 18

HARRISON

Name: Named
for William Henry
Harrison, 9th
President of the U.S.
Established:
Feb 1, 1813
Size: 403.6
square miles
Population: 15,856
Projected population
for 2015: 14,700
Persons under
5 years old: 5.8%
Persons 65 years old
and over: 17.7%
Persons per
square mile: 39.2
Average personal
per capita income:
$18,669
County Seat:
Cadiz Village
House District: 96
Senate District: 30

HOLMES

Name: Named for Major
Holmes from the War
of 1812
Established:
Jan 20, 1824
Size: 423.0
square miles
Population: 38,943
Projected population
for 2015: 48,260
Persons under
5 years old: 10.3%
Persons 65 years old
and over: 10.5%
Persons per
square mile: 92
Average personal
per capita income:
$17,591
County Seat:
Millersburg Village
House District: 97
Senate District: 22

HURON

Name: Named for
the Huron Indians
Established:
March 7, 1809
Size: 493.1
square miles
Population: 59,487
Projected population
for 2015: 64,500
Persons under
5 years old: 7.5%
Persons 65 years old
and over: 12.4%
Persons per
square mile: 120.7
Average personal
per capita income:
$22,720
County Seat:
Norwalk City
House District: 58
Senate District: 13

JEFFERSON

Name: Named for
Thomas Jefferson,
3rd President of
the U.S.
Established:
July 29, 1797
Size: 409.6
square miles
Population: 73,894
Projected population
for 2015: 74,500
Persons under
5 years old: 5.2%
Persons 65 years old
and over: 18.6%
Persons per
square mile: 180.2
Average personal
per capita
income: $20,720
County Seat:
Steubenville City
House District: 95
Senate District: 30

LAKE

Name: Named
for Lake Erie
Established:
March 6, 1840
Size: 228.2
square miles
Population: 227,511
Projected population
for 2015: 224,700
Persons under
5 years old: 6.1%
Persons 65 years old
and over: 14.1%
Persons per
square mile: 997.9
Average personal
per capita income:
$29,276
County Seat: Painesville
City
House Districts: 62, 63
Senate District: 18

LORAIN

Name: From the French
province of Lorraine
Established:
December 26, 1822
Size: 492.6
square miles
Population: 315,630

Projected population
for 2015: 224,700
Persons under
5 years old: 6.9%
Persons 65 years old
and over: 12.5%
Persons per
square mile: 577.4
Average personal
per capita income:
$25,712
County Seat:
Elyria City
House Districts:
56, 57, 58
Senate District: 13

MAHONING

Name: Named for
the Mahoning River,
a Native American
word meaning
"at the salt licks"
Established:
March 1, 1846
Size: 415.3
square miles
Population: 257,555
Projected population
for 2015: 284,700
Persons under 5
years old: 6.0%
Persons 65 years old
and over: 17.8%
Persons per
square mile: 620.6
Average personal
per capita income:
$24,095
County Seat: Youngstown
City
House Districts: 60, 61
Senate District: 33

MEDINA

Name: Named for the
Arabian city where
Mohammed is buried
Established:
Feb 18, 1812
Size: 421.6
square miles
Population: 151,095

Projected population
for 2015: 175,920

Persons under
5 years old: 7.0%

Persons 65 years old
and over: 10.5%

Persons per
square mile: 358

Average personal
per capita income:
$28,954

County Seat:
Medina City

House Districts: 69, 97

Senate District: 22

PORTAGE

Name: Named for
a Native American
word meaning
"a carrying path"

Established:
June 7, 1807

Size: 492.4
square miles

Population: 152,061

Projected population
for 2015: 160,600

Persons under
5 years old: 6.1%

Persons 65 years old
and over: 11.0%

Persons per
square mile: 309.1

Average personal
per capita income:
$24,146

County Seat:
Ravenna City

House Districts: 43, 68

Senate District: 28

RICHLAND

Name: Named in honor
of the county's rich
soil

Established:
March 1, 1808

Size: 497.0
square miles

Population: 128,852

Projected population
for 2015: 121,200

Persons under
5 years old: 6.4%

Persons 65 years
old and over: 14.2%

Persons per
square mile: 259.3

Average personal
per capita income:
$22,721

County Seat:
Mansfield City

House Districts: 73, 90

Senate District: 19

STARK

Name: Named for Revo-
lutionary War hero
General John Stark

Established:
Feb 13, 1808

Size: 576.2
square miles

Population: 378,098

Projected population
for 2015: 379,900

Persons under
5 years old: 6.4%

Persons 65 years old
and over: 15.1%

Persons per
square mile: 656.4

Average personal
per capita income:
$25,214

County Seat:
Canton City

House Districts:
50, 51, 52, 61

Senate Districts: 29, 33

SUMMIT

Name: Named for the
highest point of
land along the Erie-
Ohio Canal, Portage
Summit

Established:
March 3, 1840

Size: 412.8
square miles

Population: 542,899

Projected population
for 2015: 557,600

Persons under
5 years old: 6.6%

Persons 65 years old
and over: 14.1%

Persons per square mile:
1,314.5

Average personal
per capita income:
$29,187

County Seat:
Akron City

House Districts:
43, 44, 45

Senate Districts: 27, 28

TRUMBULL

Name: Named for
Jonathan Trumbull,
Governor
of Connecticut

Established:
July 10, 1800

Size: 615.8
square miles

Population: 225,116

Projected population
for 2015: 240,800

Persons under 5
years old: 6.1%

Persons 65 years old
and over: 15.7%

Persons per
square mile: 365.4

Average personal
per capita income:
$25,022

County Seat:
Warren City

House Districts:
64, 65, 99

Senate Districts: 32

TUSCARAWAS

Name: Native American
word meaning "open
mouth"

Established:
March 15, 1808

Size: 567.6
square miles

Population: 90,914

Projected population
for 2015: 86,800

Persons under
5 years old: 6.6%

Persons 65 years old
and over: 15.0%

Persons per
square mile: 160.1

Average personal
per capita income:
$21,708

County Seat:
New Philadelphia City

House Districts: 61, 96

Senate Districts: 30, 33

WAYNE

Name: Named for Revo-
lutionary War General
"Mad"
Anthony Wayne

Established:
Aug 15, 1796

Size: 555.4
square miles

Population: 111,564

Projected population
for 2015: 118,600

Persons under
5 years old: 7.0%

Persons 65 years old
and over: 12.2%

Persons per
square mile: 201.0

Average personal
per capita income:
$21,708

County Seat:
Wooster City

House Districts: 3

Senate District: 22

Source: Ohio Department of Development; FedStats, Ohio State University Extension Data Center
*For comparison: Average personal per capita income for Ohio: $27,171

JAN FEB MAR APR MAY JUN JUL AUG SEP OCT NOV DEC

Flora & Fauna DECEMBER

WEEK 1

BIRDS: As the last of the migrating Canada geese move south, they may be joined by snow geese, white geese with telltale black wing tips. Open water remains at most refuges and rivers until month's end. Watch for late-migrating ducks such as shoveler ducks and the fish-eating red-breasted mergansers. **MAMMALS:** Bucks' antlers become brightly polished as the breeding season continues from October and November. Territorial battles are rare, but the rattling antlers of

WEEK 2

combatants can sometimes be heard in Mill Stream Run and Brecksville reservations. When you spot a deer, look for others nearby

WEEK 3

BIRDS: If winter hasn't been too harsh thus far, some of Hinckley Reservation's buzzards may still be seen circling overhead at midday. As food becomes scarce, they will gradually drift to more southerly locations for the winter. Cedar waxwings begin to harvest the summer's crop of over-ripe berries. The fermented sugars in the berries turn to alcohol and the happily inebriated little birds occasionally lose all sense of direction, propriety and flight when the alcohol-laden berries warm their tiny stomachs. **TREES:** Many oaks and beeches will hold dead leaves on their branches all

WEEK 4

winter. Spring growth sheds the golden brown mantle of old leaves, thus allowing the forest to gain two layers of nutrients each year. The rustle of leaves in the winter wind is a sharp contrast to the quiet of snowy meadows. Certain witch hazels in sheltered locations continue to bloom this week.

BIRDS: Each year at this time the National Audubon Society sponsors a nationwide "Christmas Count" of birds remaining on the wintering grounds. (Contact a Cleveland Metroparks nature center for information on this year's Christmas Count.) If open water remains, ruddy ducks, common mergansers and goldeneye ducks should be passing through this week. These are generally the last of the fall migrants. **MAMMALS:** Cold, snowy weather and limited food resources mean the temporary disappearance of winter-sleeping mammals like the raccoon, opossum, and skunk. They may awaken from time to time to feed as winter passes. Deer tracks in the winter snow tell tales of evening adventures in Rocky River, Brecksville, Hinckley, Bedford, and North Chagrin reservations. Follow a set of tracks and try to imagine what the deer were doing there, and why.

BIRDS: Tufted titmice and chickadees should be willing to take sunflower seeds from friendly hands at Brecksville and Sanctuary Marsh nature centers from now until the end of winter. Bring a pocketful of seeds and make a new bird friend this week! As winter begins officially this week, watch leafless trees in deep Cleveland Metroparks forests for barred and great horned owls. **MAMMALS:** Chipmunks have become scarce as they "hole up" for the winter. These farsighted little squirrels depend on acorns, seeds, and nuts carefully stored in underground caches for their winter food. They remain active underground until March. The last of Cleveland Metroparks groundhogs should be carefully tucked away in their burrows and hibernating until early spring

Adapted from the Nature Almanac by Robert Hinkle, with permission from Cleveland Metroparks.

Twinsburg is in the Guinness Book of World Records for having the World's Largest Gathering of Twins. Twins Days takes place on the first full weekend of August each year, and twins have been gathering here since 1976.

MY CHRISTMAS STORY

NEIL ZURCHER

We probably all have our favorite stories of the
holiday season. The warm things we remember that
make Christmas so special each year.

In Lorain County, in the tiny community of Brownhelm Township, a Christmas tradition has been going on there for nearly 70 years. And, although Brownhelm today is dotted with expensive homes and serves more as a bedroom community for nearby Lorain and Cleveland, a tradition that started during the worst of times in the Great Depression goes on and on.

Each Christmas, every person in Brownhelm receives a visit and a gift from Santa Claus.

It started during the grim Christmas of 1931. The Depression was being felt even in farm homes along the edge of Lake Erie. The Reverend Ralph E. Albright, then pastor of the Brownhelm Congregational Church, was all too familiar with the hardships some of the members of his congregation were facing. Some fathers had lost their jobs, for farmers it had been a tough year, and what little money there was running out. But like so many farm folk of that era, they were too proud to apply for charity and the relief programs that were in place then were, themselves, in trouble.

Sunday after Sunday through that autumn, Reverend Albright saw it in the faces of his congregants. When he would visit their homes, he would hear stories of overdue mortgage payments, of lost income, jobs that had evaporated in the whirlwind of the Depression. And now Christmas was coming and he knew that many children that year would get little or nothing on

Christmas Day.

The Reverend knew that he could do little to reverse the Depression, or stop the eroding of family incomes, but there might be something they could do for the kids in the community, and for those families that were facing the holiday with little or nothing in the house.

He called a meeting of some of the community's better-off residents and spelled out what was happening to their neighbors. He did not want to offend the feelings of those who were in need by attempting to force charity on them, but he felt something must be done.

Perhaps it could be done anonymously, as Santa Claus—a little help from an elf at the holidays could not be turned down, especially if they did not know where it came from.

It was a time when people did help each other and within days a committee was formed with volunteers to dress like Santa and others to pack Christmas boxes for the children and grocery baskets for the needy adults, as well as special gifts of money and other items that might be needed in some special cases.

That Christmas of 1931 was one that residents who are still alive today remember as the year they began believing in Santa Claus.

On Christmas Eve the volunteer Santas divided the community into zones. Before the night was out, Santa had dropped in unexpectedly at every home in the township. Children received a toy, adults a fruit basket, and in special cases groceries and clothing were left for the surprised residents.

Even the most stubborn farmer could not refuse the help, especially when he had no idea of where, or who, it was coming from. Besides, who could say "no" to Santa on Christmas Eve?

It was such a success that it was repeated the next year, and the next, and now, nearly 70 years later, it still goes on even though the economic times are good for most residents there. It has become a tradition, a rich memory that is treasured by folks who live in Brownhelm, Ohio.

To be sure, it has changed a bit over the years. During the war years a committee would also make sure that every serviceman from Brownhelm was remembered with a package at the holidays, as well as the continuing visit of Santa to the homes. During the Korean War, I know of one soldier who got an unexpected leave at Christmastime and was delivered to his Brownhelm home by one of the Santas to give that family a Christmas that they still remember. Today men and women in the service from the community are still remembered along with the kids and the older folks.

For some families it has meant involvement for generations. Henry Leimbach was one of the first Santa volunteers. Years later his son, Paul, headed up the program for several years, and then it was the turn of Paul's son, Orrin, to play Santa.

The Cutcher family was another that played an important role for all the years they ran the Brownhelm store. (Aside from some fruit and vegetable stands, the little general store is the only store in the community.) Not only were both Bill and Bonnie Cutcher on the committee, their store served as a gathering place for donations and for signing up volunteers. At least three generations of their family have kept the tradition of the Brownhelm Santas alive.

No one gets paid each year; some funds are raised to keep the Santa costumes in good shape and replace those that wear out.

Unlike 70 years ago when everyone in tiny Brownhelm knew not only their neighbors, but probably everyone else who lived in the community, today with housing developments and a growing, changing population it's difficult to really know even your neighbors' names. Yet this community keeps alive a tradition that says "we care."

Maybe it's due to the simple, proud sentence that Reverend Ralph Albright wrote in the Congregational Church record book on that long ago 1931 Christmas: "There was not one lonely, disappointed, or hungry child in our Community this Christmas Eve."

That, perhaps, is the true meaning of "Merry Christmas."

Neil Zurcher reports on "One Tank Trips" for FOX 8 and is the author of four books: *One Tank Trips, More of Neil Zurcher's One Tank Trips, One Tank Trips: Road Food,* and *Ohio Oddities.*

WINNERS
~ OF ~
ANNUAL NORTHEAST OHIO AWARDS
(CONTINUED)

American Cancer Society, Lorain Chapter, Volunteer of the Year 2001: **Daniel Haight**, *Grafton Township*

Inducted into the Trumbull (County) African-American Achievers Association's Heritage Hall of Fame in Warren: **Robert Saffold**, *Shaker Heights*

Heights Regional Chamber of Commerce, Business Person of the Year: **Marv Gisser**, *President, Gisser Communications, South Euclid*

Visiting Nurses Association, Healthcare Partners of Ohio and National City Bank, Distinguished Women in Healthcare Award: **Denice Sheehan**, *Faculty, Breen School of Nursing, Ursuline College, Pepper Pike*

March of Dimes, Ohio Chapter, 2001 Franklin Delano Roosevelt Humanitarian Award for Excellence: **Carol Cartwright**, *President, Kent State University*

Ohio Interscholastic Athletic Administrators Association, Ohio Athletic Administrator of the Year Award: **Bill Schumacher**, *Athletic Administrator for Beachwood Schools*

Environmental Education Council of Ohio, Christy Dixon Award: **David Wright**, *an Outreach Coordinator, Nature Center at Shaker Lakes, Shaker Heights*

Winner, 75th Annual Ohio High School Speech League Tournament; Winner, Western Reserve Society, Sons of the American Revolution, Greater Cleveland High School Oration Contest: **Laura Juliano**, *Orange*

Ohio Association of Career and Technical Education, Special Needs Division, Career and Technical Teacher of the Year Award: **Laurie McDonald**, *Multi-Area Job Training Teacher, Cuyahoga East Vocational Education Consortium, Highland Heights*

All-Ohio Council of the American Society of Safety Engineers, 2001 Safety Professional of the Year: **Wayne Creasap II**, *Assistant Director of Safety/Education and Project Director of the Safety Incentive Program for the Construction Employers Association, Cleveland*

Academy of Medicine of Cleveland/Northern Ohio Medical Association, Distinguished membership Award: **Robert Daroff, M.D.**, *Chief of Staff and Senior Vice President for Academic Affairs, University Hospitals of Cleveland*

Medina County Educational Service Center, 2002 Homer B. Smith Teacher of Excellence: **Dave Reber**, *a Science Teacher, Black River Middle School*

Lake Erie Chapter of the Ninety-Nines, 2001 Pilot of the Year: **Bernice Barris**, *Highland Heights, Commander of a Local Civil Air Patrol and pilot for more than 50 years*

2002 RTNDA (Radio-Television News Directors Assoc.), Edward R. Murrow Winners, Region 7 (IL, IN, MI, OH), Radio, Large Market: Overall Excellence, Newscast, Sports Reporting: **WTAM-AM**, *Cleveland*; News Documentary: **WCPN-FM**, *Cleveland*; Feature Reporting, News Documentary, Writing, Use of Sound: **WKSU-FM**, *Kent*

Glen and Betty Martin of Dalton in Wayne Co. share the distinction of having driven to Alaska on a tractor—and back—averaging 13 miles per hour for 9500 miles in 126 days.